Because We Live Here
Sponsoring Literacy Beyond the College Curriculum

D0814842

Research and Teaching in Rhetoric and Composition
Michael M. Williamson and Peggy O'Neill, series editors

Because We Live Here
Sponsoring Literacy Beyond the College Curriculum

Eli Goldblatt

Temple University

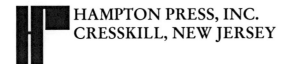

HAMPTON PRESS, INC.
CRESSKILL, NEW JERSEY

Printed in the United States of America

Library of Congress Cataloging-in-Publication Data

Goldblatt, Eli.
    Because we live here : sponsoring literacy beyond the college curriculum / Eli Goldblatt. -- 1st ed.
      p. cm. -- (Research and teaching in rhetoric and composition)
    Includes bibliographical references and indexes.
    ISBN 1-57273-768-9 (hardbound) -- ISBN 1-57273-769-7 (paperbound)
1. Literacy programs--United States. 2. Literacy--United States. 3. Literacy--Study and teaching (Higher)--United States. I. Title.
    LC151.G65 2007
    379.2'40973--dc22
                         2007026035

Cover photo by Wendy Osterweil

Hampton Press, Inc.
23 Broadway
Cresskill, NJ 07626

For Selma Kushner Goldblatt (1927-2002)
my mother and dearest teacher

and for Gil Ott (1951-2004)
poet, activist, friend

One is one alone, is one among others. However it is phrased,
it is a question. (Ott, *traffic* 83)

Contents

Acknowledgments

An author writing a book about literacy sponsorship and relationship building necessarily must thank many people. I cannot possibly name everyone with whom I worked over the years of putting this book together, and some people must not be named in order to keep school identities confidential, but I will try to mention those who made direct and significant contributions to the completion of this project. To all those I interviewed, observed, and learned from, I give my deepest gratitude.

I owe my first acknowledgment to my friend and colleague Steve Parks. He worked with me for 8 years, during which we also coached soccer together, complained about and kvelled over our kids, discussed city politics and family life. We formed ideas about community engagement as we built New City Writing; he brought an energy, intelligence, and inventiveness that made everything seem possible, even when nothing looked likely. His wife, Lori Shorr, contributed to our work as she challenged Temple and later the State Department of Education to do the right thing for all students. Steve and Lori continue to be a main source of light in the profession for me.

Other dear colleagues at Temple whose ideas and support shaped the way I think about literacy in a metropolitan university include Bob Schneider, Sue Wells, Dennis Lebofsky, Lori Salem, Jim Degnan, Michael Smith, Jill Swavely, Aneta Pavlenko, Lori Pompa, Sherri Grasmuck, Rebecca Alpert, Susan Hyatt, Barbara Ferman, Kate Shaw—each of whom has given me something precious for this book. Carolyn Adams was the dean who approved the original budget for the Institute that later became New City, and she was unwavering in her support. Morris Vogel, in his ironic and visionary way, continued his support as interim dean during a very hard time at the university. Vanessa Allen-Smith—secretary, budget manager, event arranger, and confidant—has been the anchor for New City Writing and the University Writing Program for 10 years; nothing I tried at Temple in that time would have turned out right without her. Graduate students have influenced me a great deal over the years, but I hesitate to name any for fear of leaving someone out; all have taught me more than I can explain here. The same can be said for undergraduates, except the list is longer. Single conferences with a student have taught me more than whole courses in my formal education. Setting aside the committee meetings, teaching is just learning for which you get paid.

From the Temple Partnership Schools I want to give a special thanks to Walter Jordan-Davis, who has been such a good friend and co-conspirator over the last years. I also thank his boss John DiPaolo for opening up the schools to our work and Linda Jones for making recent connections possible. I thank principals and teachers in the Partnership Schools for allowing us to join with them in working with the kids of North Philadelphia. And I thank the kids, particularly those who participated in our Tree House Books workshops, for their exuberance and pleasure in writing and art making after a day in school. Joanne Jackson and Jon Weiss at Tree House have been especially helpful in making the workshops happen.

I am duty bound not to name other folks in the regional schools I visited. I will go as far as to thank Jim, Evelyn, Mary, RG, Barry, Judith, Gail, and the many other teachers who allowed me to sit in on their classes or their departmental meetings. One welcome discovery in my study was that, despite the statistics and the news articles and the public complaints, contemporary schools still have a significant supply of devoted and skilled teachers in the classroom. I wish we had the public will to honor teachers more and to value the learning they foster over the standardized test scores they produce.

I am extremely grateful to friends and associates at the Community College of Philadelphia, especially Tom Ott, Dianne Perkins, Kathleen Murphy, and John Howe. They have been consistently welcoming to me and eager to make strong connections between our writing programs. I also want to thank Susan Darrah and the faculty of Language and Literature at Bucks County Community College for their openness to my questions.

Manuel Portillo is one of the central influences on my thinking about community engagement over the past 4 years. I hope we can work together for many more years. Edilma Franco has been a good friend, a devoted teacher, and a superb manager at Proyecto Sin Fronteras/Open Borders. I also want to recognize Father Carlos and the board of Proyecto for the hard work they have done in the neighborhood around Christ and St. Ambrose Episcopal Church. Felice Simelaro, Mary Ann Borsuk, and Johnny Irizarry were remarkable partners in the short-lived but rich collaborative we called Open Doors.

I close the book with an account of the Community Arts and Literacy Network (CALN) project. The CALN project was the last grant at Temple that Steve Parks wrote. He left me a great gift in network partners Lorene Cary, Gayle Isa, Billy Yalowitz, Karen Malandra, Nicole Meyenberg. Nicole has done heroic work keeping CALN, New City Writing, and the Press under control, and yet she always challenged us to invent better ways to serve communities in need. Mark Lyons has been a good friend and an invaluable contributor to the life of the Press.

Project SHINE, and its parent agency the Center for Intergenerational Learning, was a part of the first grant we wrote to the Knight Foundation. Nancy Henkin, Tina Kluetmeier, Liz Hayden, and Darryl Gordon have been gracious and dependable friends. I always turn to them if I need allies who truly understand community-based learning.

I owe more than thanks to the John S. and James L. Knight Foundation and especially to my two program officers, Rick Love and Julie Tarr. Knight has supported many more projects at Temple than they bargained for; they helped me create our little endowment and thus let us seed new projects continually over the years. Perhaps their greatest gift to us was that they accepted our model of university–community partnership and gave us the confidence to imagine scholarly activism beyond the campus. Helen Cunningham of Fels Foundation and Beth Feldman Brandt of Stockton Rush Bartol Foundation have helped me understand how foundations work; John Rice and Fernando Chang-Muy have been special guides in that world.

My debt of gratitude to Deborah Brandt appears in nearly everything I write. Perhaps less evident but also profound is the influence of Martin Nystrand. Deb and Marty were my advisors at University of Wisconsin-Madison, and I sometimes wonder what sort of work I might have taken up had I not run into them half way through a PhD in modernist poetry. Brad Hughes also remains an advisor and friend from Madison days. Obviously, many others influenced me there as well, but I must mention two dear friends, the poet Charles Alexander and the sculptor Chris Bruch, whose creative visions helped me see that there were no walls between art, political life, and the honest work of hard thinking.

In many ways, this book is a love song to my field. Tom Fox, David Bartholomae, Jean Ferguson Carr, Andrea Lunsford, Beverly Moss, Charles Schuster, Russel Durst, Linda Adler-Kassner, Susanmarie Harrington, Diana George read parts or the whole of this manuscript at times along the way, and their good words and belief in this project kept me at work. Linda

Flower has been a generous supporter and intellectual mentor for more than 15 years. Juan Guerra shared his enthusiasm and commitment to social justice in the last year when I most needed a lift. Special thanks to Jeanne Gunner and her staff as well as the anonymous readers at *College English* for publishing a version of the Alinsky essay (Chapter 4) and to the NCTE committee members who gave it the Ohmann Award. My editor Peggy O'Neill came along at just the right time and has been an invaluable final reader for the present text. My thanks to everyone at Hampton Press who made the published version possible.

I can't name all the family and friends who contributed directly or indirectly to this long, long process, but I will mention a few here: Chris and Ellen Hill, Alan Symonette (for baseball), Len Rieser and Fernando Chang-Muy, Bill Lamme and Robin Semer, John Landreau and Sherri Grasmuck, Julia Blumenreich and Willa Ott, Dan Osterweil and Susan Kohl. Herb Cohen taught me how to recognize my choices. My brother Aaron and his wife Laura Foster as well as my sister Sharon Goldblatt-Bloom and Nicolas Bloom gave me their unquestioned love and their questioning intelligence.

My wife, Wendy Osterweil, and my son, Leo, appear everywhere all at once in this text. Wendy's twin passions for artmaking and teaching have sustained me, pushed me, consoled me, amazed me since our first long phone conversation 25 years ago. And Leo has taught me, as only a son can, from the first day I saw his eyes.

—Eli Goldblatt

About the Author

Eli Goldblatt was born in 1952 in Cleveland, Ohio, and grew up on Army posts in the United States and Germany. After earning his BA at Cornell University, he attended a year of medical school, taught high school, traveled in Mexico and Central America, and finished a PhD in English at the University of Wisconsin-Madison. His work includes *Round My Way: Authority and Double Consciousness in Three Urban High School Writers* (University of Pittsburgh Press, 1995) and articles in *Writing on the Edge*, *College English*, *Linguistics and Education*, and *CCC*. He won the Ohmann Award in 2005 for his *College English* essay on Saul Alinsky and community-university partnerships in literacy. His book-length collections of poetry include *Sessions 1-62* (Chax Press, 1991), *Speech Acts* (Chax Press, 1999), and *Without a Trace* (Singing Horse Press, 2001). He is currently First Year Writing Director and associate professor of English at Temple University. He lives in Philadelphia with his wife, Wendy Osterweil, and their son, Leo.

Introduction

WAC programs, which have traditionally focused on micro issues, must now devote significant attention to macro issues. The first macro challenge is the need to work with other organizations.
—Barbara Walvoord, "The Future of WAC"

Even the smallest country must have both a domestic and a foreign policy. It is never enough to deal solely with the events and economy contained in one's own territory because the outside world always has a way of impinging, seeping in over the airwaves, or bursting past the border guards. Countries must pay attention to trade, immigration and emigration, pollution wafting across from the neighbor's city. They must establish alliances they can depend on in times of conflict or national emergency. They must build large-scale institutional structures so that individual citizens can accomplish goals outside the country that also further the national interest. Setting aside ideologies, successful foreign and domestic policies can further each other if they are formulated carefully and pursued with a rare combination of vigor and wisdom.

Until fairly recently, colleges and universities had the luxury to maintain a sense of autonomy to which countries such as Luxembourg, Monaco, or North Korea could never pretend. Professors labored in gentile poverty but did what they liked in class; deans had their quarrels over money with provosts but could not be compared, by training or habit, to industrial managers or government bureaucrats. Students learned what they learned, got their degrees or dropped out, but hopefuls still came knocking for entrance at the front end. State schools always had to pay attention to their legislature, but the flagship universities at least got most of what they wanted, especially if the football team was winning.

We live in an academic world now where outsiders are much more likely to ask questions about outcomes and make demands on our programs. Parents and prospective students in private schools feel more entitled to ask for certain services and curricular features in the schools they choose. State legislatures are making major cuts to once sacrosanct higher education budgets, and the federal government is considering legislation that could bring a level of accountability to undergraduate education that K–12 schools have been feeling for more than a decade. This outside attention may be unwanted but it is not wholly unnecessary. Not since the student rebellions of the 1960s have academic practices been so interrogated. Pedagogies and curricula that had come to be taken for granted are now under scrutiny; measures of student learning and retention have become major indicators of success in many schools. This time around, however, the interrogation is often framed in the jargon of professional outcomes and managerial efficiencies, and these approaches can become mechanical and formulaic all too quickly. The language of accountability alone can drive a staid faculty meeting into a state of panic and denial.

I focus on a notion of literacy education at a large metropolitan university that takes into account the inside and outside, the domestic and foreign, the on-campus and the community-based in order to make writing and reading instruction more responsive to the complex of needs that arise in urban circumstances. I call for a vision of writing beyond the curriculum not because I think writing across the curriculum has failed but because it has succeeded. I agree with Susan McLeod and Eric Miraglia that Writing Across the Curriculum (WAC) can and will survive in the new millennium (McLeod et al 3). Where they define WAC in terms of the pedagogy of "writing to learn," I propose an orientation, a perspective, a sociological vision of literacy that can help us understand the context for WAC. Like Barbara Walvoord, I believe we need to work with "other" organizations, and those organizations by and large exist outside the walls of the typical American campus. By no means do I wish to displace WAC with some formulaic Writing Beyond the Curriculum (WBC) approach. In a sense, I mean to develop a "foreign policy" for writing programs that will complement the domestic policy WAC represents.

Because We Live Here is driven by two insights about writing instruction. The first is contained in a quote attributed to the poet Gary Snyder (alas, I have not been able to find it in his essays; scholars I have asked say it sounds familiar, but they can't place it): "Perhaps the most radical thing we can do today is to live in one place for the rest of our lives." I encountered the quote in 1988 when my wife and son and I were just packing up from 5 years in Wisconsin, returning home to Philadelphia where she grew up and where I taught high school. I had grown up in the U.S. Army, moving every couple of years with my family when my father was transferred somewhere new, and the idea that staying put was radical—and thus heroically productive, in the way I'm sure Snyder meant it—seemed appealing and true. I have always admired people who have lived somewhere long enough to know the history behind local political upheavals, understand why one city councilman hates another, recall the way a neighborhood changed from Italian to African American to Hmong to Albanian, or remember when a candy store used to stand where a parking lot is now. This is a sort of genuine knowledge that all my graduate training could not match. I wanted to go back to Philly and let the baseball team break my heart year after year, meet my former students in the grocery store, have a stake in schools and public transportation and wage taxes. This commitment to the local—in my case the city of Philadelphia, which has been my home now for more than 23 years—shows itself in every chapter, in every paragraph of this book.

But this book is also about relationships among people who have an investment in literacy education across diverse institutions. What binds together most of the people I mention in the following chapters is that we all live in the Philadelphia region, and many of us have come to the conclusion that in order to make things better for our particular constituents we must take into account the interconnections among schools, neighborhood literacy centers, 2- and 4-year colleges, and universities. Building relationships is terribly demanding work, often fraught with conflict, frustration, and disappointment. And yet I want to argue that we cannot solve many of the problems we face as undergraduate or graduate instructors and researchers of writing without extensive connections to others outside the academic circle who occupy themselves with written language in all its manifestations.

Eventually, that consciousness of connection and relationship will need to reach to business, nonprofit, and government employers in the metropolitan region as well. College writing administrators and instructors need to have a clear conception of where students are going as well as where they have been. One limit of this book is that my current research has not taken me in the direction of the workplace or cyberspace yet, but others have opened up that territory for the field of composition and rhetoric. Cynthia Selfe, in her sharp little book *Technology and Literacy in the Twenty-First Century*, warns us to pay attention to the way "literacy instruction is now inextricably linked to technology" (5). Ideally, this book would also take into account the networks, programs, hardware she points us to, but in one way this book takes her call to heart. She recognizes the large-scale bureau-cracy and institutional structures that foster and maintain ideological orien-tations toward the use of technology and, ultimately, literacy in our society. What I am interested in here is the structures, indeed the technologies of schooling that segment teaching and learning to such an extent that students can be injured as they pass—or don't pass—from one institutional space to another. These institutional structures have grown up, often without a plan or with incomplete or ideologically driven plans, and what is left is an infra-structure that carries some students from stage to stage of their literacy lives with little interruption but that confronts other students with vast gaps and obstacles that make travel nearly impossible. In this I share Selfe's concern that we learn to "pay attention" far more to the institutional structures we are elaborating and upholding every day.

In Fall 2001, after the tragedy of 9/11 and during the ensuing soul-searching and patriotism of that time, I began visiting high schools in the Philadelphia area. I had a study leave from Temple University that year to begin a book project I had long contemplated but did not yet grasp; going out to local 12th grade English classrooms seemed a good place to start fig-uring out what to say about writing beyond the college curriculum. I want-ed to know where our students came from and why some of them thrived when they got to Temple, whereas others dropped out or struggled with our courses. I felt that the sky had been falling for many people in our country a lot longer than since the terrorist attacks, and the renewed political fervor simply gave more urgency to my sense that college literacy work had to extend beyond the college campus. My mother was dying of lung cancer and had lost much of her power to frame sentences, but her long-time habit of sociological analysis and commitment to social justice suddenly seemed manifest in this project. I would visit a school, look at data, read a little Dewey or Alinsky, and then visit her in the hospital and tell her what I was seeing and what I thought. She had worked for Saul Alinsky when she was a graduate student in sociology at the University of Chicago, so that pairing seemed particularly appropriate in her honor, even if she couldn't respond and sometimes could not even hear me.

One morning in late fall I went to visit a high school not far from Temple's main campus in North Philadelphia. The school, which I call North High School in this book, is a large, concrete hulk that looms over a busy street. Highly praised by architects when it was first built in the 1970s, North today seems menacing outside—despite the colorful mural on one wall—and inside its hallways combine the charm of a back stairwell in an overbuilt football stadium and the hopefulness of a cinderblock corridor in a maximum security prison. Noninstructional staff bark at students to get to class, and kids hide in nooks and behind columns to talk past the bell or fin-ish up proscribed transactions. I was standing on a kind of bridge in the middle of the school when I suddenly had an image of what it might be like to stand there as a high school kid contemplating my future. I saw roads with detour signs and potholes, narrow one-way alleys that led nowhere but ran tantalizingly close to the highway. I thought about the roads that led from suburban schools right onto the on-ramps and thruways marked with big green signs pointing to colleges and universities that would be the next stop on careers laid out for middle-class kids. Any 17-year-old is afraid of the future, and even the most privileged have obstacles and pressures to face, internal and external demons to overcome. But this imagined kid I experienced standing there in North, with the sun coming down on his head through the dirty skylight and the bell ringing in his ears, beheld a long, nearly impossible journey in front of him and no map to guide his way. I thought then that the book I write needs to be a call to all of us to draw that map and, in the process, think harder about how every person from any neighborhood can get from where he or she starts as a kid to a safe and productive place he or she chose as an adult. That is not purely a job for educators, but as an educator and researcher I must have that objective informing what I do.

I referred to a "metropolitan university," and I mean that term in both its technical and hortatory senses. Technically, the term has come to stand for a movement among state-related schools in urban areas toward a higher education identity that is distinct from the standard American dichotomy between the small liberal arts college and the large research-driven university. One article in a collection on the movement defines the term as follows:

> Although metropolitan universities are likely to share certain characteristics, such as a high enrollment of commuter and minority students, metropolitan universities are best recognized by an interactive philosophy by which these institutions establish symbiotic relationships with their metropolitan areas. In some institutions, such interaction is focused primarily in a few well-defined units, such as a college of education or a center for urban studies; however, we envision a metropolitan university as an institution where the commitment to interaction with the metropolitan area permeates the entire institution. At such universities, applying resources to improve the metropolitan quality of life must be an institution-wide commitment. (Hathaway, Mulhollan, White 9)

Thus, the term names not only a location but also a preoccupation, not only regional function but also an institutional lifestyle. But that leads to the hortatory aspect, for no matter how much a central administration or leading faculty in a university may want to identify itself with such a movement, this sort of a self-definition will be extremely difficult to maintain in any

American research institution because faculty are simply not trained to think about knowledge production, teaching, or even professional service with the requisite orientation toward either the local or the relational that this definition of "metropolitan" demands. If we feel any allegiance to this way of thinking about higher education, we must exhort and encourage colleagues to pay attention to the problems of the people among who we live. Most academics in nearly every noncommercial field—especially in the liberal arts but not exclusively so—are neither educated nor rewarded for this kind of localized problem solving.

I introduce the concept of *literacy sponsorship* as a way of making explicit a set of assumptions by which institutions in a region operate and through which they are kept isolated from one another. In order to be metropolitan, a university or college must not presume it can set the direction of research and service with its neighbors without their active participation. To partner with schools and community organizations, a postsecondary institution must be clear about its self-interests and the interests of its partners; it must be willing to negotiate with partners over the direction of a project in a way that benefits all participants. In the area of business and governmental partnerships this can lead to problematic and even unethical decision making, and so I am aware that what I am calling for is not without its very real hazards. Working for seemingly the most laudable causes— cleaning up the environment, eradicating poverty, bringing greater parity among school systems—can challenge traditional ideas of knowledge production that have great merit and deserve to continue. We don't want to lose the ability to ask difficult questions even to our friends and to evaluate the world critically even if it involves challenging a political ally. But of course "pure" research involves its own set of value judgments and unexamined choices. Only if we constantly ask ourselves why we take certain actions or teach in certain ways can we hope to make decisions that can sustain later scrutiny and can serve as foundational choices for later work. I hope this book maintains that sense of critical awareness while it also encourages academics, community activists, and educators to make common cause in mapping and elaborating literacies beyond the limit of our individual and institutional agendas.

1

Writing Within, Across, Beyond

Most mornings when I go to my English Department office, I take the stairs. Until they repainted the stairwell, I used to pass a graffiti exchange written on the wall between the sixth and seventh floors. In black ink, one person had written two lines: "From West P to North P/Never NE." In red ink, another person had put an X through the first message, ending the downward swipes with devil's pitchforks, and written underneath: "Learn to Write."

I passed those cryptic markings hundreds of times, but I could never make much of them until I began writing this book. Then one day it occurred to me that this graffiti was an instance of the linguistic drama central to the writing program from which this book is drawn. The black ink voice is exercising the time-honored function of graffiti writers to assert the primacy of home territory simply by naming where they come from and rejecting rival territory (see Stewart 206 ff. for a reading of graffiti in the context of consumer culture). West Philly and North Philly are predominantly African American, and Northeast Philly is predominantly White working class, although both North and Northeast have significant Latino neighborhoods and many other ethnic communities figure in the mix as well. But the red-ink voice, in the manner of bathroom wall interlocutors everywhere, attempts to overrule the first message by writing over it, reproving the author, urging the discussion in a new direction. Red Ink does not address the race comment or neighborhood rivalry inherent in Black Ink's message but slaps back with the implied criticism of linguistic deficit (wasn't the black-ink message *written*, after all?) and an abstracted statement of the university's writing requirement that turns rule into command. At least at Temple, professors teach "writing" (and all other knowledge and ability formations) in the context of just this unspoken conversation among students, what Robert Brooke terms the "underlife" of classroom instruction.

In my first year as a high school teacher I got a lecture on graffiti from a kid I will call Terry, a boy who still stands out as one of the brightest students I ever taught. He was in trouble with a couple of gangs in his Philadelphia neighborhood, and he was explaining to me why he had lately missed some school and might miss much more. He stood at my blackboard after school and drew various symbols I had seen on buildings in my own neighborhood. I was new to Philadelphia and did not understand the subtleties of terrain claiming and other inflections Terry talked about. He was urgent, almost feverish, as he spoke to me that afternoon, and he never returned to our school again after that lesson. Maybe he went south to stay with relatives, maybe the gang-bangers caught up to him, but Terry changed something for me with his lecture. He convinced me—a young Jewish guy who had worked with migrant farm workers in California and dropped out of medical school in Cleveland but had never lived in the heart of an eastern city—to listen closely to my students and pay attention to the walls arrayed around us all. It is worth recognizing that the marks others make have a meaning both to the artists themselves and to the uninitiated bystanders like me, even if I have to make up the sense for myself. New students must make sense of their teachers' marks on blackboards in university classrooms, and those marks are no less exotic or tinged with unspoken violence than the graffiti Terry showed me more than 20 years ago.

This is a book about the rich regional context and institutional relationships that surround, stress, and sustain a multifaceted writing program in a state-affiliated metropolitan research university, Temple University. I do not fictionalize the setting because the peculiarities of the local are too essential to literacy work as I conceive of it, but characters in the book are pseudononymous except when they have given me explicit permission to use their names. The K–12 schools or their professional teachers are not given their actual names to ensure that positive identification could not be attached to students. The book is part institutional history, part anthropological field journal, part sociological analysis, and part manifesto. Anyone interested in cooperative work on urban literacy is welcome as a participating reader.

After a team of Temple faculty published an article on our writing program in 1997 (Sullivan et al), Kristine Hansen responded in print that she would "like to hear more from the Temple group . . . after their reforms have been in place a couple of years" (264) because she thought it would be useful to see how the reforms we outlined then had worn with time. What I have realized in the intervening years is that the interesting question is not so much how our reforms have worked out—after all, any given institution changes and transmutes according to a logic of personality and power that does not follow or even respect a plan—but instead how can we better understand the details and local demands those reforms took for granted. The more we know about where our students come from and what the literacy conditions are around our institution, the better chance we have of designing a program that truly fits our environment. This book attempts to present a picture of the social context in schools, community colleges, and neighborhood literacy centers that we did not bother to investigate before we undertook program reform. In the process, I suggest that college writing and writing instruction as activities cannot be encapsulated, investigated, or promulgated exclusively through a curriculum on a particular campus, especially in an urban setting with so many large and small literacy-related institutions functioning simultaneously alongside the university.

A motivating assumption of this work is that all literacy learning is local in much the same way that, as former Speaker of the House Tip O'Neill famously put it, "all politics is local." Even when the subject matter or audience is national or international, the acquisition and exercise of language is always mediated by and reflective of conditions that can be traced to the geographical, social, and economic locations of the speaker, writer, listener or reader. In short, there is no WAC in the abstract, only individual programs enacting a vague but shared idea in their particular mix of departments, personalities, and regional circumstances. And if one pursues a vision of writing or literacy instruction that goes beyond the campus, indeed beyond the curriculum, there is all the more reason to understand that program in its very specific locale, based on the kinds of students in the university, the economic climate of the region, the state of the public and private schools in the area, and many other crucial considerations, both contemporary and historical. This book does not come near to tracking all these factors for readers, even in one school and regional setting, but I hope it does point the way for further research into the social contexts for college and university writing programs. I believe we need a more comprehensive theoretical model of the postsecondary literacy environment, and that will take many hands to assemble.

The title of this book comes from the last sentences of an article my colleague Steve Parks and I published in 2000 about our notion of "Writing Beyond the Curriculum." At that time we concluded the following:

> We are building on the insights of social theory in composition research by engaging in the world our students come from and go to, and we intend to add our voices especially in the local scene because that is

where we teach, raise our kids, and pay taxes. In this sense, writing and
literacy instruction go beyond the "beyond." This is simply where we
live. (604)

We applied this idea to a conference called "Literacy Because We Live
Here" that we organized in spring 2000 with partners around the
Philadelphia region on the connections across K–16 schools and literacy
centers (see more on that conference in Chapter 5). The idea seemed to
appeal to all involved that a broad range of literacy workers should collaborate in teaching and learning together because we share this particular corner of the planet.

In many ways, however, the idea of literacy as a local activity has been
on my mind a long time. Joe Harris, cautioning the field about the easy use
of the metaphor of "community" in an essay first published in 1989, called
for us to "reserve our uses of *community* to describe the workings of such
specific and local groups" as we might find in city life or everyday classrooms, and that we should center our study of writing on the complex and
contradictory talk of real collocations of people "with their mixings of
sometimes conflicting and sometimes conjoining beliefs and purposes"
(*Teaching* 107). He stresses the "everyday struggles and mishaps" of language use over our tendency to "abstract and idealize the workings of 'academic discourse'" (*Teaching* 106-07). This location for composition studies
gives it a messy but endlessly challenging mission.

I associate Harris' emphasis on the unkempt but vibrant local commu-
nicative scene with a moment I experienced in 1989-1990 when I first
entered the college job market with my brand new Ph.D. My wife and I had
just returned to Philadelphia after 5 years away at the University of
Wisconsin-Madison. I was working on a dissertation rooted in a few Philly
neighborhoods, Wendy was quite happy in a job that involved her with
many neighborhood arts organizations; we both had family in town who
wanted to be a part of our toddler's life. But an academic job search often
means considering work anywhere in the country, and my advisors urged
me to apply for the best jobs, wherever they might be. This was undoubtedly the most tense moment of our marriage. Wendy said I could apply anywhere I wanted, but she wasn't leaving Philadelphia. I didn't particularly
want to leave Philadelphia, but I felt I couldn't limit myself to one area only.
One of my graduate professors, a distinguished feminist literary critic, urged
me to tell my wife that she could always find something in a new town, but
a choice academic position had to take precedence. In the end, I did apply
elsewhere, and was a finalist at a job in the south, the northwest, and the
Philadelphia area.

I went on a campus interview to a research university in the northwest
and had a wonderful day with my prospective colleagues. The work was

challenging but congenial; the faculty members were smart, friendly, and supportive. By mid-morning I had privately begun to consider the possibility of commuting across country for at least a year or two. Late that afternoon my host took me to a micro-brewery off campus, and as I sat drinking a splendid dark beer I suddenly had an unflattering vision of myself at that rough-hewn wooden table. I saw that all my training had shaped me into a kind of mercenary mandarin, a skilled knowledge producer who could go anywhere—find a good coffeehouse, subscribe to the *The New York Times*, keep up with the learned journals, attend national conferences to see my fellow wizards—and the place I lived would never be anything more important than a mere personal preference, like my brand of soap or my favorite scotch. My father, an army plastic surgeon, had done the very same thing I was now preparing to do. He went where his professional skills were needed, whether that meant Fort Benning, Georgia or Landstuhl, Germany.

Even if I had set aside my personal life and the very real possibility that my choice could destroy my marriage, professional questions remained. What did moving for the job rather than the region say about the knowledge I had so carefully larded away? Wasn't there any value to what I knew about Philadelphia's schools and neighborhoods? What did it mean for me to study kids in Philly neighborhoods and then fly 3,000 miles away to teach other kids who didn't know Rittenhouse Square from Fishtown? The beer started to taste a little bitter, and I suddenly felt ashamed for my eagerness to please these people in a city I did not know.

Of course, many will say it is a luxury to be able to choose place over position, and certainly it's damned good luck that my story worked out well for me. I was offered a job in a Philadelphia area university and I pulled out of all the other job searches the next weekend. Many academics are not so fortunate as to choose where they work, but the principle I am driving at goes beyond the choice I made. Even if I had taken a job outside Philadelphia, I still would have faced a decision about how my knowledge of the local setting affected my teaching and research life. Is there something about the demography, geography, or social psychology of a region that should affect the instruction and investigation pursued inside a given campus? Our departmental and college affiliations reinforce a radical distinction between academic writing and other social forms: writing in a university may vary from discipline to discipline, but disciplinary discourse is a thing apart from region or locale. I'm not saying this separation is necessarily wrong, but at times it renders us incapable of understanding our students or ourselves as actors on a local stage, and it tends to obscure the role of our particular institutions within their regional economies.

WAC—perhaps our field's second most important contribution to literacy learning after the insight that writing needs to be taught based on an understanding of what writers actually do—has one fatal flaw. It emphasizes the campus as the unit of measure, a great improvement over the earlier habit of measuring writing purely on the basis of English Department standards, but the campus perspective is limiting nonetheless. Keying writing instruction to the college curriculum restricts the conception of literacy possible in the minds of students, faculty, and administrators. If we look beyond the curriculum, to the places students come from, the jobs they will go to, and the language and literacy needs of the neighborhoods where students might work and study, then a new picture of reading and writing begins to emerge. Indeed, many in our field have studied writing in workplaces, in schools, in poor and rich neighborhoods. But we haven't truly reconceived of writing programs in the context of all we know about the social network of reading and writing, and this is what I hope to begin to accomplish. The rise of community-based and service learning-style composition courses puts new pressure on writing programs to take the outside world into account, but I would argue here that many outside forces come into play when we consider the successes and failures of students in college writing classrooms and beyond.

PLAN OF THE BOOK

The plan for the next three chapters is based on the local circumstances of the writing program I take as my text, the one I have directed for the last 8 years at Temple University. I am not so interested in rendering for the reader the fine points of the curriculum or administrative structure, although I have to explain some of the program's details along the way. The crucial matter to consider is all the stuff that isn't in the curriculum but presses on our students' abilities to learn to write. In Chapter 2, I consider data on Temple students who come from a variety of local schools in the Philadelphia region. I then explore in greater detail a couple of representative schools to understand the gap between expectations in 12th grade and the first-year undergraduate writing curriculum. I look closely at the mismatch of curricula in two schools and Temple, but my purpose is not to trumpet curricular reform as the answer to students' difficulty in transforming themselves from high school to college learners. My approach is certainly influenced by what some educators call the K–16 movement—an effort by administrators and teachers on both sides of the high school–college divide (see, e.g., AAHE's document *Greater Expectations*)—but I have no illusions that institutional alignments can be easily built or that curricular reform alone will lead to better results for students. Indeed, I suspect that institutional connections are necessary but not sufficient; individual relationships among people in schools and colleges will probably prove to be the single most important factor in students' success, though we may never have enough data to prove that assertion.

In Chapter 3, I investigate another school-to-school connection, this time between community colleges in the Philadelphia area and Temple. The data tells an interesting story, echoing the story in Chapter 2 that students from schools with fewer resources do less well than students from schools with more. The story seems obvious and almost trite, maudlin, or despairing, like a plot line from Dickens stripped of its quirky characters, coincidental meetings, and odd moments of spontaneous combustion. Yet the deeper we look at the data, the more we must remember to remember what wealth means to real people who have it and those who do not. An institution like Temple University or its nearby neighbor, the Community College of Philadelphia, has no choice but to face the ugly fact of unevenly distributed resources directly, but obviously we must not stop with that recognition. I conclude that chapter with an account of a project to get teachers from two partner institutions to talk about the assignments they give in first-year writing, the course ostensibly common to both.

Chapter 4 considers the connection between and among a university and the neighborhood groups that students and teachers might encounter in community-based learning situations. This chapter introduces a character from the history of community organizing in the 20th century, Saul Alinsky, as an alternative guiding light to current educational influences such as Paulo Freire and John Dewey. Community-based or service learning will not thrive and cannot last if it is patched on to an unreconstructed composition curriculum and introduced into communities that have not had the opportunity to negotiate with the university or college for equal partnership in the venture. Alinsky's work forces us to see community-based learning from the point of view of the community, raising our eyes beyond the curriculum in another direction. I conclude that chapter with an account of an educational venture among partners in the area near Temple in order to illustrate the power (and frustration) of working along the lines suggested by Alinsky.

The fifth chapter emphasizes the need to build relationships across institutions, administrative structures, and social boundaries, and the final chapter focuses on the need to circulate insights and participants among the components of the network. In both chapters I highlight projects or programmatic directions that grow directly from such networks, with the hope that my stories can generate any number of possibilities for other schools with their own specific local circumstances, constraints, and resources. By being as specific as I can be about the localness of literacy learning at Temple, I intend to offer a meaningful case study to those in very different but equally compelling regional situations. Very little that I say in this book is wholly original, for good work outside the traditional campus and curriculum is breaking out all over the country as I write. I hope, however, that my stories and arguments call attention to a compelling internal logic within attitudes and approaches already found in American and international writing programs.

I hope too that I can emphasize the urgency of our work for the large number of students who seek the social and economic advantages that a college education has come to stand for. Like many in composition and rhetoric, I am unabashedly committed to providing a rich and democratic education to the widest array of people in our country. In our field, unfortunately, terms like access, accommodation, and service have—for some scholars—become dirty words in the polarized discussion of educational policy and critical writing pedagogy. I intend to use these reformist concepts without shame alongside more "radical" notions derived from the work of educators such as Freire, Ira Shor, Henry Giroux. For this reason, I start the discussion in this chapter with a consideration of John Dewey, a quintessentially liberal figure in American education, but one whose vision, if taken seriously and followed with dedication, leads to a highly activist and multidimensional conception of writing beyond the curriculum.

JOHN DEWEY AND THE WRITING PROGRAM

So many important figures in composition have written about Dewey's work that yet another reference to Dewey may seem both superfluous and presumptuous. What more can I say? Janet Emig saw him as the seminal figure in composition. George Hillocks, Linda Flower, Kurt Spellmeyer, Tom Newkirk, Sharon Crowley, Louise Wetherbee Phelps, and Russel Durst are only a few compositionists who have discussed Dewey in significant books in the field. Henry Giroux points to Dewey as an important forbearer who "talked about democracy as a way of life that has to be made and remade in every generation" (12). Philosopher Steve Fishman has written extensively about Dewey and his application to writing pedagogy, and Fishman's co-investigator Lucille McCarthy has demonstrated the usefulness of Dewey's approach to qualitative research in the writing classroom. Tom Deans' book on service learning draws heavily on Dewey, pairing him with Paulo Freire for the theoretical basis of service learning initiatives.

In this chapter, however, I want to offer an application of Dewey's thought to the design of a writing program. Encountering his ideas in *Democracy and Education* and elsewhere reframes the challenges to a writing program at a large metropolitan university. Dewey's work helped me develop a set of principles I find useful in thinking about writing instruction placed in the larger framework of a city and an economic region. His commitment to a profound and radical democratic vision has great guiding power when I consider the circumstances and goals of the program at

Temple. I view each of the following principles through the prism of Dewey's thought, not to lend a philosophical patina to administrative affairs but to render all four principles in the light of a single project: to enact democratic values through literacy education.

1. **Aim to develop a constellation of abilities that help students become both productive individuals and engaged social beings: access, reflection, and connection.** Build the university program not on a first-year course or courses alone but on the full range of activities possible in an undergraduate career, and teach both for the students' present experience as well as their future literacy needs.

2. **Bring the margins to the center, and recognize that the most stressed students serve as the best guides about what a program can do.** English as a second language (ESL) and transfer students, basic writers, and learning disabled students have needs that are not so very different from those of all students: less fragmentation, more individual support, better coordination between tutors and faculty, a technological environment that provides a maximum of resources and a minimum of surveillance.

3. **Cultivate relationships both inside and outside school to support literacy learning.** Develop partnerships, foster joint sponsorship of writing among a variety of disciplines, organizations, and the students' home institutions. Enact the social vision of composition that the field has elaborated for more than 20 years, but do not become so enamored by external projects that internal academic training becomes impoverished or neglected.

4. **Continually assess, evaluate, and study the program in as collaborative and imaginative a way as possible in order to gain perspective on the local environment.** We should know where our students come from, what they learn as they move through our program, where they go when they leave undergraduate school, and what they do over time with what they learned in college. This is a big order, but we can start by developing ongoing research that is practical and theoretical, quantitative and qualitative, focused on local detail but cognizant of national trends. We can compare our numbers and observations with partner institutions that are both alike and different from our own. We can learn more from research than from gatekeeping.

I use these principles as a set of interrelated themes in the following sections to frame my understanding of Dewey and his contribution to literacy instruction. I also return to the principles in Chapter 5 as a way of reconsidering the journey in the following chapters.

Aiming to Develop Social as Well as Individual Abilities

One of Dewey's central preoccupations seems particularly relevant to the project of this book: the relationship between student, school, and the larger society. Deans noted that Dewey called on schools to take an active role in helping "students become good citizens in the broadest sense" (37). Donald Jones recommended Dewey's conception of experience, knowledge, and language for resolving the "postmodern impasse of agency" (81) that limits even the most politically committed compositionists, such Patricia Bizzell, Lester Faigley, and James Berlin, in their ability to theorize individual students as autonomous producers of meaning. My purpose here is not strictly pedagogical or theoretical. I am interested in the programmatic ramifications of the position Dewey articulated early in his career in "My Pedagogical Creed": "In sum, I believe that the individual who is to be educated is a social individual and that society is an organic union of individuals" (429). By "programmatic ramifications" I mean to ask this question: What institutional and civic engagements does this dialogic relationship between individual and society commit a writing program to undertake?

In Dewey's view, even the youngest human beings are intimately shaped by and shaping their social world. At least two assertions follow from this basic observation. The first is that schools have a responsibility to provide a community environment in which learning grows from experience and inquiry is carried out in cooperation with others (see Fishman & McCarthy 48ff). This has formed the basis of much work that is now considered Deweyan, including some tendencies in the progressive education movement that Dewey himself felt were too casual and unfocused (Fishman & McCarthy 50; Dewey, "Educational Confusion," 242-3). A second assertion follows from the first. For Dewey, learning should be experienced as a present condition, one in which daily activities should matter for the individual at the time they happen and not simply as lessons for a later career or more advanced study. In the "Creed" Dewey describes education as "a process of living and not a preparation for future living" (430). This position may be the more troubling of the two, even for Dewey's followers, for it has been much less noticed. I return to presentness elsewhere, for it has direct bearing on writing within a first-year curriculum, across a range of disciplinary curricula, and beyond the collective college curriculum — within, across, and beyond. For now, let me just say that we must balance our desire to prepare students for the future and ensure their later success with an investment in the present, in the satisfaction and challenge their classes offer them in the moment they are taking them. This principle of a balanced approach—recognizing students' needs now and later, emphasizing abilities that have both individual and collective benefits—is crucial for first-year writing but also necessary throughout an undergraduate's career.

Dewey's "Creed," a manifesto written at the time he was most involved with Chicago schools and opening the Laboratory School at the University of Chicago (Westbrook 97), evokes the image of lively classrooms drawing on the language and understandings kids bring from home but pushing students to test what they know in the here and now context of peers, adults, and the surrounding city. It suggests pedagogical strategies such as peer review, school publications, service learning, and others that are so familiar to writing instructors today. In many ways, the beliefs stated in the "Creed" express both unspoken and explicit doctrine at the core of contemporary composition. Composition theorists have shed much ink over both the division and the bridge between expressivist and social constructionist approaches to writing, differentiation and rapprochement initiated by debates between Peter Elbow and David Bartholomae in the mid-1990s. Dewey's work incorporates both positions as necessary elements in dialectic between a conception of language use as individually based and one that is primarily rooted in discourse communities. As Jones notes, "Deweyan pragmatism retheorizes many of the sound practices of writing process and postmodern composition instructors" (99). But have we incorporated this dialectic thinking into writing programs themselves? Indeed, have we truly pursued a democratic social vision at the organizational levels above the classroom? It is my contention that we must hold Dewey's "social individual" fully in mind if we are to build writing programs tuned to the lives of actual students.

In this principle, I suggest three sets of abilities that writing programs can focus on throughout a whole student's career in any discipline.

- *Access* refers to entryway abilities such as problem framing and data interpretation as well as a knowledge base about discursive conventions. Dewey links this from early on in students' education to "doing things," attacking challenging but not unfamiliar problems, out of which will come active intellectual curiosity and engagement in the subjects they encounter in school (see, e.g., *DE* 156-7). Students need access abilities to begin functioning within the academic literacy environment in general education courses, but they also need to gain new access skills each time they enter more specialized literacy environments. If we approach the problem of "teaching fundamentals"

as a matter of knowing and doing for greater engagement—
rather than for reaching some arbitrary standard of correctness
and fluency—then we can both challenge those who make
grammar a moral battle and also describe without mystical
obfuscation the job students must face.

- *Reflection*, as Dewey defined it, is the "active, persistent and
careful consideration of any belief or supposed form of knowledge in the light of the grounds that support it, and the further
conclusions to which it tends" (HWT 6). Following Dewey,
Phelps called *reflection* composition's "first principle" (64)
because it involves a response to experience in organized
inquiry, teaching, and personal literacy encounters (72-73). I
mean here the ability to question the frame of every task and
the claims inherent within assertions a student makes or
encounters. However, this cluster of abilities would also
include less linear explorations of a topic, expressive responses
to personal or professional situations, and self-reflection on the
writer's own process.

- *Connectivity* names that set of research and networking abilities so prized in electronic environments, but it can also mean
cultivating the habit of reaching out to others who might have
a different perspective on a problem or task. For Dewey, the
distinction between the training that animals receive and the
education of which humans are capable is that a human may
learn as a "partner in a shared activity" (*DE* 13). Through this
social environment for learning, language becomes more than a
sequence of sounds: "Understanding one another means that
objects, including sounds, have the same value for both, with
respect to carrying on a common pursuit" (*DE* 15). We demonstrate connectivity programmatically when the writing center
and other components of the writing program maintain close
connections with departments and programs throughout a
campus and in the surrounding area.

These three categories do not exhaust the possibilities for literacy expectations in a writing program, but they suggest ways that a program can focus
attention on a core constellation of abilities and use them to link, sequence,
or build across levels, departments, and learning sites. Each of these abilities
has a social and an individual component, a way to build a student's sense of
a composing self (even as a "unified self" will be called into question) and a
network within which one person's composing can or must be located (even
if that network shows its limits as its outlines come into focus). Any work
on principles or categories is provisional at best, but the effort to make these

expectations explicit will serve a program well in making decisions on new project designs and in building relationships with other schools or institutional partners.

Bring the Margins to the Center

Deans points out that Dewey recognized diversity in the American population as an enriching element in American schools, even if he didn't talk as much about it as we might like now 100 years later (36). Dewey did urge schools to train students explicitly in dealing with people of different backgrounds and traditions. In *Democracy and Education*, he says: "it is the office of the school environment to balance the various elements in the social environment, and to see to it that each individual gets an opportunity to escape from the limitations of the social group in which he was born" (20). By this he means that every student brings habits of home and neighborhood with him or her to school—to this he has no objection—but that students also bring the provincialism of narrow experience with them to school; this modest scope of vision will limit how much they can learn from others. Dewey goes on to focus specifically on the mixing of groups that we now refer to as diversity: "the intermingling in the school of youth of different races, differing religions, and unlike customs creates for all a new and broader environment" (21). In order to accommodate such a wide range, Dewey urges us to use a variety of pedagogical methods to challenge all students, not just the exceptional ones, to grow as much as possible: "What is required is that every individual shall have opportunities to employ his own powers in activities that have meaning" (172). These are high expectations for public institutions to meet.

This aspect of Dewey has been cited in the work of the New London Group, a collective of literacy researchers who bring together expertise in fields such as Teaching English to Speakers of Other Languages (TESOL) and new media to introduce a powerful conception of multiliteracy education. They point out that Dewey speaks approvingly of the "assimilative force" of American schooling (*Democracy* 21-22), which they interpret as "the function of making homogeneity out of differences" (Cope and Kalantzis 18). In this sense Dewey was no multiculturalist, and I do not mean to make him out to be so. I return to the New London Group later, for they offer an exciting way to reorient Dewey's view of assimilation in the current situation where effective education must "recruit, rather than attempt to ignore and erase, the different subjectivities—interests, intentions, commitments, and purposes—students bring to learning" (18). Their perspective provides an excellent vantage point for envisioning a comprehensive writing program that goes beyond the curriculum.

Temple University has been a particularly opportune site for incorporating diversity as a key element of a writing program. Temple attracts a striking range of students—in 2004 about 18% African or African American, 10% Asian or Asian-American, 7% Latino, 3% Arab or Arab American; the Caucasian population includes many 1.5 generation (born in another country but at least partially schooled here) immigrants from Russia, Ukraine, Romania, and Croatia to name only a few. Somewhat less than half the undergraduate students are transfers; half of the transfers come from a handful of regional community colleges and the other half come from more than 70 four-year institutions. Because Temple students often come from modest economic backgrounds, they have a tremendous motivation to learn, even if their idea of an education may be more instrumental than that of their professors, and their outside jobs prevent them from studying as many hours a week as their professors would like. In short, we have the diversity that many schools claim they want, but we aren't always capable of seeing our diverse student body as a treasure because we are too busy seeing it as a drain on resources and a liability for national ratings.

Designing and funding a full-service writing program for this diverse a population is a challenge that Dewey in 1915 (when he published *Democracy and Education*) could not have foreseen, but he might have embraced it as an opportunity to introduce social context into the study of any subject matter (*DE* 67). People of different backgrounds studying together, by the nature of the social situation, force each other to ask questions about definitions and evidence that may not come up in more stratified arrangements. Too often, however, administrators picture the students for whom writing programs are shaped as either a reflection of the best prepared (those whose backgrounds, motivations, and goals are closest to the educational architects' own) or the worst prepared (those who seem most frighteningly unlike the designers). ESL, nontraditional, transfer, underprepared, or learning-disabled students can come to be considered strains on the system, contaminants in the pool of "normal" constituents; they may, on the other hand, be the target population, the uninitiated who must be converted, saved, and civilized.

At Temple we tried to move the "margins" to the center of the first-year writing program by redesigning basic writing as a challenging college-level course that would reinvigorate our standard composition course. In our writing center we employ a corps of TESOL-trained tutors to emphasize language differences as a major component of any tutoring session. Thus, we learn from those who are ordinarily the last to receive services or be considered the mainstream; we hope to avoid the common trap of calling for a diversity we secretly dread. All students benefit from such a shift because the emphasis must fall on the learning process and away from how much isolated subject material a course or a teacher can cover. Students and faculty alike can come to value what Dewey called "collateral learning" (*Experience and Education* 48), the attitudes and habits one acquires in the process of developing skills or mastering a knowledge set, because for neglected students such learning is more obvious and requires more explicit attention. We can teach in a more dynamic and democratic way if we don't teach with an idealized—and impoverished—abstract vision of our students and ourselves.

Cultivate Relationships Inside and Outside School

Dewey focused on growth in students that arises from conjoint activity drawn from specific community needs, linking the values of democracy and subject-mastery (*DE* 22). I associate this idea with Deans' focus on "writing partnerships" when he looks at case studies of three types of service learning models. Deans demonstrates that the type of writing (or conjoint activity) a teacher asks of students—whether it is with, for, or about an outside community experience, or some combination of these—also determines the type of partnership necessary to sustain the work of the course. This question of mode linked with style of partnership becomes even more crucial when we view the undertaking from a programmatic vantage point. To build writing programs that go beyond the college campus and its curriculum requires that we examine the extent of mutual benefit and understanding we have achieved in our partnerships, for that will determine the kind and quality of our projects. The more reciprocal the relationship we build with other institutions or agencies, the greater potential for the project to affect the college program as much as it affects the neighborhood center. Any college administration that mandates service learning or community participation in its writing program must recognize that this doesn't just add another wrinkle to the curriculum but alters the very relationship between town and gown.

Louise Wetherbee Phelps points out that the balance between experience and reflection is crucial to Dewey's pragmatism (73-74). As she contemplates Dewey's "method of experience" (72), she begins to picture schooling, and particularly composition instruction, as necessarily engaged beyond the classroom:

> Teachers and students alike become subjects rather than objects of reflection, so that we come to see the teacher as researcher and the student as scientist, each learning *about* written language and *with* it. Their own personal experiments with reflection and symbolic action, in and out of classroom discourses, critique knowledge about literacy and about development proposed by researchers on the basis of systematic inquiry (science). As composition moves concretely into a broader field of cultural

education (e.g., into homes, workplaces, prisons), this experimental relation is reproduced within other spheres and levels of society. (75)

This is a particularly exciting way to formulate Dewey's educational philosophy. It blurs the distinction among writing courses within, across, and beyond
college curricula because the focus is on the back-and-forth flow of reflection
and experience, wherever it may be found. This passage conjures for me an
image of radiating concentric rings in a pond on a rainy day—each individual
act of engagement in a classroom or outside one sends out widening rings of
consciousness and critique that intersect one another and reach further across
the entire plane of human engagement. But in order to follow such a vision of
experience and reflection, we in writing programs must allow the critique to
enter into our own institutional practices and question how we relate to all
partners within campus WAC programs and in ventures off campus.

     Service learning is not cheap or easy if it is to be implemented successful-
ly. In order for writing programs to incorporate community-based learning
they will need greater support and a more central place in educational planning than most colleges and universities usually afford them. But it will also
mean that we need to think about community-based learning not only from
the point of view of students and coursework but also from the point of view
of our partners in the neighborhoods themselves. For this reason, I propose
in Chapter 4 that we consider the model of community organizing developed
by Saul Alinsky during the Depression in the desperately poor Chicago
neighborhood called Back of the Yards. Alinsky's approach complements
Dewey's democratic philosophy (Dewey arrived in Chicago to teach at the
university 32 years before Alinsky started there as a student in 1926), but
Alinsky adds an element of street savvy and urgency that comes in handy
during the long struggles to make community–university partnerships work.

Continual Assessment Done Collaboratively and Imaginatively

This brings us to the fourth principle, a research-based and imaginative
approach to continuing program assessment. Kathleen Blake Yancey and
Brian Huot, in an introductory essay to an influential book on assessment
of WAC programs, claim this sort of assessment as a crucial element in the
field of composition:

> The modern, and postmodern, history of writing instruction is fueled
> by knowledgeable teachers who invite others to participate with them in
> making students the center of learning. Central to that act is assessing
> our own work with those students. (14)

Their emphasis in that introduction—and their collaborators' orientation in the whole collection—is toward "regular, systematic, and coherent" assessment (11) driven by specific research questions (9) and carried out by diverse methods (10). However, their comment about "teachers who invite others" evokes the widening set of circles in Phelps' picture of experience and reflection, and adds assessment to our obligations as partners in educational ventures wherever they occur. Yancey and Huot emphasize formative assessment—"an opportunity to learn something worth learning" (8)—rather than summative evaluation that merely judges teachers and grades students. This translates for me into a process by which we can begin to track those interactions as the rain falls on the pond. If learning is presumably going on simultaneously inside composition classrooms, in discipline-based writing-intensive courses, and at off-campus sites among people of many backgrounds and levels, then we must use our best research methods to understand this collective flow of experience and reflection, register its power, and identify its failures.

Dewey's overall vision calls not only for a particular quality of student–teacher relations, but—as Lucille McCarthy showed—a creative and labor-intensive approach to research. The same can be said for assessment. We investigate and evaluate according to the values by which we act. Dewey put a high value on moral education without allegiance to a particular doctrine. His 19th-century vocabulary—replete with quaint words such as "wholeheartedness" and "honesty"—embarrasses us today in a postmodern environment. However, such language can be translated into a concern for individual agency with a "social spirit" (Jones), Dewey's dialectical approach to the single student in the context of the group. This approach stands counter to the conservative call for greater individual responsibility among people who own little and have few prospects within the American social system, and it has a direct application to assessment.

As Kurt Spellmeyer noted, Dewey's attitude toward the measurement of learning—a quality linked to lived experience and thus never adequately measured by unchangeable standards—is antithetical to the current enthusiasm for more standardized testing as the main means of assessing both individuals and programs ("Response" 176-77). Spellmeyer does not mince words about the way standardized testing in the state of New Jersey threatens the poorest students and the schools that serve them:

> Unless my state makes significant changes in the unequal funding of its public schools, funding that starves poor school districts while engorging the ones already privileged, testing will not raise up the lowly but will help to naturalize economic disparities that grow wider every year. (178)

This specter of assessment-as-testing hangs over every program, but looms particularly over any program—college or K–12—with a sizeable population of students from underserved and economically stressed neighborhoods. Only vigorous and well-documented assessment practices have a hope of protecting students and programs from the standardized approach.

In *Democracy and Education*, Dewey indicated that schools can challenge social relations by linking the practical with the liberal arts (257). But it is not enough to assert that we are changing minds and thus affecting class structure. As Russel Durst has done in *Collision Course*, we must honor the pragmatism in American culture enough to inquire deeply into the goals students bring to the classroom and actively seek to discover if we in fact help them attain not only our goals for them by their goals for themselves (50). As McCarthy has done, we must commit ourselves to long-term and fine-grained research that will yield textured portraits of students as they pass through our programs. McCarthy, following other qualitative researchers in education, has pointed to the "transformatory power of naturalist classroom research for teachers" that "results from its encouraging them to be practitioners, researchers, and theoreticians all in one" (Fishman and McCarthy 120), and this approach can have a profound effect on the overall level of teaching in a program. Ambitious objectives like these can be terribly difficult to assess, but we cede the field to those hostile to all but the most traditional sorts of teaching and evaluation by avoiding the hard questions about programs we require students to pass through.

Dewey's conception of education places the school squarely in the social arena as one of the central functioning institutions of a culture. This seems obvious, except that educators and many others tend to picture schools in a separate sphere from work and colleges as the "ivory tower" divorced from "real life." Educators assert our importance when bond issues come up for election or a legislative committee is voting on the state university's yearly allocation, but too often we do not accept the responsibilities and obligations that follow from this claim. I agree with Deans that, compared to Freire's work, Dewey's philosophy does not seem radical (41). Yet Dewey set educators a steep challenge in his "Pedagogical Creed" when he called for schools to attend to both the "psychological and sociological sides" of the individual ("Creed" 2), to see students simultaneously as persons with unique emotions and cognitive processes but also as members of families, home communities, a national culture. Today we might add to that list both the multicultural currents and the specific global and historical circumstances that affect most students in American education. Dewey's was not a vision of weak egalitarianism or mere complicity with institutional demands. If we accept the challenges of his most inspiring words, then, in Robert Westbrook's description, we recognize that Dewey was "a more radical voice than has been generally assumed" (xiv) and that he was "radicalized by his distinctive faith in thoroughgoing democracy" (xvi). I share his commitment to a more profound democracy than our current polity allows, and this leads me to a discussion of service and access that is in many ways the impetus for writing program reforms at Temple in the last 10 years.

CROWLEY'S ATTACK ON SERVICE AND TEMPLE'S RESPONSE

Sharon Crowley weaves John Dewey's attitudes toward knowledge and experiential learning into her history of the first year writing requirement (*Composition* 163-67). She notes that Dewey had a beneficial influence on the field of composition as a whole (196-97, 273), but she suggests that an overly reductive interpretation of Dewey by progressive educators combined with the hardening ideology within Cold War rhetoric to reinforce some of the worst elements of freshman comp as it has usually been taught in American colleges (164). Hers is one of the most influential critiques of the first-year writing requirement and the "ethic of service" in the field of composition, and I introduce her work here because, quite frankly, the reforms and development of Temple's writing program benefited from our abiding but respectful disagreements with her conclusions about the place of composition in the university. I am writing for myself here and not in the name of the entire Temple composition faculty, some of whom might not agree with part or all of what I say here. I must also emphasize that I am indebted to Crowley for her ringing critiques. Her work has helped me articulate a political position explicitly designed to sustain a university writing program. In many ways I agree with her analysis of "our seedy institutional past" ("Reimagining" 192), but I oppose her recommendations for action.

Crowley holds that the immediate solution to the historical problems of first-year writing is to abolish the universal requirement. If the course would only become an elective, then we could staff it in a more reasonable and professional way, teach students who want to be there, stop mass placement testing (*Composition* 244-45), avoid complicity with a corrupt and exploitative system (240-41), and develop an elective vertical curriculum with greater academic status for the field (263). She powerfully summarizes the cavalcade of sins associated with the first-year course (241-43) and waxes hopeful and even utopian (245) about the prospects of change after doing away with obligatory freshman comp.

In my view, this misreads the central problem and doesn't so much solve anything as avoid everything. I agree with her about most of the sins, although she does get carried away when she asks: "Do we want to equip students to succeed in a culture that is devastating its natural resources, that fails to care for children, elderly, and poor people, that subjects people to verbal and physical abuse on the basis of gender, ethnicity, or sexual behavior, and that wages war on other peoples for self-serving reasons?" (248). Is she asking us to cease teaching until the society measures up fully to our criteria, no matter what motivates students to enroll? I can understand her outrage, but this overplaying of her hand reveals what I see as the major flaw in her argument. By setting up a high, even insurmountable, political standard for the teaching of writing, she can dismiss the messy work of teaching imperfectly in an imperfect world. Along the way, she obviates very real political urgencies that in my view trump the objections she raises to reforming the system we have.

The central problem for any first-year writing program is how to provide students access to academic discourse without either alienating them from their home languages or foreclosing criticism of hegemonic discourse. This problem does not fade away once students have weathered their initial year. Writing programs, by their nature, must in large measure work with the dominant uses of language in a literate culture. Writing teachers may develop critiques of the common notions of "clarity," offer alternative readings of assumed values such a "freedom" or "family," place students in off-campus sites where they will see bureaucratic language in use against disenfranchised people, but expository writing courses must contribute significantly to students' facility and sophistication with the dominant discourse or they serve little purpose in a college curriculum. What else is a canny and critical writer like Crowley teaching in her courses? Once she has set aside first-year writing as a major preoccupation of composition, Crowley imagines writing teachers in "an array of upper-division courses in creative, technical, and professional writing" as well as courses in "editing and document design" (262). Are these courses not at least as carefully designed to "equip students to succeed" as any introduction to college composition?

Crowley may call my position, as she does David Bartholomae's, "just too damn liberal" ("Reimagining" 195), but she herself has noted that a radical position cannot solve the problems she recognizes (*Composition* 235). This leads me to a second position she takes that I find unproductive for writing program design. She divides all writing pedagogy into conservative ("current-traditional") or liberal ("process") approaches (*Composition* 218-19), with a small space for radical pedagogies powerless to resist complicity with the system (235). Despite the fact that most of her history of first-year writing vilifies the "humanists" who established current-traditional practice as the universal paradigm for composition, in the conclusion she reserves her greatest sneers for liberals. She constructs them as hostile to race, class, and gender as anything but "accidental" factors (219); overly fond of the personal (220); easily duped by generic textbooks (221); and quick to blame the victim if he or she is a teacher harassed by students (223). At least conservatives are willing to look human nature squarely in the face, whereas liberals are gauzy-headed do-gooders: "While conservatives retain a healthy respect for the human proclivity to go wrong, liberals assume that individuals are either inherently good or are subject to shaping toward it by supportive environments" (219). The one apparently "laudable" trait of liberal compositionists is that they want to "empower" students, but this is too unfocused and impractical to be of much value, so that even "the most sympathetic critic of composition instruction must admit, I think, that the aim of empowering students, however worthy, is so encompassing that it can never be reached, and so vague that to articulate any usable meaning for it is nearly impossible" (234). Conservatives may hold all the cards, but liberals are apparently blithely dealing for the house with no complaint.

After the careful work Crowley has done tracing the history of failures, betrayals, and self-aggrandizement in the rise of English departments and the efflorescence of the humanist curriculum, this easy division of conservative villains, liberal scoundrels, and ineffective radicals leaves compositionists little to work with and nothing to hope for except a little higher status once we sell off the family business. What is holding us back most, in her estimation, is the "ethic of service," the idea that our students "need" us: "The discourse of needs positions composition teachers as servants of a student need that is spoken, not by students themselves, but by people speaking for powerful institutions . . . the discourse of needs interpellates composition teachers as subjects who implement the regulatory desires of the academy and the culture at large" (257). This subjectivity earns us only scorn from our academic peers, our low status a result of our lack of disciplinarity (252-4).

SITUATED LEADERSHIP AND THE NEW LONDON GROUP

It is this concept of "need" that formed one of the major themes in the article my colleagues and I published in 1997 about Temple writing program reforms. Where Crowley saw "the discourse of needs" as language that silenced students, we saw it as a challenge "to reinterpret that language, to translate needs that had been seen as deficiencies into the 'strong needs' of students to read and write critically, to reflect on how universities produce knowledge" (377). University faculty responded to this positive redefinition of need with additional support for our program, a more prominent place for writing in the English Department, and a more central role for the writing director in university-wide administrative committees. We carried out a program assessment that reinforced reforms in labor practices, instructional training, curriculum, and administrative structure. In short, we worked "to transpose the language of needs from a way of talking about student deficiencies to a way of talking about desires—what kind of writing the faculty wanted to read, what kinds of conditions students wanted for their learning" (379).

Crowley might argue that we simply had accepted a larger role enforcing the academy's desire for regulation. Indeed Tom Fox, in a clever split-screen response to our article, notes that our reform was "brought into being by the same 'discourse of student needs' that marks the history and current practice of composition in the United States" and that our article suggests that "you have to be fairly complicit" with "the system of social sorting and discipline" if a program wants "to get meaningful reform" (257). I would have to agree with Fox's analysis, at least in part. We are involved with sorting people, scrutinizing their performances, preparing them for the work force. I hope we are performing these functions with care, justice, and thought, nor do I think these are the only functions we serve, but, as Jeff Smith pointed out, we "cannot secede from the rest of the curriculum" (316), nor can we dismiss students desires to join and succeed in the economy. Clearly, there have been times when I am talking expansively about students' writing abilities at a university committee meeting, and others are nodding agreement, but I know from experience that some colleagues have a narrower, less libratory purpose in their support for our program. They are reinterpreting my remarks, just as I do theirs. My solace in these circumstances is that, for the time being, the definitions that underlie most of what actually goes on in our classrooms, conferences, and tutorial sessions come primarily from faculty and staff I trust and not from those who would like to see a return to drill, traditional modes, and sterile humanism.

I believe we are teaching reflective and critical processes as we are working to give the greatest number of students the best access we can to benefits the university may provide them. In this I agree with the approach Russel Durst calls "reflective instrumentalism," in which a writing program "accepts students' pragmatic goals, offers to help them achieve their goals, but adds a reflective dimension that, while itself useful in the work world, also helps students place their individual aspirations in the larger context necessary for critical analysis" (178). Durst emphasizes the necessity of listening closely to the desires and expectations of students in writing classes, and trying to develop curricula that take into account the mismatches between students' and teachers' understanding of what should go on in a writing course. He doesn't call for dumbing down the curriculum or following a strict vocationalism, but he does urge us "to show greater respect in composition pedagogy—and find a place in our course designs—for the more instrumentalist orientation of most of our students" (176). In this argument, Durst invokes Dewey as a thoughtful ally (175-176), in opposition to Spellmeyer's use of Dewey as an opponent of instrumentalism (*Common Ground* 12).

We can honor students' desires while still recognizing the complexity of rhetorical and literate practice in contemporary American culture if we are inclusive rather than exclusive about what connects a writing program to its university and its surrounding region. In this way, I agree with Crowley's discouraging words about first-year writing, for I believe we should not build our profession or our programs solely on one initial course in the most bewildering moment of a student's career. We are better off conceiving of writing programs that function throughout the undergraduate experience and into the graduate years as well, contextualizing that program with service learning, internships, publishing projects, public debates, anything to give literacy the life it loses in isolated classrooms.

In his book about higher education reform, Richard Miller remarks that "those truly committed to increasing access to all the academy has to offer must assume a more central role in the bureaucratic management of the academy" (46). Although I may have less faith than he in the efficacy of bureaucratic management to accomplish improvements in higher education, I do agree that we must not only complain but act within the power structure of the university and its surrounding community if we are to produce meaningful change for students' lives. In a postscript to our 1997 writing reform article, I called for reconfiguring the "ethic of service" into a conception of "situated leadership," which would commit Writing Program Administrators (WPAs) and their allies to enact three functions (Sullivan et al. 389):

1. Participate in university, college, and departmental policy decisions as much as possible,
2. Advocate for rich and reflective literacy instruction both inside and outside the university,
3. Articulate the intellectual implications of curricular and pedagogical choices from the diverse points of views within our professions.

These three functions have, in the intervening years, grown into the principles I outlined in my discussion of Dewey. As to the first function, in the years following our program reform I averaged at least 18 committees a year and led an effort to reform the university-wide core curriculum in 2002-2003. My composition/rhetoric colleagues also took on added university, college, and departmental responsibilities. This participation gave our composition group both a greater perspective on university policy and procedure as well as more exposure to players in and out of the institution we would never have known had we remained within the confines of the English Department or the traditional WAC program. The second function led us to redefine WAC in such a way that it factored in new developments in service learning, community literacy, neighborhood arts initiatives, and the conditions of learning in the city schools. This brought us to conceive of the notion of WBC.

The third function led us to take assessment as a serious element of research for everyone associated with the writing program, so that we rededicated our intellectual energies to the investigation of writing, writing pedagogy, and the rhetorical situation of literacy learners. To some extent, composition and rhetorical theorists like Crowley sound apologetic, almost convinced by the critiques of academic colleagues that composition is merely "low" work (254). We decided to embrace the picaresque "worm's eye perspective" of our historical narrative position and wear our motley disciplinary rags with honor. No other field can study the literacies found in academia, compare and contrast them with the literacies of neighborhoods and boardrooms, and still develop a direct intervention on the phenomena we study. If this is not quite the "disinterested pursuit of knowledge" that Crowley correctly identifies as the approach of disciplines rewarded with academic status in the past (254), then I accept our differences with them. The advantages of the perspective we gain by remaining not quite a discipline but very much a force outweigh the frustrations of being judged wanting by some academic colleagues.

Hoping to foster an attitude of situated leadership inside and outside the university, Parks and I published "Writing beyond the Curriculum" in 2000. There we outlined the approach we have taken since the reforms of the mid-1990s at Temple and called for an expansion of the WAC approach. In the years that the Temple program has become a unified entity—gathering together and linking basic and introductory writing, writing in the disciplines, a writing center, and various outreach and assessment efforts—Steve and I came to realize that the conception of a writing program had to be revised to account for all the centripetal and centrifugal forces at work on the people, curricula, and administrative structure involved. We were writing grants that funded more traditional services like a peer tutoring program and more unusual structures like a literacy network that linked adult basic education programs, community arts organizations, local schools, the writing center, and Temple courses. That article described our Institute for the Study of Literature, Literacy, and Culture (now called New City Writing), which has grown even more productive and engaged since we published the piece. We were writing there to clarify for ourselves what we were doing, and the conclusion we came to was that we were pursuing a vision of literacy that had its roots in the lives we and our families led in the city of Philadelphia.

Susan McLeod and Elaine Maimon published an article alongside our piece in the same issue of *College English*. They wrote there about the core values and objectives in the WAC movement that they helped to found in the early 1970s. Their rejection of the "myths" about WAC as well as their reaffirmation of its "realities" suggest that in our article we are not so much claiming to found a new movement as we are urging writing programs to be more of what they have long hoped to be: agents for pedagogical change, advocates for writing as an active intellectual pursuit, facilitators for interchange and challenge across the disciplines, leaders in the effort to assess educational programs using meaningful qualitative and quantitative methods (McLeod & Maimon 580-81). Although we intended in our article to push writing programs toward a more activist orientation than even critical pedagogy calls for, we were pleased to see this spirit reaffirmed as central to the WAC movement by McLeod and Maimon. They point out that WAC has historically worked its profound transformations within the educational system through grassroots involvement rather than through direct confrontation (578).

Yet there are new elements to what we are proposing, elements that go beyond Dewey and the traditions of WAC, although they probably don't violate the spirit of either. In closing this chapter, I would like to circle back to the New London group, the work I referred to earlier when I discussed Dewey's position on diversity and assimilation. I have no space here to touch on their very productive suggestions about a pedagogy based on design, but I think their vision of a future for schooling and work based on multiliteracies is challenging indeed for the field of composition/rhetoric. Bill Cope and Mary Kalantzis put the challenge starkly to literacy educators who are "both inheritors of patterns and conventions of meaning while at the same time active designers of meaning. And, as designers of meaning, we are designers of social futures—workplace futures, public futures, and community futures" (7). We must look closely at who our students are, what their futures will demand of them, and what sort of meaning-making will lead to equitable and productive social relations within that collective future.

Cope and Kalantzis identify two "related aspects of textual multiplicity" (5) that led the New London group to develop their concept of multiliteracy. The first has to do with the broad and constantly shifting diversity of representations not only in traditional language but also in television and film, Web-based communications, advertising, the arts, and bodily gesture. They argue that focusing primarily on a print-based standard national language must inevitably "translate into a more or less authoritarian kind of pedagogy." Thus, they call for any literacy instruction to be multimodal and dynamic, "where the textual is also related to the visual, the audio, the spatial, the behavioral and so on" (5). The second aspect they focus on is that "something paradoxical is happening to English":

> At the same time as it is becoming a *lingua mundi*, a world language, and a *lingua franca*, a common language of global commerce, media and politics, English is also breaking into multiple and increasingly differentiated Englishes, marked by accent, national origin, subcultural style and professional or technical communities. Increasingly the name of the game in English is crossing linguistic boundaries. (6)

This situation necessitates a new approach to language learning because the old idea of a stable and standard language is at odds with the swirl of local language practice one encounters at every turn.

For a writing program, especially one located in a metropolitan university, these two aspects of multiliteracies present daunting pressures on an already overburdened system. We struggle to provide enough classes and qualified teachers for just the entering students, let alone adequately oversee advanced writing courses in more and more specialties. We underpay adjuncts and overwork teaching assistants (TAs). We don't offer enough support to faculty in the disciplines who are supposed to teach writing, and we can hardly say with confidence that all students are graduating with the minimum skills to succeed in their first jobs. And now the New London group is telling us we fail to account for a changing multimodal media environment as well as a hopelessly fractured English? Surely this is a cause for the gnashing of teeth and the rending of clothes.

This book by no means solves the dilemma set by New London group, or perhaps any dilemma at all. It says too little about computers and multimedia, and merely begins to address the issues raised by the multiple ways our students have of speaking English. It should say more about what students do AFTER they leave college, but that would be yet another book. What I hope the next chapters accomplish is to investigate the conditions on which we will build a new approach to literacy in college settings by asking who our students are and where they come from, how they perform when they enter and move through our system, and what environments off the campus would best present literacy in truly equitable circumstances. I suggest a pathway, a direction for writing programs to take toward the future that the New London group as well as students from Philly high schools and adults in neighborhood literacy centers are hammering on our heads to recognize and respond to. The WAC tradition and Dewey's legacy of progressive education provide us a past to build on, but we must go beyond their admirable lessons to meet the vexing present and the miasmic future before us. The wind whips the raindrops in all directions on that pond in Phelps' model of experience and reflection, but we have to row out into the weather nonetheless.

At Temple, we hope that improvements to the literacy environment of North Philadelphia will emerge from greater involvement and participation by faculty, staff, students, and Philadelphia citizens in, as Dewey would say, "joint activity, where one person's use of material and tools is consciously referred to the use other persons are making of their capacities and appliances" (*Democracy and Education* 39). As the graffiti I quote in the beginning of the chapter suggests, such activity is not innocent of conflict and compromise, power struggles, and historical distrust. I undertook to write this book, as Steve and I wrote the earlier article, to help make sense of what we have been doing in the Temple writing program over the last 10 years. The chapters that follow indicate what we are beginning to learn, and what more we must still learn, about this new but not unfamiliar direction we have taken.

2

Continuity and Control

A university like Temple is part of a system of schools, neighborhoods, and community colleges. Every college bodies forth its history and the history of the people who pass through its sphere, but a large metropolitan institution grows and changes with its region in a way that most private schools tend to resist. Even at Temple, however, we do not always actively account for regional pressures or historical forces that come to bear on our instructional, curricular, or administrative decisions. In this chapter and the following two, I consider sectors of regional life that have direct and indirect impact on our writing program. I wanted to know more about the schools that send us significant numbers of students, and to develop out of this new perspective recommendations for our program and others like us that have strong ties to communities in a region. The next chapter takes up the question of community colleges in the area, and the subsequent chapter will look at university–community partnerships in literacy-related projects.

In Fall 1995, 42% of all Temple students came from Philadelphia County. By 2001, that number was down to 34%, but Philly students still remain a significant portion of our student population. Over these years, the suburban population from other schools—public, private and parochial—in the four Pennsylvania counties surrounding the city has held steady at about 32%. The decrease in Philadelphia school graduates came in part as a result of an increase in students from other Pennsylvania counties as near as Lancaster and as far away as Pittsburgh's Allegheny, from Mid-Atlantic and New

England states, and from the rest of the United States and an array of more than 60 countries. In short, Temple became a more cosmopolitan center in those 6 years, but the five-county area of Philadelphia still accounted for almost two-thirds of the total student body in recent years. From 1995 to 2000, an average of 5% of all college-bound high school graduates in the five-county region enrolled at Temple for their first year of college.

In Fall 2001, I began to look at Temple data on entering local students, sorted by their high schools of origin, and certain trends became apparent to me even if the reasons for those trends grew less obvious the more I contemplated them. Perhaps to the surprise of no one, students from wealthier areas did better in our university than students from poorer ones. But why does this disparity occur? What are we doing about it? And are we making the transition to college writing productive and enlightening to all our students? I realized after a short time with the data that I didn't know enough about the schools our students came from, had not been in the buildings or met their former teachers or visited the neighborhoods. I thought I knew Philadelphia pretty well, having lived here for nearly 20 years at that point, having taught high school and college here, having worked at various odd jobs before a career in teaching, and having participated in a number of political campaigns across the city. But now I felt ignorant and foolish, staring at the numbers as though they were the prophetic entrails of animals I had neglected to admire when they were alive. What could these numbers tell me, and to what larger stories could they lead?

Like Mike Rose in his book *Possible Lives*, I hope to contribute to what he calls a "capacious critique" of public education:

> one that does not minimize the inadequacies of curriculum and instruction, the rigidity of school structure, or the "savage inequalities" of funding, but that simultaneously opens up discursive space for inspired teaching, for courage, for achievement against odds, for successful struggle, for the insight and connection that occur continually in public school classrooms around the country. (4)

Like Rose, I decided to visit schools in a spirit of cooperation and openness. In my case, however, I wanted to learn specifically about the schools from which a great many of Temple students come. I recognized that I could not understand writing at Temple if I did not develop some familiarity with the schools that surround us. Regional schools—urban and suburban, public and Catholic—seemed a set of institutions I needed to know better.

Readers may reasonably object that much of the data I present in this chapter is simply not news. When my wife saw this data, she asked me: "Isn't this intuitively obvious?" My son, with the solemn patience of an adolescent to an obtuse father, said: "Dad, are you saying that poor kids go to

bad schools and rich kids go to good schools?" Both of them were absolutely right to warn me that data about urban and suburban schools will surprise
no one, and the sheer obviousness has sometimes frightened me into doubt-
ing the entire project. Yet I keep coming back to the obvious as something
the larger social and political movements of our day barely recognize and
seldom act on. As one of my wisest friends, educational law activist Len
Reisser, remarked to me about the tragedy inherent in my data: "This may
all be intuitively obvious, but what may not be so obvious is why we let such
conditions go on without doing something about them." College teachers
and administrators need to be reminded again that the "playing field" is far
from level for students entering college and that we have a responsibility to
take this fact into account when we design curriculum, train teachers, and
formulate K–16 initiatives. Perhaps more important for writing programs,
we need to understand this diversity as more than a story of deficit but as a
challenge for creating course sequences, school and community partnerships, and support systems that will help students from every point along
the spectrum of entering students. Most of the data and observations in this
chapter raise more questions then they answer, but perhaps questions are
what we most need.

AN OVERVIEW OF REGIONAL SCHOOLS

From an original data set of the 97 largest feeder schools in the region over
the period from 1995 to 2000, I chose 33 schools to include in my initial
investigation of how area first-year students make the transition into college
writing at Temple. These represent a range of schools that send significant
numbers of students to the university. The list included 13 Philadelphia public schools, 8 suburban public schools from three different counties, and 14
Catholic Archdiocese schools (some co-educational and some single-gender
enrollment). It included both comprehensive high schools and magnet
schools in the school district of Philadelphia, and schools from all the major
sections of the city (west, south, north, northeast, and northwest). I did not
include charter schools in this study because there are still relatively few
graduates of these new, small quasi-autonomous schools, and their graduates
have not been at Temple long enough to track them adequately. I also did
not include in this study private Catholic, Quaker, or secular schools; they
are highly selective and tend to focus their placement efforts on private colleges and universities (13 students from private, non-Catholic schools in the
Philadelphia area enrolled in Fall 2001 out of 3,334 first-year students that
year). Indeed, the geography of language arts education in the public, charter, parochial, and private schools of the Philadelphia area is quite varied and

probably deserves a book-length study of its own, but for my purposes I wanted a manageable group whose data I could analyze and from which I could draw a smaller list of schools to visit intensively.

For each school and category of school—city public, suburban public, city Catholic, suburban Catholic—I chose three measures between 1995-2000 that would indicate or describe students' transition to college. These measures were as follows:

- Average grade point average (GPA) of students in their first Fall semester.
- Percentage of students who did not return to school in the Fall semester following their entering year.
- Percentage of students who placed into basic writing.

These struck me as measures that might indicate general high school preparation, ability to handle the transition during the initial shock of entering college, and financial or emotional support available for students' staying in school.

I could see, of course, that no numerical data would untangle the complicated web of causation that surrounds the ultimate academic success or failure of a college student. These numbers cannot tell us what happened in specific class sessions to particular individuals or track interactions among students or between a given student and his teacher. We can't know from this level of study whether one person left because he or she couldn't pay the tuition, another couldn't pass calculus, or a third could no longer stand to live at home and so dropped out to pay for an apartment. However, we can make some general observations about student populations that may serve as an opening point for further investigation with a smaller subset. These observations turn out to be intuitively obvious in some ways, and yet they remain striking to me. They are well worth considering in some detail before we proceed to a finer look at a school–university literacy continuum.

One more note before we consider each of these three factors in turn. I divide the city public schools into two distinct subgroups based primarily on enrollment patterns. Over a 6-year period, from 1995 to 2000, the 13 representative schools drawn from the school district of Philadelphia sent 2,084 students to Temple. Of these students, 1,526 (73%) were graduates of five schools: three magnet schools and two comprehensive high schools in the northeast section of the city. The magnet schools are relatively selective, put a high premium on school performance, and draw students from families with a higher socioeconomic status (SES) than many other city schools; an average of 47% of students from magnet schools in this study are classified as low income (according to Pennsylvania Department of Education's figures for 1999–2000), as opposed to the district average of 76%. The two schools in the northeast I chose share a similar SES profile with the magnet schools (46% and 45%) and are somewhat selective in the students they take from outside their home area. Thus, I grouped these five as one distinct category of feeder schools.

Of the 33 schools I studied, the balance of Temple first-year students who came from district schools in 1995-2000 (556 or 27%) graduated from 8 other comprehensive high schools scattered throughout the city. These schools sent us on average many fewer students per school than the magnet/northeast group (69.8 over the 5-year period as opposed to 305.2 from the magnet/northeast group). The SES profile of each school varies more within this group than in the magnet/northeast group; the poorest school in the group has 87% of its students classified as low income while the lowest percentage of low income is 62% (again with a District-wide average of 76%) but all together the average of this group (75%) is 29.3 percentage points lower than the magnet/northeast group. As we look further, it becomes clear that that these two groups perform differently along the other chosen indicators as well.

FIRST-YEAR GPA AND RETENTION

Figure 2.1A and 2.1B represent a comparison of median GPAs for each school category after the first semester at Temple. City schools, both Catholic and public, do less well than the other categories of schools. The averages, of course, reflect more than ability in writing, for they represent grades in all the students' subjects. Early GPA need not be a predictor of later performance in classes, but it probably does indicate something about both the preparedness of students for college work and their ability to make the adjustment to the demands of college-style note-taking, studying, and time management.

As with all other considerations in this chapter, however, other factors may rival preparedness as a causal factor in GPA. In an in-house study done on the Temple class that entered in 1996, Jim Degnan and Tim Walsh suggest a number of economic and emotional factors that were likely causes for students to leave the university in addition to poor academic performance at Temple and poor academic preparation. Their list includes failure to establish a sense of belonging at the university, poor study habits, dissatisfaction with aspects of the Temple experience, working at a job too many hours, and stressful family situations. Clearly, economics matters a great deal; students who worked more than 25 hours a week persisted at a rate of only 32%, whereas students who work less than 20 hours a week persisted at a rate of 60%. Students who reported family earnings of less than $15,000 persisted

Fig. 2.1A and 2.1B. Comparing first semester grade point averages (1995-2000).

Category	First GPA
City Comp	2.34
City Catholic	2.58
Magnet Northeast	2.80
Suburb Catholic	2.80
Suburb Public	2.89

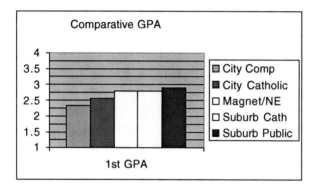

at a rate of 47% whereas students who reported a family income of at least $45,000 persisted at a rate of 58%. In general, Degnan and Walsh say that students "who reported that most of their first year expenses would be met by their parents were more likely to persist than student who reported that they would have to provide for themselves" (4). These statistical observations match the anecdotal evidence from Temple writing instructors, the teachers most likely to get to know their students personally in that first semester. They often note that students who struggle the most in their classes are often also the most on the edge financially, work the longest hours at their jobs, and have the hardest time finding reliable access to a computer for school work.

Another major factor in overall college performance at Temple may be the significant number of first-generation (FG) college students in the population. In the period from 1997 to 2001, more than 40% of first-year students reported that their fathers had received no more than a high school education; the average is only slightly lower for students whose mothers had no college education. As Anne Penrose noted in a review of the literature on FG college students, parents' education may or may not be a factor for academic achievement by those students who persist, but it is implicated in the differences for retention and for students' sense of belonging in a college setting between FG students and their peers who come from college-educated families. It may be that emotional factors mentioned by Degnan and Walsh, such as developing a sense of belonging and appreciating the Temple college experience, may be related to parents' educational background.

A factor that may indicate even more strongly the financial character of the transition from high school to college is the rate at which Temple students return to classes in their second year. Figures 2.2A and 2.2B suggest a general separation between city and suburban students in return rates, with the exception that students from the magnet/northeast schools have rates closer to suburban public schools, and suburban Catholic schools have a lower rate of return than do their public school neighbors. My experience with visits to both magnet schools and northeast high schools suggests to me that students from those schools are among the most motivated students to enter Temple, often coming from immigrant or minority families of modest means but tremendous drive to move up socially and economically. In trips to these schools, I met a number of African-American, Ukrainian, and East Asian students who were at the top of their classes and strongly compelled to succeed in school, and career; Temple was a top choice for them because their parents did not want them to leave the city and could not afford to send

Fig. 2.2A and 2.2B. Percentage of students not returning in the fall semester after their initial enrollment.

Category	% Not Returning
City Comp	30%
City Catholic	26%
Suburban Catholic	20%
City Magnet Northeast	17%
Suburb Public	15%

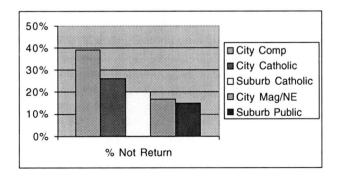

them to more expensive private schools in the area. This is an area for more research, but the data leave us with some important questions in academic policy. How can we link financial aid counselors more closely to academic advisors or instructors? How can lower-income students avail themselves of services and supports that come ready-to-hand for middle-class students? Can writing programs in particular help address retention problems in crucial ways?

One should note that many Temple students do not "drop out" as much as "stop out" of school. They also "swirl," meaning they may leave Temple to attend one or another community college in the area and then return to finish, or they may bounce back and forth from Temple to other schools before they finish or leave off their undergraduate studies. I have more to say about this phenomenon in Chapter 3, but to underline this point I mention that, in the Degnan and Walsh study of the students who left the class of 2000, 48% of the people on which they had transfer records went to a community college after leaving Temple. This suggests that there may well have been both economic and an educational preparation factors involved in their leaving the university.

When I see low GPAs and high failure-to-return rates, I remember a student I taught at Temple in a basic writing class a few years ago. An African-American man who recently graduated from a Philadelphia public high school, Scott was clearly one of the brightest students in the class during the first few weeks of the semester. His writing was ambitious but underdeveloped. Our first conference lasted longer than usual because we talked first about his high school experience in the city, the possibilities in his paper, and then about his intellectual interests in liberal arts as well as his vocational aspirations in business and computer science. But soon after this first paper he began to miss classes, and when he finally showed up again he said he had been very sick. Later he told me that his family had somehow been forced to leave their home—he was vague as to whether it was because of fire or finances. At the end of the semester he managed to turn in only an incomplete final portfolio, and he explained to me that he could not do much homework because he was squatting in a house until he could find a better place to live. Scott never showed up on days when I had hoped to talk to him about his work, and in the end I had to fail him without ever talking to him about what had become of his semester. I have no way of knowing if his stories to me were true, but I can assure you that, on the strength of the writing I did see from him and the two long conferences we had, the problem was not that he wasn't capable, or even unprepared, to fulfill the academic demands of the course. Scott remains merely a statistic in the 1995–2000 data, but his story persists in my mind; we cannot dismiss the nearly 40% rate of attrition among city school graduates as merely a matter of unsuccessful high school preparation for college.

PLACEMENT IN BASIC WRITING

The First-Year Writing Program at Temple consists of two courses and ESL versions of each course. Over the 8-year period from 1989-1996, approximately 38% of entering students were placed in basic writing courses, mostly in a remedial course entitled ELECT. In 1996-1997, we instituted a reorganized curriculum and placement process to bring basic writing, renamed and reconceived as English 40, into greater coordination with English 50, the introduction to composition most other students take. At the same time, we were streamlining and rationalizing our program, the admissions office was effecting a rise in average SAT combined scores of around 10 points each year; thus the entering classes were probably getting somewhat stronger academically over the years 1997–2000. In that 4-year period, we averaged about a 30% placement rate into basic writing.

What do placement rates tell us about the students who enter a school or about the high schools that prepared them for college? The traditional approach is to see basic writing as remedial and thus to see student placement as a measure of the failure or success of high schools to give students the training they need for college academic demands. In recent years, the emphasis in basic writing circles has been away from a remediation model and more toward a transitional approach that gives students the opportunity to understand writing as communication and discovery rather than performance and mannered submission to the authority of the teacher (see Enos as a collection that represents this sea change). English 40 certainly follows this latter direction, and we have some data that suggests that it is doing a better job than the previous ELECT course to prepare students for later courses. But a transition is a bridge from somewhere to somewhere, and as I stared at the data summarized in Fig. 2.3A and 2.3B I began to wonder what the numbers really told us. The years covered by Fig. 2.3, 1995–2000, represent a year of ELECT, a year of change to the new curriculum of English 40 and placement, and 3 years of the new approach.

Unlike the data in Fig. 2.2A and 2.2B, this data tends to link all city school students as needing more transition than those students from both Catholic and public suburban schools. Even the magnet/Northeast students place into basic writing at rates closer to the 1989–1996 placement average (38%), whereas students from both types of suburban schools place into 40 at nearly the 1997–2000 average (30%). Is the phenomenon here similar to the dynamic Shirley Brice Heath identified 30 years ago, when she noted that the middle-class students in her study seemed more accustomed to the cognitive tasks set by schooling than did their poor and working-class peers? I cannot answer the question of causation here, but I can suggest that we address the situation with a more systemic approach than we have heretofore.

Fig. 2.3A and 2.3B. Placement of first-year students in English 40 (basic writing).

Category	% in English 40
City Comp	63%
City Catholic	41%
City Magnet Northeast	37%
Suburb Catholic	31%
Suburb Public	31%

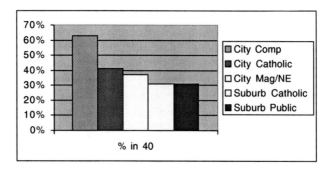

I began thinking that we do no one any good by mourning the 63% placement rate for city public students in English 40. In fact, if we claim that the English 40 and 50 course sequence is a worthwhile college experience—we attach college credit to the courses and require students to take them—then we need to view all composition placements as part of a positive effort to make a partnership with schools to educate students along a literacy continuum. We can think of students placed in English 40 as people who need a full year of college composition rather than one semester to reach a level of comfort and familiarity with academic discourse. There are those, of course, who suggest that universities should not be in the business of educating anyone who needs a full year of college composition, that the investment is just too great and that community colleges should do this work if any institutions should do it at all. But I would answer that the beauty of a school like Temple is its fortunate position as a gathering point for the diversity that most schools talk about but cannot sustain. Yes, there may be students who need a more developmental approach and would do better starting in a community college, but experience suggests that a good many students need a transitional course in the beginning of their college careers but then can go on successfully in the 4- or 5-year program offered at Temple. For compositionists, the numbers in charts such as these represent the greatest challenge for sustaining true economic and social diversity in postsecondary education.

The history of admissions at Temple in the last 20 years is instructive on the question of diversity as well. Temple suffered two faculty strikes, one in the mid-1980s and one in 1990. For the years leading up to the second strike, Temple had maintained a population composed of a wide range of students, primarily drawn from the region but encompassing poor African Americans from North Philadelphia as well as wealthy Caucasians from the outlying school districts. When the second strike occurred, applications from the suburbs dropped precipitously and the number of suburban freshman that year fell by half. The admissions office, at the prompting of the university president at the time, responded by taking many more students from the most stressed urban schools, but this put a greater burden on the remedial and support system and reinforced the fear in the suburbs that Temple was "lowering its standards." Many of those underprepared urban students admitted did not persist to graduation. Over the last years of the 1990s, however, Temple began to attract more out-of-state students who wanted a school with an urban environment—after all, not everyone could get into and pay for New York University or Columbia—and, when the economy started seeming shakier and high tuitions looked less appealing, the number of applicants from outside the metropolitan area began to pick up. Suddenly, Temple admissions could increase its average SAT scores from a steady average of 990 over the years 1991 to 1996 to 1,012 in 1997 and 1,046 by 2001. By 2004 that average was up to nearly 1,090.

I fear this kind of trend will exclude students from all but a few city schools, and pleading to administrators to uphold the traditional Temple mission is not persuasive enough. However, even administrators driven by SAT numbers and tuition dollars can see that the university must draw a mixed population, partly because of our geographical setting and partly because the university cannot compete with Penn, Villanova, Swarthmore, or even Penn State for the bulk of the students in suburban areas. For all the demographic shifts, Temple has a reputation for training FG college students—Black, White, Asian, Latino—either for their full college careers or for their last undergraduate years. Economics could shift again, small liberal arts colleges could come again into vogue and cities become passé, but the strength of a school like Temple is in the abiding fact that it educates such a range of people.

What became clear to me, as I lived with this data and thought about admission shifts in the university, is that writing at Temple could not be an isolated step in a mechanical process. We could develop the best possible first-year courses, train teachers with the best mentors and the most thought-provoking articles in the field, but if our classrooms remain mere way-stations, disconnected from what has come before or what will confront students afterward, then we are doing little more than practicing a more efficient way to tighten a single bolt on an assembly line. Perhaps, after all, we deserve those shrill attacks on us from teachers in the major who complain we didn't "fix" their students' writing in the first year. Their complaints make sense if we continue to frame what we do as a value-added function independent of other literacy experiences in and out of school. Even when we ask students to write about their lives, their home neighborhoods, their histories as writers and readers, the first-year course itself stands on a hill with other college courses taught by instructors whose allegiance is to a university employer, not a region. But what if writing administrators, instructors, and students understood writing across the levels of instruction? What if our program were designed to take into account the types and varieties of instruction students received in the high schools from which they graduated and the neighborhoods out of which they grew? Would a more textured understanding of literacy education in the region help us improve our program or reframe it in productive ways? My next step along the way was to learn what I could about the schools in our region and how their students were doing at Temple.

VISITING SCHOOLS

At first glance, the data I have already presented suggests that students from different schools of origin are relatively distinct in their academic performance once they come to college. A large part of the motivation for this next phase involved discovering what was truly distinctive about these schools and what was a common element in high schools where Temple students come from. I visited a set of schools as a way of looking more closely at what students and teachers do in English classrooms in preparation for college writing and reading. I also hoped to initiate conversation with high school English teachers about what further relationship the university and schools might develop. Of the schools I visited, I chose five to highlight and two to describe in detail here.

First of all, it is clear from looking at Fig. 2.4A that a grave disparity exists among the schools. Practically everyone graduates from Fields High School, a predominantly White suburban school north of Philadelphia. St. Mary's is also a largely White middle-class school, although it draws from a more diverse population base than other suburban schools in its county, and their graduation rate is comparably high (no official data was available to me for this study). Boulevard has an extremely diverse student population of White ethnic minorities, African-American, East Asian, and Korean students. There is a significant difference between the entering and graduating classes, but not nearly as severe as at other District schools. At the same, time North and Somerset high schools—both in poor neighborhoods near

Fig. 2.4A and 2.4B. Five schools compared.

School	Total Average 1995-2000	% Low Income 1999-2000	% No Return	% in English 40	First GPA	PSSA Reading 1999-2000	12th/9th Ratio 1999-2000
Boulevard HS	243	45.2	15	45	2.81	1,150	543/910 = .60
Fields HS	126	7.2	17	23	2.89	1,320	855/853 = 1.0
North HS	63	85.0	30	58	2.41	1,030	212/950 = .22
Somerset HS	45	86.7	49	63	2.54	1,010	439/1341 = .33
St. Mary's HS	62	not available	16	30	2.84	not available	Not available
Phila School District Ave		76.4	29	49	2.53	1,130	9997/20098= .50
All TU Freshman		State Average 31.1	27	35	2.68	State Average 1,300	

GPA, grade point average; PSSA, Pennsylvania System of School Assessment; TU, Temple University

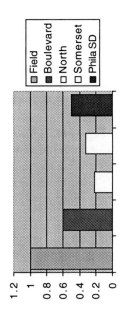

12th/9th   Ratio   1999-2000

47

Temple, the former almost entirely African American and the latter mostly Latino—lose an appalling number of students between Grades 9 and 12. They are hardly the only schools in the District with such a frightening difference between Grades 9 and 12 (witness the 50% difference between the two classes district-wide), but a graduating class one-fourth or even one-third the size of the entering class is a sign of a distressing problem, practically an educational genocide in certain sections of the city. Similarly, the first GPA of students at Temple from Fields is nearly a half a grade higher than the GPA for students who graduated from North. As I have said, this may have something significant to do with working to pay for college, but combined with the differences between the schools in the state reading test results and the placement rates in basic writing, I can be pretty confident in saying Fields students are more prepared for academic writing in college than their counterparts from Somerset or North. In perhaps the most dramatic difference between schools in this study, the percentage of students classified as low income at Fields is almost 80 points lower than the percentage at Somerset. Thus, when we think about the entering class of Temple students, we confront the gaps and injustices of American society generally.

But this picture becomes a bit more focused (if no less complex) when we consider who decides to attend Temple from these schools. Only among students from Boulevard is Temple a common first-choice school. There, and at other northeast Philadelphia schools, when I asked a classroom full of advanced placement (AP) or rapid-track English students how many of them applied to Temple, nearly every student raised her or his hand. In a school like Boulevard, a number-one ranked student in the graduating class who gets into University of Pennsylvania and Temple is quite likely to choose Temple, partly because of finances and partly because more of his or her family and friends already go there. Many of the students at Boulevard come from immigrant families that left the former Soviet Union, India, or Pakistan. These families discourage their children from applying to schools out of town; for them Temple is ideal.

Some St. Mary's students probably choose Temple for its large Catholic population (a typical entering class for the last 20 years is between 16% and 20% Catholic; only LaSalle, among Philadelphia schools, is better at attracting working-class Catholic students). St. Mary's draws primarily from a suburban county, however, and is therefore more like Fields in sending Temple fewer of its top-ranked students. The highest ranked students from North or Somerset may or may not be admitted to Temple at all, or may enter through a special admissions program, but many college-bound students from those schools choose to go to community college first before attempting a 4-year school. Others choose to go to the small state schools in central or northeast Pennsylvania, schools where faculty teach more and are not rewarded for research, schools that recruit rather heavily in the Black and Latino communities of Philadelphia because otherwise their student population would be almost exclusively white. According to a New Student Questionnaire (NSQ) that Temple administers to first-year students in the Fall, over the 5 years between 1997 and 2001, an average of nearly 42% of entering students report that Temple was not their first-choice school, and we can guess that that percentage is somewhat larger for students who come from the area and regard this university as their "home" school, with all the affection and ambivalence that label implies.

This is not to say that a Temple entering class is full of disgruntled, resistant, or apprehensive students. On the contrary, they are optimistic about their future. Responding to the NSQ in the last 5 years, more than 96% of entering students report that they expect to earn a B or better GPA in college, 99% say they expect to be satisfied with Temple, and more than 98% expect to find a job in their chosen field. Students come with a wide range of preparation, coaching, support, and fore-knowledge about what college will be, but they mostly seem excited to be here at the start. However, going beyond even the arguments Bartholomae, Bizzell, and others have made over the years about initiating students into academic discourse, the demographics at a school like Temple make it imperative that we provide a learning environment where students can acclimatize themselves to college reading and writing and to the speaking and listening habits of each other. An associate dean from an Ivy League school once confided to me at a conference in 1998: "We have a writing program at our school. It's called the admissions office." That struck me as cruel but honest at the time, although since then his school has put new resources into a writing program, following a new trend in the Ivies and other elite schools. Schools like Temple, however, must solve the crucial American problem of how to educate a rich mix of people who share an enthusiasm for "getting ahead" (if not for "advanced learning") but who bring to the classroom a bewildering and intriguing array of skills and background knowledge.

Contrary to the bad reputation teachers get in the American press, most of the teachers I met in the schools I visited seemed to like being in the classroom. At Boulevard, St. Mary's, and Fields I had a greater sense of regularized professional life—faculty acting as part of an overall plan, working with students who moved in an orderly fashion from class to class and, in due time, on to college. Nearly every teacher I met at those three schools was knowledgeable, self-assured, and comfortable with the kids, and some were among the most organized and thoughtful teachers I have ever witnessed in a classroom.

At Somerset and North teachers seemed more sensitive to the public perception of teachers as not doing their jobs, not competent at their subject matter, not caring about the children. I saw no teachers who fit the public's stereotype of the burned out or intimidated teacher, and I met a number who had worked out effective courses for their kids, kept a decent classroom decorum, and clearly enjoyed most of the students. At North, the most stressed school I visited, English teachers expressed enthusiasm for their jobs and commitment to the kids, although all of them spoke also of how difficult conditions were and how far they felt their students had to go to be prepared for college. The department chair at North described her English staff as "dedicated, intelligent, and compassionate." Teachers at North tended to frame their work in more political terms than any of the other schools' teachers, whereas teachers at Somerset seemed to talk about developments in their curriculum as personal triumphs. On one visit, the department chair at North told me that teachers in the English office had been in tears that morning because a newspaper article had suggested that the central administration might not replace 500 retiring teachers in the district. These were not people who did not care. They felt acutely their short-handed conditions and the great needs of their students, the lower pay they received compared to peers in the suburbs, the competent principals who jumped to outlying school districts, and the general hostility toward city teachers among the newspaper-reading public.

Every school follows certain principles for how to divide students into classes. Fields, Boulevard, and St. Mary's have highly explicit tracking systems. Students are sorted early, know what track they are on, and seem to take up the behavioral patterns and expectations of those tracks. Teachers, of course, are well aware of the track labels too. In all three of these schools I heard much talk about the appropriate books for college preparatory, rapid, or AP classes. Two of the dullest classes I sat through were in lower track English classes dealing with demanding texts, one a Chaucer class at Boulevard and the other a class on *Rosencrantz and Guildenstern Are Dead* at St. Mary's. In both cases, the teachers were nice and thoughtful people, but they felt the need at least on those days to plough ahead in the texts without much comment or intervention. The time dragged. In the Chaucer class, students at the back of the room started passing notes and mouthing messages quietly enough not to get caught while students in the front read uninspired prose descriptions of the pilgrims from the Prologue. The teacher tried to enliven the class with some pictures from a medieval art book she had brought from home, but only the first two rows paid the book any attention; the rest of the class simply passed the book from hand-to-hand, unopened. In the other class, students read parts in turn, but the teacher—having apparently given up on explaining jokes or correcting misreadings—let them roll on while three, four, five students put their heads down and tuned out. I spoke to her afterward, and she was quite lively, knowledgeable about literature and film and with a great commitment to her students, but apparently the need to cover material and other circumstances of the day produced that slow class. Sitting in those classes, I remembered just how dull high school life could be sometimes, filled with unspoken longings and long waits for the saving grace of a bell.

On the other hand, two of the liveliest classes I visited were lower track English classes at a school near Boulevard in the northeast but not on my final list. This school is less highly rated than other northeast high schools, largely because its population is poorer (60% low income) and its curriculum more vocational, but the kids were engaging classic high school texts— *1984* and *Streetcar Named Desire*—in an interactive and personal way. The former text was taught in a class whose teacher was a large White man who had been a fireman for a full career and then decided to retire and teach school. He was gruff and somewhat prescriptive about what the characters represented, and he had warned me privately beforehand that only a few students in the class were planning to go on to a 4-year college and some had already gotten into union jobs through connections of their fathers. But he clearly liked these kids and felt that *1984* had an important message for them, especially in the aftermath of the 9/11 attacks earlier that semester. Everyone listened, many asked questions, and only one student had his head down (he later turned out to be the only one applying to Temple, but for all I know he had been working late the night before, as Temple students often do). In the *Streetcar* class, students read aloud just as they had in the *Rosencrantz* class. But here the young African-American teacher set the scene extensively, stopped people who did not deliver their lines with proper emotion, and generally cajoled the class onto an imaginary stage where they could picture Blanche meeting Stanley. The two ingredients I found most compelling in both these classes were the expectation that students would engage in the material and the familiar, sustaining relationship both teachers built on with students that they saw every day.

Of course I saw some marvelous advanced track classes at the schools, too. Every school except North had a section or more named AP, and many had more than one labeled rapid or accelerated. In most of these classes, the relationship between students and teacher was particularly warm and the expectations were high. Some of the teachers tended to want specific kinds of answers from their students, wanted them to follow a certain procedure in order to produce what they thought of as college-level analysis, but the students were almost always quite willing to go along with the process. The department head at Boulevard, sensing perhaps my reservations about the tracking system, explained to me that the school had resisted pressure for years from the district to do away with tracking. She argued that tracking was what kept many of the highest achieving and middle-class students at the school, for without it parents would have withdrawn their kids and sent them to one of the magnet schools or Catholic schools, or the families would have moved out of the city altogether. Her argument reminded me that politics is never far removed from a school curriculum.

Neither North nor Somerset divides classes by a tracking system, although as I describe later Somerset did have two sections of an AP senior English class. Both use what are called "small learning communities" (SLCs) to break the total population into more manageable units for scheduling classes and following themes. Both separate ninth graders into their own SLC, including the significant number of ninth graders who must repeat the grade. The SLC system not only hinders tracking but also undermines the departmental structure most other schools use. Students and teachers are meant, in this system, to identify more with the SLC than with a track or a department, respectively. This can work well if the SLC functions as a unit and has an enterprising leader who encourages participants to become invested in the theme of the community but, where the SLC is merely an administrative unit or a holding tank, it has a chilling effect on school life for everyone. The organizing themes tend to be specific, such as mechanical careers, business, TV/radio communications, or art, but Somerset also has a unit called Motivation that is devoted to "College Preparatory and Health Careers." This is a bit misleading, because students can work toward college entrance from any SLC in either school, but it is true that some SLCs tend to be more vocational than others. Students generally request the SLC they want to enter at the end of ninth grade; they take no entrance exam and are not selected on any particular basis for entrance, but students don't always get their first choice of SLC. Again, I will have more to say about this arrangement when I look more closely at the programs at Fields and Somerset high schools and contrast the tracking system with the SLC system for English education.

Another major area of comparison that has a direct affect on the English curriculum and instruction is physical plant and supply budget. All five of these schools occupy impressive buildings. Fields is the oldest—parts of it at least were built as early as 1953—but it is probably the best kept, having been renovated recently. St. Mary's was built in the early 1960s, Boulevard in the late 1960s, and North in 1970. Somerset is the newest and perhaps most attractive from the outside, built in the mid-1980s. But clearly the Philadelphia schools do not have the budget to maintain the buildings the way Fields' school district does. This is not all a matter of money, for the Archdiocese—with its slender system-wide budget—is able to keep St. Mary's blocky yellow brick and glass buildings in better repair than the school district keeps most Philadelphia schools. Somerset has problems with a leaky roof, Boulevard is a bit drab and marked with some graffiti, but North looks the most worn. Despite the fact that it bragged a striking and controversial design when it opened, the building badly needs paint and roof repair now and had a major boiler problem on one of the days I was scheduled to visit.

On the subject of supplies, the story is similar but not so easy to understand. Fields has a beautiful book room and a large store of books for every grade and track. Some classroom sets are old and patched (I remember particularly some well-worn copies of *Heart of Darkness*), but generally the books are in good shape and readily available through the English Department head. Other schools do not have as nice a storage facility but seem to have books for classes. Some schools have invested in large anthologies, but teachers who use them often keep the texts in the classroom and make photocopies of short stories they want students to take home. In schools where kids are not so compliant and focused on school, heavy books tend to sit in lockers and don't get read; North and Somerset, for example, depend on smaller paperbacks almost exclusively for reading assignments.

But money or even staff support are not really the biggest problems English teachers seem to be wrestling with. Sure, North stopped its literary magazine because they didn't have a budget to put it out, and the chair of the department just could no longer help with the magazine while still administering English, Spanish, and social studies courses and teaching her own load. The North Humanities Department has a miniscule book budget, not enough desks, chairs, or supplies for classes that are chronically overenrolled beyond the state- mandated maximum of 33. And certainly, substitutes are hard to come by in city schools, so that teachers cannot easily take field trips with a single class or even make phone calls during the day in order to set up trip arrangements. One teacher I spoke to at Somerset was distraught because she had set up a field trip to the University of Pennsylvania museum that morning, but the trip hadn't come off. Even though she had gotten her other classes covered, settled the times with the museum guides, gotten the permissions signed, and arranged for the buses to come, somebody in the office hadn't submitted crucial paperwork to allow the bus company to be paid, and so the buses never arrived.

But the abiding problem I saw in North and Somerset had to do with establishing a curriculum that could be preparatory for college but appealing to students with a very skeptical view of what they need to learn. Curriculum is caught between the needs to produce higher state test results but also foster independent thought, in line with the changing demands of a school district in constant crisis but stable enough that the books you ordered last spring would also serve you next fall. Somehow, the feeling in Fields and St. Mary's is that both for students and teachers one step will follow another, even if that may mean an occasional dull class or stressful night of grading. The system feels like it works in those schools, and both students and teachers have some faith in its solidity, if not its ultimate wisdom. There is an atmosphere of continuity at the schools that are functioning best, while at the most struggling schools there is a constant striving after a modicum of control. I return to this idea in the following chapter when I talk at greater length about literacy sponsorship.

At Boulevard, this sense of continuity feels present but at risk, like a set of bells going slightly out of consonance. Two violent incidents occurred at Boulevard in 2000-2001, first white-on-black and then black-on-white; I could still notice a trace of tension as I moved in and out of the college prep classes that were relatively integrated by race and class. The departmental head assured me the incidents were isolated and not reflective of the school culture as a whole, and I saw little evidence to refute her claim, but I left feeling I had really only begun to understand this school. A teaching position there is highly prized, and so it takes teachers of fairly advanced seniority to get jobs there, and those that receive assignment at Boulevard seldom leave before retirement. As a result, the department head herself characterized the school as quite attached to an older curriculum taught by an aging faculty. This gives classes solidity, and the curriculum is stable enough that the required books are always in stock. Every student gets an anthology, a grammar and vocabulary book, as well as the small single work paperbacks that are the stock of most high school curricula. However, the reading list would have fit in my high school curriculum of 30 years ago; on the day I visited I saw Chaucer, Shakespeare, Poe, and Arthur Miller being taught. The only work I saw discussed that broke with the old canon was Kate Chopin's "The Story of an Hour," taught by a combative, digressive, endearingly maddening teacher who also taught college introduction to literature courses part time.

At Somerset, and even more at North, the music begins to turn dissonant, a cacophony of demanding voices, each pitch clashing with the next. I discuss Somerset in greater detail in the next section, and I cannot say very much more about North here. There had been an effective, energetic principal at North in the mid-1990s, but she ran afoul of the central administration during a period of highly publicized school reform that was not greeted warmly by many teachers and some administrators in the district. The principal went to a suburban school, and she was replaced by a much more circumspect administrator. Temple has had programs with North off and on, but connections haven't been smooth or far-reaching, probably for a lack of sustained commitment on both sides. Indeed, on this project I was not allowed to pursue more than initial visits to the school despite my assurances that I would not study individual students.

I cannot blame the principal at North for his wariness. Yet another major reform was about to be imposed on the system, and his school—with 83% of the students scoring in the lowest quartile on the state assessment test in reading—might well have been among the group considered for a takeover of troubled schools. Temple has not been a particularly good neighbor, whatever the historical reasons, and he had no confidence that my visits would do anything for the school but publicize its faults and gain me professional advantage. I can only report that the principal, teachers, and students at North seemed quite willing to make further joint efforts with Temple but at all levels they acted with caution: the principal out of protectiveness for the public image of his school, the teachers because they had entertained visitors before who could not deliver on their promises, and students because even the seniors had a fairly vague sense of what college would really ask of them or what they themselves wanted from postsecondary education. No school is easy to understand, even after many visits and observations over a year or more. However, I walked away from North after my last interview with the principal feeling that only a long-standing commitment to such a school—no matter what changes reform and administrative turnover produced—would ever yield a relationship where research could go on freely, without the suspicion of self-interest, and where students could have a more informed conception of the college life going on right down the street from their classrooms.

I want to say a word more about the difficulty of this sort of research before turning to a closer look at two schools, one suburban and one urban. For decidedly different reasons, the Catholic Archdiocese schools are nearly as difficult to observe, analyze, and write about as troubled city schools. The gaps in Fig. 2-4A under St. Mary's is largely because, although some information is available on all public schools in the state, this is not true for test scores and other vital statistics of private and parochial schools. All Pennsylvania public schools are now required to administer the Pennsylvania System of School Assessment (PSSA) in Grades 5, 9, and 11 but non-public schools can administer whatever standardized tests they choose. In Philadelphia the Catholic schools administer a test called Terranova, but the scores are used for internal purposes only. I had a delightful conversation with the principal of St. Mary's in my visit there, during which he told me that I wouldn't be able to write extensively about his school unless my work was cleared by the Archdiocese itself. He went on to give me a great deal of interesting information about the system and his school, but our conversation went on with the understanding that I could share no specifics in my book. This seemed reasonable to me, for I began to see that looking at the Catholic schools in Philadelphia was a major undertaking on its own, and that I could only pursue it after proving that my university was willing to engage on the Archdiocese's terms with its schools. They do not, for instance, reveal publicly the SAT score averages of individual schools, and although I have access to St. Mary's SAT scores through Temple's databank, I promised not to discuss their scores. One public school partisan commented to me that Catholic schools didn't reveal their scores because they didn't want people to know how low they were, but—having looked at the data—I see no evidence that Catholic schools do less well on these tests than their comparable neighbors. St. Mary's principal said they didn't publish the scores so that people would not compare Catholic schools from different parts of the city and different demographics with one another. I cannot evaluate their decision at this point; I can only report it.

Again, my experiences with St. Mary's and North, and in fact with all the schools I visited for this chapter, taught me that research in this context must be done to support relationships and develop mutual understanding. People in every school were far more willing to talk to me if they thought I might be back to converse and cooperate with them more fully once my book was finished. And I began to see that no matter how much time I spent at any one school, no matter how much data I collected on how their students did once they entered Temple, I could not hurry my understanding of these schools. I could only develop a more textured picture in my mind from which to construct our programs and our half of whatever projects we develop with the teachers and students in these schools. Perhaps that makes for a somewhat less satisfying polemical position for writing, but I suspect it makes for more fertile ground eventually for research that will lead to productive improvements in schools and meaningful social change in a region. In short, the most productive working knowledge must come over years of collaboration and the building of mutual respect. University researchers rarely have the time for that kind of commitment, but a more geologic timeframe will produce better results.

TWO SCHOOLS

Somerset High School

Somerset High School occupies a green and well-kept campus on a road otherwise lined with working factories. You drive past a city compound for abandoned cars, and then you see the stately brick and metal fence enclosing grass and trees, a parking lot, and a large, modern, orange brick building. Unlike other city schools, this one does not give the impression of being a factory, with its rambling wings and levels studded with ample, dark-framed windows. The roofs at various levels are accented with a stylish gray metal siding. Around the side is a soccer field, also used for baseball in the Spring, and tennis courts. A bank of wall ball courts lines the side of the building beyond the parking lot. Wall ball is a sport kids in this Puerto Rican area of the city enjoy almost more than basketball; it's a game you can play with just a tennis ball, a wall, and your bare hands. Kids play here on the courts mornings and afternoons. The building is imposing but not uninviting, giving the impression that learning is serious but not necessarily regimented or grim. You might almost believe that school can be engaging even if it's required by the state.

I entered through the front doors along with arriving students, but there were no lines to get past the metal detectors. I put my bag into the x-ray machine, and I signed in with the guard, but everyone was quite pleasant to the students and me. Later that same week I would visit another school where the attending aide yelled—even screamed—at kids on the metal detector line, but I saw no indication of that atmosphere here. I signed in at the office where substitutes report for work and teachers pick up mail, and they directed me to the library upstairs where I would start my day. Before I took the stairs up, I paused to look at a series of self-portrait paintings hung in the office and two magnificent tile murals on the walls of the entrance atrium. The students' work was broad and colorful, the faces expressive and the tile cityscape sophisticated but not slick. It felt good to stand in that place and look up at the balcony running around the second floor. Intermittently along the balcony windows were hung beautiful stained-glass windows that, I was told later, had been taken from the old Somerset building when the school moved to its present site in 1988.

A recent grant proposal written by the Somerset staff and cooperating faculty at the University of Pennsylvania describes the school as

> an inner-city school in North Philadelphia with a population of 2,700 students, 75% of whom are Latino, 15% African-American, 9% white, and 1% Asian. The school's neighborhood, which is in Philadelphia's Empowerment Zone, is extremely disadvantaged. 92% of the population lives below the poverty line. Violence, drug dealing, teenage pregnancy, and AIDS in the neighborhood are rife. Many students dropout before graduation: the 9th grade has 1,000 students and the 12th grade 330.

Indeed, the area around Somerset High School is one of the most economically distressed portions of the city. Yet the school does not have a desperate or besieged feeling, as some schools in poor neighborhoods can have, but feels bright and cared-for inside and out. In the halls, school police and nonteaching assistants urged students into their classrooms, but there was little of the yelling and confrontation that I have seen elsewhere. Students, teachers, and staff seemed genuinely comfortable in the building.

Comfort in a building means a great deal for morale, but of course it doesn't solve all the problems. One of the first school officials I spoke to, a former Somerset teacher retired from the school district now but working as a language arts consultant in Somerset, described what the school had been like in the original building during the 1970s. "The halls belonged to the students, and the classrooms belonged to the teachers," Peter said, "The first thing you learned when you started teaching there was to lock the doors when class began, and you didn't open the door for anyone who couldn't show a valid pass." Now he believed teachers and students love the school and feel safe in it. Yet, Peter noted, student achievement on standardized measures or in classroom activities hadn't improved significantly. "Not enough full commitment to school," he said, even though he felt the school is a success story in other ways.

Next I spent a good hour with the principal, a vigorous Latino man who had been at the school for some years. He agreed with Peter about the challenge of the school, saying about the students: "There's not the same anger at school, but the problem we still haven't solved is to make them enthusiastic students." Dr. Fuentes, by all accounts among teachers I talked to, had been instrumental in bringing calm and order to the school. He grew up in the neighborhood, went to school in the old building, and experienced a disappointment as harsh as any high school student might face. When he was finishing at Somerset he attended a ceremony honoring the top-achieving seniors, during which it was announced that he had earned a 4-year scholarship to Temple. Afterward the vice principal held him back from the crowd filing out.

"Fuentes, you can't have that scholarship," the man said.

"Why not, sir? I earned it, sir."

"You're only in the general track. Those scholarships are reserved for students in the college preparatory track."

"I took all the college prep courses along with the others. I got higher grades than they did. Why shouldn't I be entitled to it?"

But the vice principal was adamant. "We'll have to give the scholarship to someone in college prep. A general student just can't have it. That's the rules."

So Dr. Fuentes went to community college for 2 years, made high enough grades to receive a scholarship to Temple for the last 2 years, and began to teach school. He worked his way through the system, finished a doctorate at Temple, and was eventually asked to take the principalship of his old school. He took it only under the condition that he could run the school as he saw fit, and he has a reputation for going against district policy on occasion. Sometimes he is stricter than they would like, sometimes more lenient. Unlike most other principals in the district, for instance, he stood at his school door and turned away kids who were not wearing the school uniform at a time when the District decreed that all schools should require uniforms. The beauty was that students he sent home came back in uniform; they wanted to come back. If Somerset is going to have a policy, Dr. Fuentes told me, he is going to enforce it, and students respond well to his hands-on approach. He talks to every parent who calls to complain and is privately as kind as he is publicly stern. His strength is that he knows the kids and their parents, he knows the neighborhood, and he is driven by the desire to see his students have the opportunities they deserve and earn.

But a principal can only do so much, as important as he or she may be for the general tone and direction of a school. I interviewed, in addition to Peter, a number of other teachers in English across the different SLCs to get a feeling for the curriculum and the expectations for the students. I also talked to the librarian, the art teacher, the video production teacher, and one of the electrical construction teachers, all of whom have done work with students that bear on writing, reading, and postsecondary schooling. I visited classes, had a chance to talk about college prospects with a number of students, but I focus here on what a few teachers told me about their curriculum and their attitudes toward college prep. Like the principal at North, Dr. Fuentes was wary of my focusing on students without a more developed context in the school, and I agreed to his restrictions. Part of the purpose for my visit to the schools was to develop a relationship with teachers so that over time Temple and Somerset could cooperate on projects together. Thus, the time getting to know faculty seemed to me well spent, no matter what I could include in the book.

Before I turn to the language arts curriculum in one SLC, I review a few more comments made by Peter, a White man in his mid-60s, elegant in his bow tie and precise manner. He had helped in an effort by five teachers in the English Department a few years back to outline their 4-year curriculum and agree on a portfolio assessment model they would all follow. This was a literature-based program drawing on a reading-journal approach to encourage the "continual interaction between reader and text," and students would demonstrate their literacy maturation through archival and presentational portfolios ("Somerset Language Arts Course of Studies"). Drawing on the National Council of Teachers of English (NCTE's) "Statements on Standards" and "Principles of Assessment," the document set out an organized and hopeful program of instruction and evaluation for the whole department to use. It has the feel of work that comes out of research by a committee, but it exudes the optimism of a staff setting its own priorities.

Peter told me that the younger teachers embraced the document and older teachers warily accepted it. About half the department had been teaching for more than 15 years, at the time, and of the other half at least four or five had taught less than 5 years, arriving at the school after the document was formulated. He was satisfied that "most of the teachers are participating in most ways," especially in regard to the portfolios. He stressed that in this effort they wanted to "set achievable goals" and design alternative assessments rather than worry about the standardized tests both the city and the state were stressing. Their students historically have not done well on standardized tests, and they hoped to devise assessment approaches that did show students they were making progress and did give them a sense of accomplishment. Peter felt that in this endeavor they had succeeded; the archival portfolios documented that more writing was going on in classes and presentational portfolios documented that students were better able to prepare finished, acceptable papers. I asked him if he didn't feel concerned about the increasing pressure coming from Harrisburg for higher scores on the PSSA math and reading test, and he answered that he was not. "The tests make students feel awful about themselves," he said, "If we can show some progress, some evidence of more complex responses and a greater amount of writing, that means more than small advances on a standardized test."

My conversations with other teachers revealed how complicated curriculum reform can be and how the best-intentioned pronouncements of even a well-informed consultant can oversimplify a situation. One of the most enlightening conversations was with George, a White man who had been at Somerset for 30 years and was the official chair of the English Department, although that was a more honorific title in a school organized into SLCs. He was passionate and lively as he talked to me in his SLC office, with students coming in and out asking for this or that. He agreed with Peter that archival portfolios were being kept throughout the school, and that the presentational portfolios were being factored into final grades, but he said the document itself had lost much curricular force as the school moved away from a departmental system and toward an organization based on SLCs. He said that many teachers who had worked on the document had now moved out of the school, some support that had been promised the school never materialized, and as a result "many things we planned didn't happen." As to Peter's dismissal of the PSSA, George simply asserted that in the current environment teachers had no choice but to pay attention to standardized test results. In George's estimation, "alternative" assessment methods meant little to the state officials now influencing school policy. However, Somerset's relative laxity toward the test was, ironically, an advantage these days. They had so downplayed the PSSA when it first came in (during those days the city was pushing its own test as the standard) that with only a little concerted effort, he felt, they could probably raise the test results each year for the next few years. An increase in PSSA scores could mean significant additional money for the school budget and a chance that Somerset might not be taken over by the state or some private educational management company. Yes, George assured me, the PSSA was nothing to dismiss.

One important factor in curriculum planning at Somerset was that the school ran on a block schedule. This meant that classes were about 90 minutes long, and most courses lasted only one semester. Thus, students usually had math or English for one semester a year, but the classes were relatively more intense. Students took four classes each day; teachers taught three. The teaching load under this system went from more than 150 to 165 per teacher in a five-class day to about 90 to 100 per teacher in a three-class day. There were some real advantages to a schedule like this for teaching writing and reading, but the greatest disadvantage was that students in the school had language arts for fewer than 5 months out of 12. Presumably, students were reading and writing in their other classes, but a lack of year-round English instruction could have been a significant academic problem, particularly in a school where many of the students did not speak English at home or in their neighborhood. Some basic students took math and foreign language in year-long courses offered in 45-minute daily periods, but most subjects for most students were taught under the block schedule.

One exception to this block schedule rule was the way George taught 11th and 12th-grade English in the business SLC to which he belongs. His load was reduced to two blocks a day because of administrative duties, but during his two 90-minute blocks he taught in tandem with a colleague in history. On the books, students have a single 45-minute period for English and a subsequent one for history, but in practice, 66 students met with both teachers for the full two periods each day. Eventually, they hope to have a large room and a small room so that sometimes they can divide the class up into smaller groups, but in recent years they have been teaching the whole group every day in a single room. When one of them gave an assignment, he read and graded all 66 papers. The arrangement suits them, however, because the two teachers worked well together, providing insights from history on the literature they read and writing assignments on the history they studied. The business SLC had the dual mission of preparing students for 2- or 4-year colleges, especially in business, and for entry-level jobs in the retail or service sector. His colleague was particularly interested in economics and, given the theme of the SLC, this allowed them some latitude to bring in money and marketing as a background to other studies.

The curriculum George followed in 11th and 12th grades was based on the interdisciplinary interests he and his colleague shared. In 11th grade they both drew on a collection called *The Civil War: A Historical Reader*, which included primary sources and literary works from the era as well as historical commentary on the era. In that class, they required a four-to six-page research paper and four of five additional papers of four pages or longer. They read a Shakespeare play in that class (usually *Othello* but lately *Macbeth* instead) because, like many high school English departments, they planned on including one Shakespeare play a year no matter what else they were teaching. They don't read the whole play, however, but go over a detailed summary, read selected speeches, and see a movie version. In this, George seems to be following the recommendation in the curriculum overview Peter showed me:

> The teacher is advised not to teach a Shakespearian play in the traditional manner—i.e., studying the text for comprehension of the 17th-century English language. While this language is early modern English, it is, as a reading experience, tedious and off-putting. Instead, the text should

be used as a script (which it literally is). The play itself is not fully rendered unless it is transformed by actors assisted by a director and turned into drama. The students should experience the play as drama by any means the teacher prefers—acting out scenes, showing videos, etc. The goal is to have the students experience each play as a stirring drama that they can comprehend and remember with pleasure. (Language Arts 9)

This attitude is in keeping with the general pragmatism I found among many Somerset teachers, emphasizing involvement and pleasure in reading and writing over considerations that might be thought technical or strictly disciplinary in character. This is not to say George didn't prize challenge or hard work. About the philosophy of education generally held in his SLC, he said: "We try to run our seniors through the most rigorous program we can. They moan, but they come back later and tell us we weren't hard enough." About writing in particular, he considered himself a demanding teacher both in terms of correctness and content: "They fight me the entire first year, and somewhere in the second year the gain comes." He served as chair of English for the whole school, but that was primarily an administrative job involving book orders and covering classes; his main identification as a teacher was with the SLC because, as he noted, "We like each other," referring to the other teachers in the unit. More than anything this de-emphasized the broader curriculum document, for most English teachers spent little time working with other English teachers in the school. They practically never met as a department.

George's 12th-grade curriculum was roughly centered on American literature, but included books that the district requires or urges teachers to teach in the grade. Many of the books listed here also appear in the departmental curriculum document Peter showed me. Here is the reading list:

Baldwin, *If Beale Street Could Talk* or Crichton, *Rising Sun* (read on their own)
Golding, *Lord of the Flies* or Card, *Ender's Game* (whole class assigned the same book, but some years it is one and some the other)
Shakespeare, *Hamlet*
Kafka, "Metamorphosis"
Miller, *A View from the Bridge*
Lee, *To Kill a Mockingbird*
10-15 American poems (a Longfellow narrative poem, Service's "Cremation of Sam Magee," perhaps some e.e. cummings, no African-American or Latino poetry)
Three of four articles on companies traded on the New York Stock Exchange

George handled many of these readings in one of two ways. In books like *Ender's Game* or *Lord of the Flies*, he gave students a detailed worksheet to fill out on each chapter. They might do some silent reading in class or he might assign a chapter or more to be read at home; students would start filling out the sheets as group work in class and finish them for homework. For other readings, such as *A View from the Bridge* or *To Kill a Mockingbird*, he gave open-ended questions in response to a chapter or scene, such as they might find in the Pennsylvania state test. They might answer the question "What would you have done in this situation?" or respond to the prompt "Write a letter to the editor on this problem" in their literature journals and share their writing with the whole class or small groups later. In both approaches students would get credit for doing the assignment but keep their work to be used in answering questions on tests.

For longer pieces, George assigned various activities meant to keep students reading and interacting with the text at least at the level of plot, character, and setting. He administered regular quizzes—two or three questions on setting or plot at the beginning of the period—to be sure students were reading what was assigned. Midway through the text unit and then at the end, he gave a short answer/short essay test, often drawing on the literature journals to add personal reflection. Students also wrote short compositions of one or two pages on topics like "compare and contrast Piggy and Ralph in *Lord of the Flies*" or "characterize Ender as a leader in *Ender's Game.*" For books read independently, students wrote guided book reports with a set of general questions to answer about the book—list characters and describe them, identify setting and tell any changes that occurred during the book—then they summarized the plot, and ended with their own test on the book, including answers to their questions and where these answers might be found in the book.

The stock market articles were perhaps the most novel element of the curriculum. This arose in the interdisciplinary character of the course, when the history/economies teacher assigned students an imaginary fund with which to buy stocks, and they followed their stocks for a certain length of time, keeping journals and doing research on the companies in which they had chosen to invest. This was apparently a popular part of the course, but it didn't seem to be associated with anything else they were reading or writing in the English portion of the curriculum.

The senior portfolio required for graduation from the SLC was impressive. Here is a list of the required assignments, to be selected from the archival portfolios accumulated in the course of their high school careers:

Resume
Two letters of recommendation (written by others)
Business letter

Letter of complaint or appreciation
Letter of application
Personal essay for college
Character description from a film or a story
Two compositions based on readings from English, social studies, or
science courses
Persuasive or point-of-view essay
Senior business plan
Investment and Wall Street research paper
Stock Market Game journal, research, and article summaries
Senior business project
Printout of major PowerPoint project (done for a presentation)
Book report
Awards or certificates received

This portfolio represents a reasonably wide range of rhetorical challenges
and a mix of personal, professional, and disciplinary genres. I did not review
the quality of portfolios submitted by the students, for that was not within
the purview of this particular study. George told me that most of the SLCs
in the school required some sort of senior portfolio, but he felt that the business SLC certainly had one of the most extensive, more extensive than the
portfolio for the motivation SLC, the other unit whose purpose is primarily college preparation.

I discussed writing and reading with a number of other teachers and
staff at the school in the course of my visits there. Daniel, perhaps the most
anxious and worried teacher I met at any school, wanted very much to talk
to me but did not want me to visit his class. He was a White man who had
been at the school for 16 years, and he worked with ninth graders, repeat
ninth graders, as well as 10th and 11th graders. Daniel feared that he might
not be able to control his classes while I was visiting; although this seemed
painful for him to report, he did not appear ashamed to tell me about it.
Writing seemed impossible for him to teach, he reported, because every time
he stopped to talk to one student about her writing everyone else stopped
working, even if he had assigned them work to do. "I was just putting out
fires," he said in an earnest voice, "when the rest of the class was going down
in flames." He told me that many students made no attempt to write at all,
seeing writing as "a hellish experience" or "a monumental task." Like other
teachers I talked to at Somerset, he found that students regularly did not
complete writing assignments for homework, that they would rather receive
a bad grade than write outside of class. In earlier years, he had tried to teach
more than one sentence answers, but that hadn't worked. He said, "I never
got to the essay because it's too deep, couldn't get past the second step in the
writing process." By this he meant that he could start them drafting, but

they refused to revise. When I asked if he ever used computers to make revision easier he answered: "They don't perceive computers as a writing machine but as a pleasure machine."

He was far more enthusiastic about teaching reading, which he viewed as more basic than writing. He felt himself a salesman for reading, often telling his students what he was reading and trying to frame reading as an "everyday experience." He said he gave them a brief assessment at the beginning of the semester and then suggested books at their reading level. But he was struggling with a dilemma about how to get at the reading; he felt that reading aloud in groups was "artificial" and not suited to their age, but silent reading didn't work because silence made students "nervous." He wanted help thinking through the issues of reading and writing instruction, but he admitted that he had not sought out any graduate classes or teacher development sessions because he doubted more training would help him. "I'm the only one going into that classroom day in and day out," he said with a mixture of sadness and resignation.

I must mention a few other staff members I met who seemed, above all, to have a fierce devotion to their students. Dorothy, an African-American woman who had been at the school several years, taught one of two AP sections of senior English. Her class happened to be nearly all girls, an unusual situation but not entirely surprising because so many kids who drop out are boys. Dorothy had a quiet authority in the classroom, and at her urging nearly all the class had, by mid-November, developed a list of colleges and made their applications. Brian, a young African-American man new to the school, taught video production with incredible energy and devotion. Some of the most important equipment in his shop was his own because the school had invested too much money in outmoded equipment before he arrived, and now he had no budget for updating the system. He was working with his classes on a video promotion to be run on the closed-circuit school TV, selling a fund-raising holiday CD so that they could buy a new video camera for the school. The school librarian, Lynn, was a White woman near retirement who had been at Somerset more than 10 years. She had a long record of writing and receiving grants for the school—developing projects with colleagues in history, English, communications, and art—and had worked closely with the University of Pennsylvania on an enrichment project for the AP classes. She held a PhD in educational technology from Temple, and her library had become a hub of activity for research and academic computing. Like George, Dorothy, Brian, and Peter, Lynn would have been valuable faculty in any school, but in Somerset her work took on tremendous urgency. In a school where two out of every three ninth graders will not graduate on time or at all, teachers who work hard to make the school supportive and positive for kids are precious indeed.

I close my account of Somerset with a story from the art teacher Sara, a White woman who had taught at the school for more than 12 years. I visited her class because the librarian Lynn told me I had to meet her. Sara had done the tile mural project with her kids, funded by a grant Lynn helped write some years before, and Sara made a point to incorporated writing and reading about art into her semester's work. But Lynn wanted me to meet her primarily because she was such a remarkable and devoted teacher. I found her directing a life drawing class in a classroom packed with materials, student work, easels, and large wooden tables. Although the room was ample and had a high ceiling, the 20 students present seemed like quite a crowd for the space. Sara said this was an unusual day because eleven students were absent; normally students would be jammed on the tables as they drew. She is one of two art teachers in the school. However, the other was a teacher who would soon retire, and she worked exclusively with profoundly disabled students. Once her colleague leaves, Sara will be the only one offering art instruction in a school of nearly 3,000 students.

Sara told me a story about one of her best students, a Puerto Rican boy who graduated a few years ago. He had studied earlier in another part of the state and had only come to Somerset in his sophomore year. He was a highly talented artist and had scored a combined 990 on the SAT — an exceptional score considering that the average combined SAT for students entering Temple from Somerset, nearly all of them on special admission but still among the best prepared in the school, was an 820. In his senior year, she worked with him to develop his portfolio for art school. When the time came to visit the Temple admissions office, she drove him there herself. She dropped this kid from one of the roughest neighborhoods in Philly in front of the administration building and told him she'd meet him inside once she'd parked the car. He said, "You're not going to leave me, are you?"

"Ten minutes to park the car," she yelled through the window, "This is a bus stop! Go in and I'll join you soon." But when she returned from the parking lot, he was still standing on the street corner, waiting for her to walk him in.

He was accepted into Tyler, Temple's art school, and began that September. She kept getting calls from him saying "They're all white! They're all rich!" and she would answer him that it was ok, that he could do it. But by the fourth week he was already in trouble in art history. The course required a $60 book, and he kept putting off buying it, but that meant he had nothing to study for the class. He flunked the first test. He finally bought the book, but by that time he felt hopelessly behind. He gave up and dropped out. I asked her what he is doing now. "He's cutting hair and working at the Acme supermarket," she said. She still knew his phone number and had some hope he'd eventually get back to an art program in town, but she knew he needed to work to keep living on his own, and that might make school impossible.

Fields High School

Fields High School is about an hour's drive north of Temple, but it feels much further away than that. Only 1 mile off a busy highway, it sits on a campus of fields and playgrounds, a part of a complex of buildings that also houses the township offices and a middle and elementary school. Before I parked, I needed to consult an outdoor map, such as you see on a college campus, to understand where I should leave my car and enter the school. Inside the front door I found a modest foyer with a trophy case, announcement board, and student-of-the-month display; I had seen grander entryways in many city schools I visited. But there was a quiet sense of prosperity and confidence in the halls, and in the office — smaller than many I had seen — I signed in and was directed to my contact with friendly efficiency.

Fields is a large sprawling one-story facility of brick, stucco, and glass, at least part of which was built originally in the 1950s. The hallways are paneled in a calming dark wood, not the beige tile block that covers most school halls. One walks down long, crisscrossed corridors with rooms off to one side, but the building is kept from feeling warren-like by regular walls of windows down the other side of the hall, windows that look out on small courtyards. Even when the halls are crowded with talking, hurrying students, the atmosphere remains cheerful and businesslike. No one yells at the kids in the halls, nor do kids show an inclination toward horseplay or hanging out in the hallways, and very few people remain in the halls when classes are in session. There is an expectation of order and seriousness in the air, but no whiff of repression or coercion. This is a school where sports teams do well, the highest ranked students get into "good" schools, and average or even below average students enjoy hopeful educational and occupational prospects. It is neither a wealthy nor a poor school by county standards, for it has a low-income student rate of slightly more than 7%, compared with 1% at one neighboring school and 15% at another. Teachers have an average load of 140 to 150 students over five classes, somewhat fewer students per class when they teach an AP or honors section.

The school utilizes a four-track system for placing students into courses. The highest track includes students in AP and honors courses, although these are not exactly the same; an AP course is weighted to receive 5 "quality points," whereas an honors course receives 4.5 and a regular course 4.0 in the calculation of GPA. Students in the highest track take a mix of AP and honors courses, and even in their junior year, some students take an English course marked AP. Approximately 45 students in a class of about 850 take AP English in their junior or senior years, but students in those sections do very well on the AP exam; in 1999-2000, more than 86% of students taking the College Entrance Examination Board AP exam in English scored 3 or higher (the Pennsylvania average is 72.4%). Apparently, few students from this track apply to Temple, preferring to use Penn State as their "safe" school and often attending small private colleges or larger well-known universities in the mid-Atlantic or New England regions. A typical student in the AP classes, for instance, might apply to Penn, Princeton, Swarthmore, Haverford, New York University, Boston College, Boston University, Maryland, and Penn State. Others apply to Pennsylvania private schools with a more regional draw such as Lehigh, Lafayette, Bucknell, Drexel, or Carnegie Mellon.

The next track down is called college preparatory, and students in this track are usually expected to go to college but either are judged to be less than exceptional academically or have chosen not to take the more demanding honors track courses. Many in this track see Penn State as one of the harder schools to get into, and they apply to schools in the Pennsylvania system that had originally been teacher-training schools. These include East Stroudsburg, Kutztown, Millersville, West Chester. Some apply also to private schools in the area or the state such as St. Joseph's, Arcadia, Albright, Philadelphia, or Elizabethtown. More of the students who attend Temple from Fields are in this track rather than in honors/AP. In one college prep class with whom I spoke in November 2001, three students had already applied to Temple and others were thinking about it. One was quite enthusiastic about a specific program in communication but most seemed merely to know Temple as a large university in the city, an alternative to the Pennsylvania system schools or Penn State, all of which are in rural or small town settings.

Below college prep is career preparatory. Students in this track may also go to college, but the expectation is that they are more likely to go to the county community college or perhaps one of the smaller state schools. The lowest ranked track is basic instruction, reserved for a student who (in the words of the school's Web site) is "undecided about post-high school education, but wishes to keep open an option for further education including community college, business school, trade school, technical school, military service, or full-time work" and is "in need of directed instruction and remediation." Some very good and enthusiastic teachers I met in the English Department chose to teach primarily in this track, but I could not help but gain the impression that the upper level tracks were regarded as the plum assignments by most of the faculty.

One distinction among the tracks seems to be that the two upper tracks require students to be capable of "independent reading," whereas the career prep and basic students are felt to need more in-class guidance. In talking with teachers, I found that "independence" was really one of the most important academic traits, often not recognized in any but the AP students. It seemed to be a measure of how much a teacher can trust students to complete an assignment without much explanation, but it probably reflected both a level of abstract thinking that some students reach earlier than others and also an ease with academic discourse that may come with family background as well. Students are placed in tracks by recommendations of teachers from the previous year, but students can request shifts in track from year to year. Apparently, few do change tracks once they have been placed in 10th grade.

I met a number of the English teachers in a departmental meeting before I visited classes. I found these teachers to be a thoughtful, committed group with a sense of themselves as a faculty working on a collective project. They spoke at one point about an effort a few years earlier to overhaul their 10th grade English curriculum in order to prepare students better for the rest of the sequence (this school has only grades 10 through 12, unlike many high schools which start at grade 9). These teachers said that they had attempted to determine where their students were coming from and what they had learned in elementary and middle school classes, but they had met with very little response when they made contacts with colleagues in the lower grades. Thus, they concentrated their efforts on what they thought 10th graders should know to engage their later courses based on American and British literatures. A committee worked on the changes. They were approved by the department and passed on to the principal. Although in the last couple of years their number of meetings as a department had decreased, and some teachers felt they were losing cohesion as a department, the group felt fairly engaged with each other and invested in the language arts curriculum. The faculty is mixed by age, with both a significant share of teachers who have been in the school for 10 or more years and a number of younger teachers in the early stages of their careers. The principal and chair told me they planned to hire at least two or three new English teachers in the coming year.

My contact in the school was Kate, a White woman who had taught at Fields for 11 years. In recent years, she had been teaching primarily honors and AP English to juniors and seniors, but she was teaching a section of college preparatory that year and frequently taught one section in the nonacademic tracks as well. She was extremely conscientious and organized, and had been deeply involved in various department-wide initiatives such as the development of the end-of-year exams that are given to each track in each grade as a check on competencies across different instructors and curriculum variations. Lately she had begun to develop a writing center, staffed by honors student volunteers. I visited her AP, honors, and college preparatory courses as well as others taught by her colleagues, but I describe her college prep curriculum as an example of the 12th-grade experience a Temple student from Fields might well have had. I must say it was a rigorous curriculum, quite as demanding as many of the AP courses I saw in other schools, and yet the 30 students seemed also to be enjoying her class. Kate often remarked on the differences of approach between her AP, honors, and college prep classes, but here I maintain a focus on the college prep class. I close with references to the parallel projects in her upper track courses.

The 12-grade curriculum was built around British literature, especially in the first semester. In the fall her class read a traditional canon, as cited in Table 2.1.

The three large writing assignments in this semester each require a bit of explanation. The "Hero" essay was one in which students compare and contrast modern ideas of heroism with the hero they find in *Beowulf*. They close with thoughts about their own personal heroes and how these fit in with the ideas they discussed in the rest of the paper. She prepared students for this essay with pre-writing exercises and journal entries on heroism and details of the text. The essay on the *Canterbury Tales* asked students to imagine that Harry Bailey has led the pilgrims back to the Inn after the journey. Students group 12 pilgrims at three tables of 4, and suggest what the dynamics and interactions at these tables might be like. In the end, each student must argue for which tale would have been the most entertaining. Because they read only one tale in full, they have to guess based on qualities of character described in the Prologue. The medieval newspaper assignment has students working in groups to produce a newspaper based on research about the Middle Ages in England and their own fanciful invention. Each student must produce the equivalent of one page of text in the form of features about the pilgrims, ads for products medieval people might need, even horoscopes pertinent to the characters and their stories. Kate reports that this last assignment was the most popular. Honors students wanted to do it too, but they had other projects that squeezed out the time for a newspaper.

After the new year, they shift gears, taking at least a month or more to develop a research paper following the Macrorie model of the "I" Search Paper. The papers may be on any topic of personal interest to the authors. Each paper must include at least one interview and must begin with a narrative describing how the author became interested in the topic, what obstacles had to be overcome, and how the project came together. Kate emphasizes research methods, avoiding plagiarism, proper paraphrasing, and thesis writing. She requires the students to turn in every bit of documentation they collect and all their notes, not just the final paper. It is a thorough process, although her weakness is that she knows little about computers and can neither help students with web research nor fully evaluate the process her computer-savvy students follow.

She follows this research unit with a return to literature, now centered on the 19th and 20th centuries as shown in Table 2.2.

In the course of a year's work they investigate the traditional canon, developing some kind of historical framework for literary study. They write some 20 to 25 pages of finished prose in eight or more formal assignments as well as another 35 to 50 pages of informal journal entries, pre-writing

Table 2.1. First Semester Grade 12 Curriculum

Text	Classroom/Homework Activities	Evaluations
Beowulf: Four translated excerpts	Daily reading journal Written exercises on the nature of heroes	"Hero" essay (five to six paragraphs)
English folk ballads	Classroom reading and discussion	Quiz
Canterbury Tales: Prologue and the Pardoner's Tale, in modern English	Classroom reading and discussion	"Entourage returned to the Inn" essay (five to six paragraphs)
Macbeth: Full text, all scenes read in class over 4 weeks, followed by excerpts of Roman Polanski's filmed version	Classroom reading and discussion Scenes acted out Group quizzes Debate on film	Identification and essay test Medieval newspaper

Table 2.2. Second Semester Grade 12 Curriculum

Text	Activities	Evaluations
A Doll's House, Ibsen	Classroom reading and discussion	Test Opinion/argument on gender (five to six paragraphs)
Night, Wiesel	Classroom reading and discussion	"Director/ Photographer" paper (5-6 paragraphs) Analysis paper
British short stories Joyce, Lawrence, etc.	Classroom reading and discussion	
British poetry Coleridge, Wordsworth, Tennyson, Browning, Yeats, Thomas, etc.	Classroom reading and discussion Presentation and analysis of current song	Short explications/analysis

exercises, and test preparations. They stand for a dozen quizzes and half a dozen tests, not to mention the SAT. They spend many hours discussing literature or their reactions to literature. Most of them also write at least one or two versions of the college essay, many of which Kate or another teacher reads and critiques before the applications are sent off.

At the end of the year, the students stand for an exam taken by all seniors in every section of college prep English. The exam includes passages from literature none have read in classes previously, minimizing, as Kate put it, the "trivial pursuit" aspect of literature tests. This exam is designed to test the use of literary terms and assesses the ability to analyze texts, organize impromptu essays, and connect readings to personal reflection. Although she was one of the authors of the exam, Kate worries at times that its nonspecific nature allows some teachers to skip literature she regards as essential, but she concedes that more standardization would do no ultimate good and variability is probably in the nature of literary studies at every level. She is, by and large, comfortable with the focus on skills and abilities she regards as most crucial for students as they go on to future studies.

The Fields English faculty was quite generous in sharing thoughts on the curriculum, but the AP teachers especially allowed me to sit in on classes and talk to students about their hopes and fears about college. Rob, a White male who had been at the school for more than 15 years as a teacher, administrator, and a coach, taught the Grade 11 AP classes. At least two other teachers before him had worked to establish a high-functioning AP curriculum, and students at the school have regularly done well on the exam. Rob's curriculum is quite impressive, involving practically no literature but a tremendous amount of reading and writing, much like an introduction to academic discourse version of first-year college writing course. He had read enough of the composition literature on his own, and talked to people at the College Board enough, so that he had a very clear idea both of what the AP examiners were looking for on the composition tests and what first-year writing teachers were looking for in English 101. By the time they started 12th grade, the students had already written a carefully crafted college essay in the second semester of their grade 11 AP English class.

Susan, a White female with about the same classroom experience as Rob, allowed me to sit in on her 10th-grade honors class and her 12th-grade AP class. The latter was filled with science students who were a bit disdainful of writing in college, and she asked me to talk to them about what would be expected of them in terms of communications in engineering programs or medicine. They were a bit shocked to learn that they could not leave writing behind, but I think the strict divisions between English and science, even in a school with a fairly active writing in the disciplines approach, did not serve them well; they could not quite picture a world where writing would continue to matter to them. In the grade 10 class, students were preparing to write their first large-scale research paper. One student was actively curious about American Psychological Association format, even though their paper was supposed to be written in Modern Language Association form. It turned out that he and his entire shop class had been assigned a three- to five-page paper in APA format as punishment by the irate teacher. He was an oddity for taking shop in this upper track world, but he regarded the assignment as a kind of affront to his character. In the context of an English curriculum stressing meaning-making, response, and curricular continuity with college, the assignment struck me as an anomalous voice from another world, a world where school teaches obedience to external authority and writing assignments are mere extensions of the rule of law. This 10th grader had heard a message addressed to a different social class, and he could not parse it except as pure hateful control.

This brings me to the last class I observed at Fields, Kate's last period senior AP class. Through some accident of scheduling and times, Kate was only assigned 12 students in this class, and the day I visited 5 of them were busy with other projects or sports events that period. I later learned that 4 of the 12 students were on the front board as students of the month—one girl was a superb runner, another starred in school plays, a third girl had set up and managed a service project in a distressed community, and a boy was president of the student council—but what struck me about the students in this class was that they were more than ready to step into a college classroom. Many had already been admitted to the school of their choice, and others felt certain that they would get into at least one school they wanted. Not that this group had chosen the most elite names; except for one student who wanted very much to go to Bryn Mawr, most were expecting to go to small liberal arts colleges like Lafayette or Ursinus, or larger schools some distance away, like the University of Cincinnati or the University of Richmond. No, I was impressed with their self-possession in the classroom at that moment. I had spent most of the day talking to students about learning that the locus of control in college must be within them, and many students were far enough along to understand the concept even if they couldn't yet live it. This group simply did not need to hear the sermon.

I passed a delightful 40 minutes with them, talking about what they hoped to major in, what they had studied in high school, what they expected college to be like. I was struck by the naturalness of their knowledge about the relationship between schoolwork and life's work, about the way college seemed to fit effortlessly into their picture of themselves. Of course, I was a visitor from the world to which they were going, and you would expect the top students in a school to be on their best behavior with a college professor. The students in Dorothy's AP class at Somerset had also been on good behavior, and we had had an equally delightful hour talking about college and majors and life. But whereas the Somerset girls were struggling hard to imagine themselves at Kutztown and Millersville and Slippery Rock, hoping that they would find a place that would accept them and not make them feel awkward and alien, these students were self-assured and eager, certain that the world they were going to was made for them to join. I do not mean to mock either class of kids—after all they were young people trying to find their way based on what they had come to know about a world swathed in amplified imagery and false dichotomies—but I felt at that moment so hemmed in by the walls of class and privilege, so boxed up by the barriers that separate people in our country, that I could barely express to the Fields students my contradictory emotions. I urged them to seek out ways to recognize their privileges just as I complimented them on their very real accomplishments, and I said goodbye to Kate with a mixture of gratitude and grief.

CONCLUSIONS

When I step back from all this data and observation, and from notes I took on school visits I could not fit into the present account, I hesitate to offer conclusions for fear they would seem overly definite or impossibly hasty. After all, in addition to homework on the data, I visited only seven schools. If I combine that with previous visits I made to regional schools in the last few years, I have recent first-hand experience with little more than 15 public, religious, and private schools in the Philadelphia area. I have met with teachers and administrators at district policy conferences and data-sharing events regularly since 1996, but these meetings tend to be quite removed from the day-to-day experiences in the classrooms and hallways of the schools themselves. One can hardly get to know a school in a couple of visits, a school system in a few years, or a local educational geography in less than a lifetime. Yet, I think in this study I did learn something about high school experiences in Philadelphia area schools and their relationship to our college writing program. As much as it is impertinent to draw conclusions about the schools from my small sample, it is irresponsible to hold my tongue just because I will never know enough.

I want to avoid judgments and condemnations of individuals or specific schools, but I do want to share my outrage at the large number of students who drop by the wayside or persist only to find themselves unprepared for college when it actually comes. Some of the data on Philadelphia schools is simply frightening—such as the difference between the number of ninth graders and the number of seniors in a given year—and I wonder how civil life goes on in this country while such inequalities remain in children's lives every day. The disparity between the number of city school graduates who leave Temple after a year and the number of suburban public school graduates who leave—39% to 15%—brings the inequalities within my own work place starkly into focus. I have no simple solution, but I do feel the responsibility to accept this as a problem in which I have a personal and professional stake.

In 2001, a top student at Somerset applied to Temple for admission. She had a very high GPA, earning As in every subject. The essay she submitted was extensive, well-organized, and compelling. The director of admissions knew I was working with the school and called me in to review the application because, despite her school qualifications and convincing essay, her SAT scores were extremely low, a combined verbal and math of little more than 600. Should we take a chance and admit her? Would admission to Temple be an opportunity to succeed or an invitation to fail? Would rejection scar her or help her find a surer path? No one wants to create another story like the one Dr. Fuentes tells of his own schooling, but no one wants to add to the number of students who do not return to the university after their first year. I went back to my contacts at Somerset and asked what the teachers who knew her best would advise. As it turned out, none of her teachers thought she was ready for Temple, and they cited her writing as especially underdeveloped. When a teacher who was particularly close to her asked the young woman herself about her school choices, the student admitted that she felt she would be better off and more comfortable starting at community college. As a result of this information, she was rejected from Temple but invited to come back under the articulation agreements we have with the community college.

I do not think anyone in this scenario was acting in bad faith or out of prejudice, but why did the situation work out this way? Did the system respond well or poorly in this situation? I think in the short-run, for this particular person at the time she was applying for college, the system probably did serve her well. Even in the special admissions program we operate, she might not have been comfortable navigating through a large university with its many demands; after all, many top students choose not to begin college at large state schools. But in the long run we certainly don't want such situations to be common. It isn't fair or just social policy to say that most or all students from certain schools should go to a community college before entering a university or 4-year college, even if you believe—as I do—that community colleges serve their students well. I discuss this matter in greater detail in the next chapter, but here I emphasize that neither individual decisions nor systemic solutions can be formulated purely along ideological lines. We need to learn more about root causes for problems, allowing for considerable good will on the part of many participants, but still we must devise reasonable responses that really do improve the educational opportunities in people's lives.

Evidence of faulty connections or indefensible gaps isn't found exclusively in data on the most highly stressed schools. I found myself thinking, in all the schools I visited, that I wanted my friends and colleagues in college writing programs to see what I was seeing and talk with the teachers I met. On the one hand, this was because I thought that the specter of college often hangs over the heads of students and teachers alike in the high school classroom. Sometimes, this leads to overly serious discussions of literature and excessively formal or prescribed assignments, and sometimes it just manifests itself as a palpable fear for how students will do in their next stage. A greater familiarity with college teachers and curriculum might make everyone in a high school feel a little more realistic about what is and is not expected at the next level, and learning in schools might be a little more fun and productive as a result. On the other hand, college curriculum is seldom formulated with a very rich sense of what students' high school experience has been like: What the students studies and reads, what the student's teachers stress in writing assignments, how they discuss texts in class. The best high school teachers have a great deal to teach college instructors about how to pay attention to individuals in the face of large classes, many preparations, and looming standardized tests. Most of all, I have been impressed with the verve and commitment many teachers bring into their classrooms every day, even after years on the job. Too often, graduate instructors have as models professors for whom teaching is, at best, an intellectual performance or, at worst, a debasing chore.

The question of tracks and SLCs is particularly striking if we see it as emblematic of the divisions that keep language arts teachers at every level from seeing all students as their students. The way we sort students is also the way we classify teachers. Honors and AP teachers work together on curriculum and tell stories about kids at Fields the way history, math, and English teachers hang around and talk about students and classes in the business SLC office at Somerset. Breaking into smaller units can be good for teachers, but it can also produce attitudes that do not help students. As much as tracking does focus instruction and allow for appropriate pacing for students of different ability, it is also notorious for typing students and lowering expectations for those who are not counted in the highest group. At the same time, Kate had developed the medieval newspaper for her college prep class, and her AP class begged to be able to try that too, but she couldn't spare the time for them to have fun because they were doing a demanding project involving a set of three nonfiction essays. Her AP class was probably getting something that might prepare them for college writing, and I wish the college prep kids could have had that too, but the newspaper assignment fostered such a sense of pleasure and inquiry that I'm sorry the AP students missed it. George was having a good time team-teaching with his colleague in history, but the English faculty as a whole was no longer pursuing the excellent work they had started in the language arts document because they no longer had any identity as a departmental faculty.

These same trade-offs occur across the levels, in language arts and many other subjects. Sometimes the debate is framed as a conflict between rigor and motivation, sometimes between basics and enrichment, sometimes between product and process. The dichotomies strike me as false, but manifestations of these conceptual differences are very real and present in classrooms. College is figured as rigorous, and therefore college prep courses more rigorous than career preparatory courses, and honors courses must be more rigorous still than college prep. But every student at every level needs both sides of that fearful polarity, and conversations across levels would allow students and teachers to recognize both the need for motivation and process in more advanced coursework as well as the rigor of preparation possible in courses often thought merely basic or standard. In the next chapter, I offer a somewhat different analysis of these contrasting approaches, based on a theory of literacy sponsorship. Dialogue across boundaries and levels appears daunting, even impossible, but when we look at the sponsoring interests of schools, colleges, and universities, we can understand what is at stake in dialogues across educational differences. For now, however, I want to detail these differences, map the contours in these contrasting school terrains.

We see one version of the contrast when we compare the two curricula I have presented from Fields and Somerset Grade 12 English classes. Kate teaches a tightly sequenced course with extended writing assignments and independent reading as unquestioned components of the experience. George requires a reasonable amount of work from his students, but all the reading and writing is broken into small pieces and specific outcomes. The students write very little in that class longer than two or three pages, and almost every sentence must answer a question posed by the teacher. Reading in his class is a highly purposeful activity in that students read to pass quizzes and summarize "what happened," but books are not heavily embedded in a narrative that binds them together; much depends on students' personal identification with characters or plot events as the class takes up each book. In Kate's class the readings represent high points in a cultural story presented as one the students have some part in, or at the least one that they know will be highly valued in the college settings they are expected to enter. Yes, students in Kate's class are probably more willing to work "independently" on assignments than students in George's class, but Kate's curriculum offers a comforting collective identity to participants who are willing to accept the British tradition—however distant—as somehow antecedent to their own.

Again, I am not presenting one curriculum as exemplary and the other as inferior. I do think that students coming out of Kate's class are more likely to catch on to the writing task a college teacher might set, with its more abstracted problems and less explicit prescription for what should go in each paragraph. In some sense neither of these curricula look very much like either English 40 or 50 as it is usually practiced in Temple classrooms. The theme base in our first-year writing courses might be a little more familiar to the students in Kate's class, but they are used to national character and chronology as the binding narrative forces, not theory or ideological positioning. The tendency, especially in basic writing courses, to draw on personal reactions and history might be more familiar to George's students than Kate's, but the emphasis on nonfiction academic texts, often proposing a theoretical model for assembling facts into a meaningful construct, will be foreign to both.

Perhaps the most telling difference between the two curricula is not evident in the books or assignments themselves but in the overall attitude represented by the particulars. The students in George's class are posited as individual agents who will succeed if they work hard and stay out of trouble. The books, stories, and articles, the worksheets and journal entries, are meant to support them as individual thinkers and actors on their way to engaging with a system that may or may not have a place for them. George is positive in the way he presents this structure, and students who accept the expectations can earn high grades and develop a sense of achievement within the school. But the curriculum does not present a cultural narrative that tells a collective story about these children in this time, and it does not indicate a clear connections between what the students are reading and writing now and what they will be asked to write in college classes or beyond. In all honesty, there is no cultural narrative in a language arts course that could be devised for the children of Somerset that does not speak of strife and struggle, disjunction and discrimination, as well as heroism within the particular setting of Latin American history; it would take a highly committed and community-affiliated teacher to teach such a curriculum in a way that would not be discouraging or overly polemical for the kids, and even then it would be a challenge to make such a curriculum preparatory for a standard college curriculum. And students in this alternative curriculum would be at a disadvantage when they took standardized tests based on the traditional college prep curriculum. This is a conundrum that needs to be addressed by high school and college teachers together, because the issues lie athwart the divide.

Kate's course may not prepare students for a first-year writing course that requires students to critique class-bound perspectives in the use of food in the film *Babette's Feast,* or has students read Bruno Bettelheim on fairy tales before asking them to compare and contrast two tellings of Cinderella. Her students may also not be prepared for the wide range of people and perspectives they will encounter in the classrooms at a place like Temple. Yet the Fields students will enter any college classroom with a feeling that school can make sense not only of their own individual experience but of collective experiences that are highly valued by the dominant society. Because they are Americans, they too will be trained to see themselves as individual agents working for their own economic and spiritual betterment. But they can also assume that their efforts fit into a framework of efforts, that their little school stories repeat a commonly told school story, even if they themselves come from families that have never sent children to college before. The curriculum they experience is coherent, even if the canon on which it is based is ultimately more arbitrary and politically determined than they or their teachers recognize. The confidence they bring with them is a shared collective confidence, and that provides stronger ground for young writers and readers to stand on.

The vision of an intact and coherent pathway from K–12 to college and beyond has been one that haunted me from the first time I stepped into the booming, concrete building at North High School to the last time I drove off with the Fields football stadium in my rearview mirror. What do students see when they pick up their heads in English class, or when they trudge down the hall for one last period before the final bell for the day rings? I repeatedly had the impression that kids in some schools see their way to college and a job and a house so clearly that they do not notice the road at all. They simply know, in that unconscious way humans comprehend everyday life, that if they turn in this assignment, read that book, give the teacher what she said she wanted in class yesterday, the future in all its vague promise will somehow come to pass. College is scary at Fields or St. Mary's or Boulevard—no mistake about that—but "going on" has a solidity derived not from the individual algebra of "Sally's going to X and Max to Y" but by the relentless teleology of "*when,* not *if.*" In other high schools, college shimmers ahead like a mirage on a hot road. The road itself winds and loops; at points the paving may have washed out entirely in a flash flood or uniformed officials may hold up traffic indefinitely. The quantitative data I gathered and the observations I made speak one lesson clearly: From some schoolhouse doors the college campus just looks a lot further away.

I return to this question again in the next chapter, but I conclude with a few words here about what college writing programs could do in response to the story I have told here. First, no amount of theoretical or pedagogical sophistication substitutes for writing instructors visiting the schools that send us students. I used this chapter as a way of initiating contact with schools I felt I needed to know, and now I have begun a dialogue that must continue and broaden. Second, we must help in any way we can to define and pave the literacy path from school to college for students and teachers through collaborative work with the schools. This would probably involve students from K–16 and into graduate school working with one another on academic research as well as experiential projects outside the traditional classroom. Third, we must draw on this richer knowledge of school literacy experiences when we design and revise college programs, particularly taking into account the variety of tracks and groupings within which students learn to read and write. In short, in every wall we must install new doors and then use them to pass more freely from room to room.

3

Deep Alignment and Sponsorship

If Temple's partnership with Philadelphia regional schools is conflicted and class-based, its relationship with regional community colleges is publicly cordial but privately troubled. In a school with at least 44% transfer students in the undergraduate population, about one-third of the entering transfer students bring credits into Temple from the five largest feeder community colleges in the region (Schneider "Transfer"). The university has core-to-core agreements with at least 10 Pennsylvania and New Jersey 2-year county colleges, allowing students with associates degrees from those schools to transfer to Temple with few general education requirements to fulfill. These agreements are signed with ceremony and a great flurry of handshakes, but, after the celebratory wine and cheese reception, much unfinished business remains to make the transfer process smooth for most students.

The most pressing business involves making connections across programs and departments at the partner schools to assure that students really get the preparation they need to succeed in upper level courses and the support they need to graduate with a bachelor's degree. Writing is a key competency for transfer students, and WPAs bear responsibility for understanding the journey students make across these boundaries and smoothing the transition for them. WPAs are also likely to have the requisite interest and experience to see the progression in all its glory and shame—more than any other academic performance (with the possible exception of math), writing provides a window on students' achievements and challenges over time. We must investigate the data related to writing and transfer students, asking ourselves who is succeeding, who is failing, and why. And we must help writing instructors on both sides of the divide recognize that they share a constituency and a mission, whatever social roles their respective schools must play as institutions in the hierarchy of American higher learning.

This chapter begins to do that work. I begin with a review of literature on the nature of the community college as a social institution and a component of an educational system. What functions do business, government, and university officials expect community colleges to fulfill? What challenges does our system of transfer put on community college students? Moving from the general to the specific, I review data on the whole population of transfer students at Temple in recent years, then the data on two quite different community colleges and how their students fare at Temple. I take a step closer to the classrooms and concerns of writing programs by telling the story of a project that Temple and Community College of Philadelphia (CCP) pursued together. WPAs at CCP and I recognized that if we were to accomplish any significant alignment of writing and reading instruction, we needed to encourage greater collective conversation. After a number of preliminary meetings, exchanges, and seminars, a group of teachers from each institution shared writing assignments from Temple's English 50 and CCP's English 101—courses that, on paper, are equivalent to one another. In the process, we discovered central characteristics and preoccupations of the two programs that separate us and work against our providing comparable training to beginning college writers.

In order to imagine what I call *deep alignment*—a shared understanding of students' needs that would encourage common approaches and sequential coursework across the 2-year/4-year college divide—I conclude this chapter with a return to theory. The concept of *literacy sponsorship* provides a lens to analyze the differences I have identified between English curricula at Field and Somerset as well as the differences between first-year writing curricula at Temple and CCP. Those large-scale social expectations that I identify at the beginning of the chapter manifest themselves in the nature of literacy instruction by the end.

According to the American Association of Community Colleges' web site (statistics uploaded in 2004 were taken from a 2000 publication of *National Profile of Community Colleges*), 44% of all undergraduates in the United States were attending community college—10.4 million students in more than 1,100 2-year schools, almost 1,000 of those publicly funded ("Fact Sheet"). In that year, 46% of all African-American undergraduates and 55% of both Hispanic and Native American undergraduates were enrolled in community colleges. The Web site reported that the community college population was nearly 60% female, and the average age of the students was 29 years old. Advocates of community colleges assert that these schools serve an extremely important democratic function in offering a pathway to college for people who might otherwise be left out of postsecondary institutions. Critics warn, however, that these schools only serve to funnel away less qualified students from 4-year colleges and that in the process many students who began by aspiring to a bachelor's degree and pre-professional training settle for vocational training and lower paying employment.

Community colleges are a major feature in the geography of postsecondary education, but too often university administrators and faculty pay little attention to their partners in this *de facto* system. At Temple, the partners are only now beginning to cooperate on a plan to ensure students a clear and well-marked path to a baccalaureate degree, despite all the articulation agreements and public displays of cooperation. Frequently, everyone involved with transfer, including the university faculty who may or may not realize that many of their students studied somewhere else before arriving in their classroom, develop attitudes toward transfer students that don't particularly help those students succeed. These ideological stances—some formulated to protect jobs or status, some merely grown out of long-held class prejudices—look increasingly anachronistic in an era where the economy is so fluid. Education has become crucial for nearly all meaningful employment, and tenure-track as well as nontenured faculty lines have become contingent on enrollments and "value-added" accountability. No matter where we teach, writing instructors and college teachers must ask fundamental questions now about what exactly we are teaching and why, how our teaching does or does not mesh with the teaching in partner institutions, and what impact our labor practices have on the learning of students who move through the system we maintain.

VOCATION AND ITS DISCONTENTS

Before I enter into the discussion of data from Temple and its partner schools, I want to consider what educational sociologist Kevin Dougherty refers to as the "contradictory" nature of community colleges. Dougherty begins a review of critics and the advocates of the community college movement by highlighting the variety of institutional functions they identify:

> [T]he community college is a hybrid institution, combining many different and often contradictory purposes. It is a doorway to educational opportunity, a vendor of vocational training, a protector of university selectivity, and a defender of state higher education budgets (by providing an alternative to expanding the costly 4-year colleges). Such eclecti-

cism can breed synergy. But in the community college's case it has sown
contradiction. (8)

He argues that this contradictory character has become a major problem, a
"crisis" for the schools themselves and especially for those students who set
out to earn baccalaureate degrees by starting in community colleges (269).

The advocates and critics of the community college sound as if they are
talking about two entirely different institutions. Arthur Cohen and Florence
Brawer, for example, write of an American educational system that, well into
the middle of the 20th century, was focused almost entirely on elite young
men headed for the professions and selected young women intent on gain-
ing the marks of the cultured class; for them community colleges "contributed the most to opening the system. Established in every metropolitan
area, they were available to all comers attracting the 'new students': the
minorities, the women, the people who had done poorly in high school,
those who would otherwise never have considered further education" (20-
21). Cohen and Brawer identify many problems that the community college
movement faces today, such as rising costs of labor as a result of collective
bargaining (119) and the increased number of less-prepared students (138),
inequities among state and county funding patterns (129), faculty resistance
to innovations in instructional techniques (155), and greater demands for
student services (194). But they see these problems as challenges to educational leadership rather than symptoms of decline or failure.

On the other hand, critics of community colleges can be quite harsh in
their denunciation of a system they see as failing students and exploiting faculty. Describing the system of 2- and 4-year colleges as "educational
apartheid" rather than "democracy," Ira Shor asserts, in an interview with
Howard Tinberg, that the "segregation of lower income students into community colleges has not only produced about two dropouts for each graduate, but also greater exploitation of part-time teachers than on four-year
campuses" (Tinberg 52). In his view, community colleges were originally
designed to maintain the status quo, preserving the 4-year schools as the
precinct of the middle and upper classes. "The policy princes at that time,"
he says, "had no intention of democratizing education" (52). Shor sees community college students saddled with repressive tuitions, enrolled in classes
driven by repressive testing (53), and subjected to a system whose major
function Burton Clark referred to in 1960 as "cooling out" those with ambitions to rise in social class and economic status (567). Shor advocates "promoting the needs and interests of the *majority*" by refusing to accept the
lesser accommodations of this tracked system, by getting rid of remedial
courses in basic writing, and by fighting against funding education through
part-time employment and inadequate facilities (55).

Dougherty takes the advocates' democratic rhetoric seriously in order to press for the critics' reforms. He urges major structural changes in the system (260), but he recognizes that idealistic motives contributed to the founding of community colleges at the end of the 19th century as well as their expansion in the early 1960s. The focus of his attention is clearly on getting students to the bachelor's degree level, an attainment that brings significant benefits both in terms of earning power and civic engagement. He notes that "[w]hereas about 85% of 4-year college entrants aspire to a bachelor's, only 20 to 35% of community college entrants do" (53), and that people who do not want a bachelor's degree when they start college tend to do better in the 2-year setting than in the 4-year college (57). These observations tend to argue for a mission in the 2-year colleges other than transfer. However, he argues, if we are to accept the democratic access justification for these schools, then we must care about the transfer function of community college. In a review of six studies done in the 1980s that examined baccalaureate attainment in community college and 4-year college entrants, even after controlling for many socioeconomic and other factors in the populations, he shows that the studies indicate a significant difference between the two types of colleges: somewhere between 11% and 19% fewer bachelor's degrees in community colleges among similar demographic groups (53). He sums up the studies grimly by saying that "Baccalaureate aspirants clearly fare less well if they enter a community college than a 4-year college" (56). The reforms he calls for have most to do with strengthening the link between the early and later years of a student's undergraduate education.

One of the main culprits Dougherty identifies is the tendency in community colleges to emphasize vocationalism, thus funneling students out of the undergraduate stream and into middle-level jobs from which they cannot progress. He complains that the quality of preparation for a bachelor's degree in 2-year colleges does not equal that in 4-year schools:

> A major reason is that the community colleges' strong emphasis on vocational education interferes with effective transfer education by seducing baccalaureate aspirants from their original plans, by reducing the chances they will be accepted by 4-year colleges (especially with full credits), and by distracting community colleges from mounting academically rigorous transfer or university-parallel courses. (248)

He does not accuse anyone of a conspiracy to hurt students, but he identifies the expectations inherent in the origins of the schools and the continued gulf between 2- and 4-year schools as contributing to the large number of students who either expect not to achieve a bachelor's degree or give up along the way.

Dougherty is particularly helpful in identifying the main obstacles that prevent students from completing a baccalaureate. He details challenges at each stage in students' progress toward graduation:

1. Staying in school during the first 2-years.
2. Transferring to a 4-year school.
3. Surviving in the 4-year school.

Dougherty is very careful to stress that even when he is recounting the most emotional or psychological difficulties that students face in the transfer process, the causes of attrition "are anchored in institutional realities" (92). In all three of the stages of what he calls "the pilgrimage to Zion"—from matriculation to graduation—"aspirants are beset by certain institutional features of community colleges and of 4-year colleges that threaten their progress" (106). Students from many community colleges face similar gaps and fissures in the educational road as do students from the more stressed high schools I described in Chapter 2; the various institutions students must pass through may not give them a clear sense of the road ahead of them nor assure them that hard work will yield good results. A vista of a fully paved and unobstructed road is what 4-year native students at private colleges usually get, especially if they have been prepared beforehand by middle-class school systems.

Shor's critique of the community college as an oppressive structure designed to produce failure has a brooding explanatory power that contrasts strikingly with the bright appeal of Cohen and Brawer's democratic rhetoric about these schools. But neither view will help us address the patchwork of institutions as it unfolds today: vastly disparate physical facilities, inconsistent curricula and policies, unexamined histories, and unpromising futures stretch out before us and our students. We have to find a way to make working partnerships within this contradictory landscape in order to provide a truly hopeful environment for the students who must shape lives from what they find there.

TEMPLE AND REGIONAL COMMUNITY COLLEGES

At an urban university like Temple, retention is constantly a major concern. According to a 2004 *U.S. News & World Report* ranking of top schools, the 2003 graduation rate at Dartmouth was 95% and at Lafayette College it was 86%, but at a more urban institution such as the University of Minnesota-

Twin Cities, the rate was 54%. The national 6-year graduation rate in 2002 was 63%, with high-income students graduating at a rate of 77% compared with low-income students at 54%; Latinos graduated in 6 years at a rate of 47% and African Americans at 46% (Carey 2). With an extremely diverse student population, Temple is no exception to this trend. In an October 2000 internal study on retention at Temple, the 1993 entering cohort of transfers and original students showed 6-year graduation rates of about 55% and 48%, respectively. At first glance, this would seem to suggest that transfer students do better at persisting to graduation than original students, and there is probably some truth to the observation. The comparison is not quite fair, however, because transfer students have been in school at least one semester longer than original students in the same cohort. More important to our present discussion, the population of transfer students includes about half who started at community colleges and half who left other 4-year institutions to attend Temple. In both cases, these are the survivors, the ones who were not discouraged by their first college experiences or by the rough passage to a new school. In some cases, Philadelphia area residents who went away to small liberal arts colleges far from home decided to return and attend Temple for its relative affordability and proximity, its extensive offerings and specialized coursework, or its urban setting and diverse student population. In other cases, Temple represents a dream for those who knew few people with a bachelor's degree; they entered community college with the goal in mind of eventually attending Temple. However transfer students arrive at Temple's campus, they are a considerable component of the population and their fates and outcomes have much to teach us about how the university functions and what we need to offer all students to keep them on track for a diploma.

Schools like Temple present a promise of democratic access that is similar to the one advocates see in community colleges. As in community colleges, developing skills and qualifications for the work world is a big motivation for students seeking a diploma. From 1997 to 2001, 80% of students entering Temple each year reported on a new student questionnaire that one important reason for their decision to attend college was "to be able to get a better job." Like community colleges, Temple still provides access to a college education for many students who might otherwise have difficulty affording college. Although at Temple the students' reported parental family income has inched up over the last few years—in 1997, 59% reporting an income of less than $45,000 while only 47% reported the same in 2001—still more than 64% of students at Temple were on financial aid in 2001, and 73% of students that year reported some or major concern about their ability to finance their college education. Temple has traditionally been a place for FG college students, and still in 2001 42% of new students reported that their fathers had only a high school education or less; 37% report that their mothers had this educational background.

At the same time, Temple has some of the contradictory character that Dougherty identifies in community colleges, although the contradictions themselves are different in nature. Our retention rates put us in a category of educational institutions much more like community colleges or even urban high schools, especially if we compare ourselves to small private schools where nearly every one who matriculates will leave with a baccalaureate degree. And yet, unlike community colleges or even most state-funded universities in Pennsylvania, Temple is a research university with a faculty tenured and promoted largely on the basis of their publication and research record. Categorized by the Carnegie Institute as Doctoral/ Research Extensive, the university "received over $109.4 million in sponsored research, training, and service awards in 2000/01" according to its official profile. Teaching matters in faculty evaluation, but because the university decided to achieve Carnegie I status in the late 1970s, the culture among faculty and graduate students has become more like what can be found in the departmental halls at Penn State or Rutgers than in the halls of 2-year county schools or at 4 year regional colleges where faculty teach four courses each semester. Despite a great many faculty development efforts and campus-wide conferences on undergraduate education, most faculty still define themselves more as scholars than teachers. Many cheer every rise in average SAT score for the new entering class reported by the admissions office, and not a few shake their heads at the prospect of teaching ESL students who can not compose perfectly in English or urban students who never encountered Sophocles or trigonometry in their high schools.

Within this setting, transfer students can sometimes become the scapegoats for faculty frustration. Although our data shows that transfers persist and graduate at a higher rate than original students, faculty conversations often portray transfer students as the ones who slow up classes, bring down academic standards, and clog the popular majors. The School of Communications and Theater is overrun with majors in its film, TV, and journalism departments, and it has taken to scrutinizing the records of transfer students carefully before letting them into the school. The faculty senate committee assigned to oversee academic policy considered articulation agreements with eight community colleges from 1999-2001, and there was much debate in these sessions about lowering our standards and admitting students with inferior training. I was on that committee and participated in most of the conversation during that time. In the end, the committee voted to approve the agreements one by one, because no interpretation of the data on students could show significantly lower performance by transfers, but the data was a little thin and inconclusive, and few critics in the debate were fully persuaded. The debate was not held widely enough to change the minds of the faculty who simply do not view transfer students as having the background to complete a demanding major at a university. Transfer students are important for enrollment numbers in many majors, and so faculty thought it prudent not to resist the articulation agreements. Still, we have done little to address our fears or reservations about transfer students and practically nothing to link the curricula of community colleges with the programs in the university students will eventually enter.

A list of institutions from which entering students transferred in 2001 names more than 50 schools in the Philadelphia area and beyond. This list includes nearby universities such as Drexel, LaSalle, West Chester, Widener, and St. Joseph's, as well as small local colleges such as Arcadia, Cabrini, Harcum, and Holy Family. Students that year came from large state universities such as Penn State, Delaware, Maryland, and Pittsburgh, as well as smaller state-funded colleges and universities such as Kutztown, Millersville, Shippensburg, and East Stroudsburg. However, the largest single sources of transfer students in 2001 and in most recent years are three 2-year schools: CCP, Bucks County Community College, and Montgomery County Community College. In that year, these three schools combined for a total of 774 students registered in an entering transfer class of 1,688. No other college came within 100 of each school's contribution; most other schools contributed less than 20 students, and many sent Temple less than 10. It is fair to say that a significant portion of the story about transfer students at Temple can be told through the experiences and performances of students from these three schools.

Table 3.1 presents one important aspect of this picture. I use data from the 1996 cohort of entering students, the last group for which I have a relatively complete long-term record. The two suburban schools show graduation rates within 4 years of 10% or higher than the graduation rate of CCP; this spread is only a little narrower by the fifth year. A great many factors come to mind when we see this data, but of course it parallels data we saw in the previous chapter about students from regional high schools: socioeconomic status (SES), early schooling, and future expectations all must figure in an explanation of the gaps in persistence to graduation. Yet, community

Figure 3-1: Graduation Rates for Transfers and Originals: Fall 1996 Cohort

	N%	Graduated by Year 4	% Graduated by Year 5
CCP	353	45.0%	50.4%
Bucks	121	55.4%	57.9%
Montgomery	131	58.0%	62.6%
Total Transfers	1,848	50.3%	55.9%
Total Originals	2,216	20.7%	41.5%

college transfer students do represent a different population to investigate than entering high school students because, on the whole, people who start off in community colleges—in the suburbs or the city—are older and tend to come from lower economic circumstances than their counterparts entering 4-year colleges as first-year students.

As discussed earlier, Dougherty says that studies indicate students who initially report wanting a baccalaureate degree but start out in a community college do not achieve their stated goal as often as students who start out at a 4-year college, even when those studies control for SES and other factors. To me, many of his posited reasons for the discrepancy distill into one challenge for the partners in the transfer relationship: The way must be smooth and clearly marked from one level of education to the next, with much effort put into preparation for students and communications among partner institutions. On the whole, students at CCP come from families of more modest means than students at Bucks County Community College. In the Fall 2000 semester, more than 67% of full-time students at CCP received financial aid, whereas only about 19% of Bucks students received financial aid in the 2000-2001 school year. This is an impressive difference, but the students at Bucks are not by and large the highly prepared, motivated students of wealthy parents; I met very few students in the upper tracks of Bucks County high schools who reported that they were planning to attend their local community college. Montgomery County Community College is similar to Bucks in population and funding for the institution, and later in the chapter I use Bucks as an example of a suburban school in comparison to CCP, in order to understand what factors may lie beneath the differences between the success of urban and suburban students at Temple.

Before I take a closer look at the two schools, I linger a moment on Table 3.2, which represents perhaps the most compelling reason for greater cooperation among writing programs in universities and community colleges. This table focuses on the GPA in all designated writing courses (WGPA) at Temple of transfer students at our three leading partner community colleges. Setting aside the differences between GPA of CCP students and students from the two suburban schools, we can make a few useful observations about all community college transfer students from this data. First, students who graduated after 5 years had higher WGPAs than those not graduating. At first this seems perfectly predictable because one would expect students who graduate to do better than students who do not, but research on retention and persistence has identified a number of factors such as social and academic integration, student engagement, financial conditions an demographic variables, and satisfaction with the college environment (see, e.g., Ahlburg, DesJardin, and McCall; Astin; Pascarella and Terenzini; Tinto; I'm also indebted to an internal Temple report by Alexis Drake). Strength or confidence in writing may be a factor in students surviving the transition and

Table 3.2. Median WGPA for Transfers Who Did and Did Not Graduate after 5 years: 1996 Entering Cohort

	Graduated				Did Not Graduate			
	N1	45+ Transfer Credits	N2	44 or Fewer Transfer Credits	N3	45 + Transfer Credits	N4	44 or Fewer Transfer Credits
Bucks	43	3.21	22	2.91	5	3.00	22	2.61
Montgomery	41	3.16	26	3.05	16	2.79	12	2.41
CCP	87	3.12	51	2.82	41	2.55	78	2.32
Total	688	3.15	533	3.08	251	2.66	426	2.58

Students included from the three community colleges earned 100% of their transfer credits at the named institution.

completing their studies. If that is true, then it is incumbent on writing directors in partner schools to ensure, just as within the curriculum of a 4-year college, that the courses students take in one school truly prepare them for the challenges they will face in later courses at the next school.

Second, students who remained at their first school for at least 45 credits or more earned a higher WGPA than those who left their first school with less than 45 credits, whether or not the students graduated from the university after transferring. This is perhaps a more surprising observation. It seems to suggest that students do benefit from enough time to develop a sense of belonging in their first institution before they transfer to a new one. The group that stayed in community college longer and those who persevered to a degree appear to be stronger writers than the group that transferred in from a 2-year school earlier and those who did not graduate from the university. We cannot make an argument about causation from this data, but we can consider it another indication that writing programs could have a powerful and positive effect on students if they were designed with an intention to support students as they move from early to late in their undergraduate career. The stepwise shape of these numbers suggests that coordinated writing programs across partner schools might make a difference in the overall success of transfer students in their quest for a bachelor's degree.

DEEP ALIGNMENT: PROGRAMS IN CONVERSATION

Motivated by the recognition that we each have a stake in the success of our common students, writing instructors and administrators at Temple and CCP have been carrying on a conversation about the objectives and pedagogy of our respective writing programs. As early as 1997, we began with a series of presentations that Temple colleagues and I gave to CCP English faculty about the writing program at Temple. At these events, we shared syllabi, guidelines, and student work from Temple and held our first discussions about what introductory writing meant for Temple students. We then negotiated an exchange program between the two institutions, with one instructor from Temple teaching a basic writing course at CCP while a CCP instructor taught a basic writing course at Temple. We followed these first attempts at collaboration with a series of discussions and pedagogical seminars, held at one or another of our schools, that have been bringing the two writing faculty together since 2001.

Much of this public conversation was facilitated by regular informal meetings I had with people at CCP and Temple committed to writing and undergraduate education. Tom Ott, director of Developmental Studies and a professor in the English Department at CCP, met with me regularly at a local coffee shop in the neighborhood of the city where we both live. We had gotten acquainted at one of my early visits to CCP, when we discovered that not only did we live near one another but our children also went to the same school. We started to get together for wide-ranging conversations about the quirks and strains of our programs as well as the challenges and possibilities each institution faced. We laughed and schemed, commiserated and vented about teaching writing at urban schools where nothing administrative ever seemed to go smoothly and students often arrived in classes with much greater needs than could be adequately addressed by our budgets or institutional habits. We also shared stories about our children as they grew into adolescents. Through it all, we worked out the remarkably knotty details of union restrictions on the teacher exchange, discussed the controversies at CCP about sequencing and exit exams, and brainstormed ways to improve reading instruction at both schools. We shared data about our respective programs and argued about the merits of various kinds of pedagogies, while we also learned each other's personal histories with writing and teaching. In short, we built the growing relationship between the two programs on our own growing relationship as teachers, administrators, and parents.

In Spring 2003, Dianne Perkins was named writing director at CCP. There had never been a position quite like this at CCP; she was given a course reduction but a heavy charge. They asked her to develop greater consistency in the first-year college composition courses as well as coordinate WAC with 28 departments at the college. That summer, Dianne and I began meeting to talk about ways we could pursue the relationship between Temple and CCP further, and we decided to focus on assignments instructors give in the two programs. Temple Writing had facilitated three year-long projects to gather assignments in the areas of social science, humanities, and social work; participants in all those projects had been enthusiastic and proud of the resulting documents we had assembled in each effort. Dianne and I wanted to use this idea to facilitate conversation about expectations for writing in the two schools, and we started to send out requests for assignments from instructors in the two courses that were supposed to be equivalents, English 50 at Temple and English 101 at CCP.

An important working relationship at Temple also fits into the story. During the 2002-2003 academic year, I was deeply involved with general education curriculum reform at Temple University. As chair of the task force drafting a new general education plan, I worked closely with Bob Schneider, the associate vice provost for general education and transfer issues. Bob and I had been friends ever since I arrived at Temple in 1996, but we had never worked so hard and so long at one seemingly endless problem as we did that year. I defer discussion of the general education experience until Chapter 5, but one pertinent idea that came out of our collaboration in 1996-1997 was *deep alignment,* a connection between institutions that goes beyond articulation agreements and the automatic acceptance of course equivalencies. We wanted to find a way that faculty from many disciplines in partner schools would know each other's curriculum. Faculty in both institutions should feel confident that what was being taught in community college prepared students for what they would find in their university majors. We wanted to promote deep alignment not by having the university faculty dictate what the community college instructors would teach, but by fostering a true dialogue that could make courses on both sides of the divide better. If the dialogue worked, then at least some faculty in both schools would know what students should be able to do at any given level, at least in writing, math, and certain liberal arts subjects like psychology and biology that were crucial to professional degrees. The dialogue would also raise fundamental questions about what is being taught, how topics were sequenced, and what students should know at different points in their careers.

Bob organized two conferences that brought to Temple's campus professors and administrators from at least three or four of our community college partners to talk to Temple faculty about transfer students. In the first conference, held in 2001, we talked primarily about what we called "transferable skills and abilities": competencies that we could all agree students need for success in later college classes. But we soon realized that the formulation was too abstract and inaccessible. The conversations that began that day involved actual elements of curriculum, assignments professors made in specific classes, experiences students gained in internships or community-based projects. In the afternoon, faculty from math and science, writing, and social science programs talked about their particular disciplines in separate break-out groups, but the conversations had just gotten worthwhile by the end of the day. Too few Temple faculty took part, and no whole departments on either side of the line left the conference feeling that they had an on-going commitment to continue the dialogue.

After our year together in general education reform, Bob and I knew we had to pursue deep alignment in a more sustained way. His transfer conference in Spring 2004 used this term as title and theme. We focused on two topics for alignment discussion: data and teaching approaches. Under the first topic, participating faculty from both environments got to see data on how students from community colleges did once they arrived at Temple. Although we did not share publicly any data that compared community colleges with one another, each school received a packet containing data about their own students' performance at Temple. The data shown in Table 3-2 on WGPA & students were among those we shared, emphasizing especially the difference between people who had completed more than 45 credits before entering Temple and those who had transferred with fewer credits.

The data sparked lively conversation at the Deep Alignment conference, and many of the questions raised on all sides could not be answered except by more data and more intensive study of how students move through their undergraduate careers in transfer. As we talked, we realized how truly complicated the picture was. Many students do not move in a straight line from one school to another; a significant number (no one can know quite how many) "swirl" from Temple to CCP to other schools and back to Temple. Many drop out or stop out (leave coursework for a semester or a year) because of financial or family problems rather than because of academic failure. Numbers tell only a small piece of the story, but case studies could be misleading in a population this diverse. Unfortunately, none of the participating schools, including Temple, had enough of an investment in institutional research to sustain the kind of investigation we all recognized we needed. We discussed the need for writing a grant and took volunteers for a committee to pursue the possibilities.

The second topic in the Deep Alignment conference involved the teaching staffs of the respective schools. Faculty present nearly as complicated a picture as the students do; in some ways faculty represent more intractable problems rooted in institutional inequities and conflicting self-interests. For many university research faculty, the teaching part of their job translates into little contact with first- or second-year undergraduates except in large or vast classroom settings. Some university faculty who are no longer producing research may be carrying a heavier undergraduate teaching load. Sometimes these professors are real gems, but they can also be tired of the subjects they teach if not bitter about their profession altogether. Community college offers faculty a more limited range of teaching possibilities, but—at least in many social sciences and humanities-based courses—faculty resist being told what or how they should teach. Obviously research and teaching expectations differ markedly for full-time faculty at a university or a community college, but what tenured or tenure-track faculty in the two institutional settings share is a measure of autonomy in their classrooms and a measure of security in their jobs.

Tenured and tenure-track faculty from all the schools participated in this conference, but we knew we needed to hear from year-to-year contract or part-time adjuncts, as well. Nontenured instructors, either full or part time, come to both academic settings from many different life histories (see Schell and Stock). Graduate students teach primarily introductory courses in the university setting, and they usually teach what they are told, although in some departments they are given chalk and a grade book and left on their own to teach mid-level undergraduate courses, with little supervision or mentoring. Graduate students are not absent at community colleges, either, because they serve as adjuncts when they run out of funding in their university departments. Adjuncts teach at the 2-year, 4-year, and university levels and notoriously must stitch together a work life that might include three or four schools, multiple courses and preparation, no offices, low pay, and little respect from anyone. From this variegated and sometimes distracted faculty—some detached and distant, some green and enthusiastic, some worn out and world weary, some perpetually on the road—undergraduate students in both institutions must, in their first 2 years, learn basic skills and approaches that they can use to enter their chosen disciplines. If we add to the complex labor picture the miscommunications and prejudices that keep faculty of various castes and affiliations from speaking to one another, we might well wonder how students manage to cross the gaps and fissures in the higher education landscape at all.

In the Deep Alignment conference, we addressed the question of teaching by presenting a panel of faculty who had taught on either side of the community college–university divide. One speaker was Dianne, my friend who was the writing director at CCP. She had been a nontenured full-time instructor at Temple in years past, and she had been involved in our teacher exchange across the two institutions. As the CCP participant, she taught basic writing (English 40) at Temple while a Temple instructor taught basic writing (English 98) at CCP. What she emphasized at the conference was that although the students were somewhat better prepared at Temple, even in the basic writing courses, the biggest difference she could see between the two courses was the expectations of the Temple instructors and the program for the kind of writing students would be able to produce by the end of the semester. She felt that the assignments in Temple's English 40 were significantly different from what students encounter in CCP's English 98, and she suggested that the same might be true in the next level writing classes. Her comments were intriguing, and they convinced me that we needed to collect assignments from faculty in the two programs and explore this difference in expectations.

In the next section, I present the results of our study of these two sets of assignments. Our experience with discussions of deep alignment taught us that only sustained, long-term efforts in specific programs such as writing, math, basic sciences would make a difference to anyone. Conferences are pleasant—an occasion for warm feelings, sweeping pronouncements, and full bellies—but only when instructors of similar courses sit down together and look at topic sequences, assignments, and examples of student work is there hope for real understanding and change. Both sides must be willing to listen and to reevaluate their own practices and goals in light of what they learn in the dialogue. The time and energy needed for such efforts is not negligible, but the results may be worthwhile if we not only develop better understandings of our common work but we make the way more rational and planned for students who must traverse great distances to gain their degrees.

Before I leave this discussion, there is one other consideration I want to mention about teachers who share the job of educating this regional pool of students across the levels. As with schoolteachers in the Philadelphia area, many college instructors and professors who teach in and around the city received at least some of their education Temple, and I take it this is a common situation for many metropolitan research universities and their region. But training faculty for regional postsecondary schools is trickier politically than training regional K–12 teachers.

Schools of education are designed to train teachers, and if their teachers don't perform well on certification exams or in the classroom, frequently there is a public outcry and the training schools are held responsible, at least for a public moment. But noneducation departments in research universities seldom feel the same responsibility toward regional colleges who hire their graduates. A department in a research university is ranked by the publication output of its faculty and by the "quality" of job placements for their graduates. This can cause great tension within research departments, especially in a school like Temple. Many of our graduates do not get jobs in more prestigious research universities, either because their credentials make them less competitive than students from more highly ranked schools or because our graduates have ties to the area and wish to find work nearby rather than go on the national market. From the point of view of training faculty to be best suited for positions in community colleges, state schools, branch campuses of state universities, or small liberal arts colleges, metropolitan universities could do much more to give students the experiences and breadth of knowledge that would make them excellent teaching professionals. But this is too often seen as a capitulation to mediocrity by faculty who identify themselves primarily as researchers and scholars, and even a mention of the problem can cause departmental strife. I return to the training controversy in the conclusion of this chapter, but I doubt any broad solution is possible. It would take careful negotiations within the specific dynamics of a given department to unravel this particular knot.

THE FIRST-YEAR WRITING ASSIGNMENT PROJECT

Dianne and I met one June afternoon at a coffee shop near her apartment in Center City Philadelphia. I brought with me a set of assignments from Temple's English 50 course to show her, and she carried with her assignments from their equivalent course, English 101. Collecting assignments proved difficult for both of us, but I could get assignments from advanced graduate students more easily and I could share the assignments required in the teaching practicum for beginning TAs to use in their classes. CCP at the time had no administrative structure specifically for first-year writing the way Temple does, and they do not have graduate students who must follow a standard syllabus. Although the CCP English Department handbook published "exit criteria" for English 101, it was less clear about how faculty should meet these criteria, a source of frustration for Dianne. She was hoping to use our discussion about assignments to get a conversation going in her department so that instructors would be more likely to accept guidelines and even some standard expectations for the course.

Our conversation turned to comparing the teaching force in each program. Both use part-time faculty, but CCP's are unionized and fiercely hold on to their autonomy in the classroom. Although as a whole about 40% of CCP instructors are part time, in the English Department a larger proportion of part time teachers teach the developmental courses below English 101; 101 and its second semester research writing course, English 102, are taught largely by full-time tenured or tenure-track faculty teaching four courses a semester. The faculty is deeply divided about how writing should be taught. They all teach developmental writing or composition, or both, and they regularly use the Teaching Center on campus to talk about pedagogical approaches (their offices and hallways are too cramped for discussions, but the English Department reserves the center for discussions more than most departments in the college). Dianne explained that the problem in their meetings is that people tend to harden their positions and reading lists along ideological lines: some see pedagogy purely in political terms, following a line they associate with Ira Shor; others argue for a more traditional curriculum built on rhetorical modes; some take a more expressivist or cultural studies approaches; still others urge a more holistic approach tying their teaching to preparation for later coursework. Dianne said that their discussions seldom move beyond long-held positions and anecdotal evidence. When they do talk about classroom practice in composition, pedagogical approaches tend to transmute into something akin to religious convictions that also reinforce chronic political splits in the faculty.

They do not often discuss recent professional articles or conduct research themselves on the issues in their classroom. Only Tom Ott, as director of Developmental Studies, has persisted in raising issues about data he collects in developmental and other classes. For him, the issue is whether first year writing is a stand-alone course with its own agenda or a service course meant to help students succeed in later courses. He works tirelessly for the latter position but recognizes that many others don't agree with him. Every summer he goes through course reports, painstakingly collates data on grades and student progress, and then publishes it in a newsletter for the department. Few people either among the faculty or the administration pay his data much attention. For instructors, close attention to data would force them to recognize the need for a more uniform approach to first-year writing courses, which would curtail their traditional autonomy. For administrators, data suggests a need for more course release time for directors of programs and more support for students; this means greater demand on a budget that is already woefully thin.

Dianne estimated in our conversation that 60% to 70% of the assignments in 101 were drawn from fictional texts. Some regular faculty members teach courses that are literature-based and quite traditional in respect to assignments, grammar instruction, and grading. Others assign nonfiction or academic texts as well as fiction and develop a sequence of writing tasks through the semester, whereas still others use little reading material, preferring to base their assignments on personal narrative and opinions. Some part-time and full-time teachers value the five-paragraph theme and rhetorical modes highly, whereas others disdain formal requirements and ask for a more impressionistic approach or one that puts a premium on rhetorical analysis of texts. Faculty teach in a wide array of special programs with acronyms like TOP, HEP, CAP, ACT NOW, all meant to address and motivate a certain segment of the student population, but to some extent these multiple programs work against any collective sense of outcomes or purpose. Some of their recent hires, including those from Temple, are young and deeply committed to the student population in an open-admissions college but may have a limited sense of how to begin teaching less-prepared students. Some who have been teaching at CCP a very long time take a somewhat cynical view of their students and administrators. Most are committed to teaching and are wary of the greater privilege research brings to faculty at universities. They hold conferences in tiny, windowless offices shared with one or more other instructor. There is no shared departmental office or faculty lounge space, and the large open student cafeteria is usually too noisy and crowded to hold conferences there.

Temple's program is built largely on graduate students who must move through the pipeline quickly because of limits on funding. Unless they have taught in their previous life, the longest serving graduate student veterans have taught less than 5 years. Most of these students do not choose composition as their specialty, and they hope for the chance to teach literature in their specialty fields. Another portion of graduate student teachers is the creative writing master's contingent. Although some literature and creative writing students fall in love with composition teaching, and many simply do their jobs well, a few each year find the work dull and demeaning, a necessary evil at best. Even among the students who declare for composition/rhetoric, not all are strong teachers. Still, the graduate students in composition usually walk off with the awards in the college for teaching, and the student evaluation ratings in the program are uniformly high (we are one of the few departments that requires a full course and provides mentors for training purposes). Some graduate students in literature and creative writing are encouraged by their advisors to focus more on their studies than their teaching, and especially at times when course loads rise to two-and-two this is not entirely inappropriate advice. Two or sometimes three students share an office, some of which have windows and all have computers with Internet access.

But under the seeming unanimity of a program administered by a central director, associate director, an administrative assistant, a TA, graduate mentors, and a practicum teacher, approaches to writing instruction are far from uniform. New teachers are struggling just to survive each class day and still do their studies, veterans are forming their own styles based on personal experiences and what their friends are doing, and the demands of high theory and literary research remain the standard for accomplished intellectual work. Few teaching assistants have experience doing any other kind of writing besides literary criticism or creative writing, and fewer still will have experienced first-year writing classes as difficult or demanding themselves. Many will concede that they were exempt from such classes when they were undergraduates, and the new ones admit that the hardest writing adjustment they have experienced is the one they experience in their first graduate classes, even while they are also expected to give guidance to classrooms of tentative undergraduates. Either they make the leap and develop an empathy for their students based on self-identification, they grow impatient with these young people who can not seem to do what looks like comparatively simple tasks, or they find themselves bewildered by the whole discourse mess and hope desperately that things get better eventually.

Many Temple part-timers are often former TAs who know the system and hang on to adjunct composition teaching for a few years until they find more full-time employment, whereas others are teaching in multiple schools to earn some modicum of a living wage. Another major source of teachers in the Temple program is the corps of full-time, nontenure-track jobs we call dean's appointments (DAs), who cannot stay at their jobs for more than 6 years.[1] DAs are either postdoctoral Temple graduates hoping to find professorial positions elsewhere eventually, or they are PhD's from other universities who needed temporary postdoctoral work because they have not yet found permanent positions. Some of these individuals have significant training in composition; usually they are willing to teach according to program guidelines, and they bring new life to the common materials. Few if any tenured or tenure-track faculty—including those in composition/rhetoric—taught even a single course in the first-year writing program during the years 1996 to 2004.

---

[1] The system for full-time nontenured employment has changed at Temple since I wrote this, but all the data from this study was compiled under the system I describe here.

At this stage in our collaboration, Dianne and I did not have enough information to begin drawing any conclusions about the assignments in the two programs—we could only marvel at the institutional circumstances and the complexities they caused in creating a program with a defined vision and pedagogical approach. The differences in labor conditions and work force between our two programs seemed themselves a barrier to cooperation and understanding, but we felt compelled to continue trying to make the connections. We generated a number of questions we had about assignments in the two programs. Here are four we noted that day:

1. What genres of readings generate the required writing tasks?
2. What reading/writing functions are required by course topics (summary, analysis, synthesis)?
3. To what extent are formal considerations primary in the assignments?
4. What sort of specificity do teachers put into assignments? Have organizational patterns or rhetorical modes been prescribed by the instructors?

We agreed to hold at least two events, one at CCP and the other at Temple, where we could share a more complete collection of assignments with participating instructors and have them talk about the differences they saw.

The first of these events was hosted by CCP. More than 20 community college faculty, 8 Temple DAs and graduate students, and 3 Temple WPAs attended. At this meeting, we began to look at a collection of assignments and four mixed groups of instructors discussed what they saw. We could not get very specific because people had just received the packet of assignments; the CCP assignments caused the faculty from that school to talk a great deal among themselves about how representative the assignments were and what the various questions said about their program. Because we were on CCP grounds, we focused primarily on their assignments and what motivated them. Faculty expressed a passionate desire to help their students learn the expected form of essays, to help them understand what kind of written language college teachers want to see in papers. They felt frustrated by the level of preparation their students bring to their classrooms, and they saw themselves as teaching language, skill, and technique in short assignments, usually six to eight papers. Expanding the students thinking mattered to many around the table, but there was no consensus on how to demand more critical or imaginative engagement from the students. Most faculty require some revisions in 101. Dianne typically assigns seven short papers and has students revise all of the first four, some more than once, but her practice is apparently not usual. With so many papers and so many students—22 in each of four writing classes—reading and grading revisions is a fearsome addition to their teaching load. Faculty must be selective in requiring revisions, so they also can have a life.

When we talked about specific assignments they saw as typical, some felt an assignment like the following was too simplistic and did not reflect what others did in the program, but many thought it did represent what a significant portion of 101 instructors were doing:

> Essays on *American Mosaic* anthology, readings by Panunzio, Rolvaag, Hurston, Morrison, Thomas, Cofer, Sone and Yamamoto.
> Develop a thesis on one of the following topics:
> - Choose three characters—from three different works—who are becoming assimilated into the American mainstream. Show how. *Please note: for all topics choose three different characters from three different works.*
> - Choose three characters who are alienated from others in the same ethnic or racial group. Illustrate how.
> - Choose three characters whose yearning for the American dream is very apparent.

These assignments were accompanied by the following stylistic notes:

> Remember the form of the standard college essay: an introductory paragraph with a thesis near the end. (Use good parallel structure in that sentence; it guides the essay.) The middle paragraphs should have innovative topic sentences. Pull together your points in the conclusion.
>
> Support your points with examples from the work, but don't give summaries. Your audience, the class, has read the material.
>
> Use at least two parenthetical documentations: (author page)
>
> Use at least one short quote, no more than two lines. Weave in and out of the quote smoothly.
>
> Make notes and outlines for this paper. (It's helpful to experiment with several outlines to see which one you like best.) The outline and notes will be handed in with the paper.

There were more subtle assignments, some that pointed directly to issues in the readings, and some that gave students a better chance to form a debatable thesis, but almost all were followed by specific instruction about form and style. This question, taken from a sequence of questions that worked students through summary, response, and comparison/contrast on the theme of adolescent psychology, seemed to the community college faculty both representative and exemplary:

> Both Laurence Steinberg, in *Beyond the Classroom*, and Judith Harris, in Malcolm Gladwell's article "Do Parents Matter?" address the influence of parents and peers on children's lives. What similarities and differences can you identify in their views? If one writer's perspective seems more persuasive than the other's, analyze why.

Like the assignment about the *American Mosaic* readings, this one included carefully worded reminders about form and style:

> As usual, your introductory paragraph should provide full context for your discussion, and there should be a clear thesis by the end of this first paragraph.
>
> The body of your essay will require at least three paragraphs to identify a few similarities and difference between these writers' views. (In each body paragraph, discuss only ONE similarity—or ONE difference—between the authors' views.)
>
> If you have done a good job locating similarities and differences and used the principles of good paragraph development (examples, quotations, analysis, and other "modes of development" that we have discussed this semester), you will already have achieved a lot, and your grade will likely be a good one.
>
> If you can also ADD a final paragraph or two about why one writer seems more persuasive than the other, it will add "the icing to the cake," so to speak. (You do not HAVE to add this final evaluative segment to your essay, but if you do so thoughtfully, it will make your essay all the more interesting.)
>
> Finally, a clear topic-sentence outline before you start drafting your essay will assure a clear structure for the essay. If you produce one by Tuesday, I will take a quick look at it and provide some feedback.

Perhaps the most demanding assignments in the packet we collected were part of a sequence developed around Deborah Tannen's linguistic work in *That's Not What I Meant!* and applied to a play called *Brother* by Mary Gallagher. Here students wrote a series of one-page papers, and each time they turned the papers in they were immediately collected and redistributed to the class as a photocopied anthology of student work called *Essays on the Language of Mary Gallagher's* Brother. Here is the first assignment for that sequence:

> In a one-page essay (typed, double-spaced, 1-inch margins, 12 point type) analyze the language in some particular piece(s) of conversation in Mary Gallagher's play, using Tannen's concept *metamessage*.

As with the other two assignments, the sheets that students received give advice about approach, but the comments are much more aimed at process and less on specific organizational form. There is an accompanying set of assignments called "Notebooks" that has students taking notes and freewriting on the texts in preparation for each of their essays.

As I look over the CCP assignments now, two characteristics strike me. The first is the directive and intervening relationship the teacher takes toward the student in all three instances. Expectations are spelled out, at least in terms of form and organizational pattern, and in terms of process in the Tannen/Gallagher assignment. In the first two assignments, a premium is placed on getting the shape of the essay right, and the teacher gives specific advice about how that can be attained. We do not have the oral instructions or class discussion that accompanied each assignment, but the assignments themselves announce approach and value in the course. Second, ideas do matter in these assignments, but they are always in the service of a particular formal objective, even in the case of the linguistics analysis. Students are invited to think, but their response to the material is constantly being focused and sharpened by teacher guidance. In the first assignment, student choice is primarily restricted to what characters to highlight, and there is little chance to say anything meaningful about relationships or expand the organizing concepts such as "alienation," "yearning," or "assimilation." Here the intellectual invitation is merely a pretext to perform a stylistic turn in the "standard college essay." The second assignment looks like a classic comparison/contrast essay, but in the context of an ongoing sequence of essays on the same subject students can begin to use what they have written to build a real concept rather than to demonstrate facility with form using an idea. The third assignment takes the sequence further and downplays the formal characteristics as the dominant objective. It still limits students by length and specified mode, but it goes further in emphasizing an interaction with the text, and it emphasizes the nature of language itself, a common trope in progressive basic writing classes (Adler-Kassner and Harrington 26).

This was the sort of commentary running through my mind as we sat in the meeting at CCP. It would be easy to critique these assignments in terms of debates in the basic writing literature, placing at least the first two in the camp of those invested in a language ideology Brian Street calls an "autonomous" model of literacy: "individuals, often against their own experience, come to conceptualize literacy as a separate, reified set of 'neutral' competencies, autonomous of social context" (114 and quoted in Adler-Kassner and Harrington 6). The stress on form was characteristic of most assignments we collected from CCP, and this suggests a conception of literacy researchers have characterized as context-independent and radically separated from notions of literacy that students may already carry with them from previous experiences inside and outside of school. Adler-Kassner and

Harrington warn that such an approach to academic conventions concentrates "on developing acumen with those conventions, but not necessarily understanding of them" (20). They worry that the model of autonomous literacy prevents basic writers from adopting one of the most crucial functions of authorship: "authors simultaneously participate in individually rooted acts of inspiration and creativity and situate these acts within the discursive conventions of larger communities" (20). The fear is that students will participate in a show of conventional mastery without participating in the purposes for that mastery.

And yet this analysis of these assignments does not take into account the institutional environment and the rhetorical situation under which the assignments are made. The composition literature has emphasized student product, knowledge, and experience in almost every level of writing and reading research, but a harsh critique of these assignments leaves out the circumstances and intentions of the instructors and the particular institutional framework in which instruction takes place. We tend to be understanding about our students but hard on our colleagues. What Linda Adler-Kassner and Susanmarie Harrington say about basic writing instruction goes also for the balance in college writing instruction among disparate schools: "arguments for making basic writing a political act are grounded in the realities of the constraints in which basic writing teachers, and basic writing students, must operate" (8). These assignments do not arise in a vacuum, and they are not devised by people who care only about students writing in Standard English. They want their students to be ready for courses after their own, and they want their students to be able to succeed at Temple, but they have little information to tell them how to accomplish those objectives.

I have more to say about how these assignments arise in the concluding section of this chapter, but for now let me note in retrospect that one aspect of the rhetorical situation I was struck with in the meeting at CCP is that teachers write assignments for their students, but they have their colleagues as an audience at the back of their minds. Not that they show each other their assignments, but there are definite tensions among colleagues that came out in our discussion—worries about autonomy in the classroom, differences over reading material, controversies over the forms students must learn to manipulate—which have great influence over what sort of assignments teachers write. You stake out a position, decide what your function is in the classroom, predict what sort of work will push forward the agenda you and your allies have developed, and assignments serve as one of the primary expressions of that intellectual work. This is by no means a bad thing but, when this rhetorical dynamic unfolds without the benefit of extensive and supportive collegial conversation as well as regular consideration of recent research, it can also produce stale or ineffective tasks for the students to perform.

Later in that same semester, 5 CCP faculty members came to Temple to join about 15 graduate students and DAs to discuss the assignment collection again. This time, the discussion centered around Temple assignments. The Temple examples were mostly much longer than the CCP assignments, and they tended to be embedded in sequences, more elaborate versions of the third assignment cited from CCP. The assignments associated with the syllabi written for new instructors had fewer instructions related to the form of the resultant essay, but examples from other instructors did detail formal concerns. Following is an example from one recent syllabus that all new instructors were required to use as a part of their practicum experience. The tenured faculty member who taught the practicum class wrote the syllabus but did not grade the papers that came from the assignments, although he did discuss the introduction to the assignment and the grading with the graduate instructors and their mentors. The following is the first assignment in a sequence aimed at getting students to think about intellectual work in their own lives and about the responsibility of an intellectual to his or her home community.

> Both Chinua Achebe's "Dean Man's Path" and Mary Louise Pratt's "Arts of the Contact Zone" focus on the power relationships between two different worldviews, two different intellectual definitions of how the world works. Achebe uses fiction to explore the relationship between a European-trained teacher and a tribal priest. Pratt uses a work of political theory to explore the relationship between Guama Poma and the king of Spain. Both ask us to consider in greater depth what it means for someone to gain recognition of their intellectual work and attain the social position and power of "recognized intellectuals."
>
> For this assignment, we would like you to continue to develop your own thoughts on this issue. Carefully read Pratt's essay. How might Pratt's term "contact zone" allow you to reconsider your understanding of Achebe's story? How might her solution, exemplified in Poma's text, critique or extend Achebe's vision of community? That is, do you see Pratt offering an alternative vision of community to Achebe's? Finally, we would like you to also consider what the responsibilities are of an individual to his or her community. What might it mean, for instance, for someone to be considered an intellectual representative of the community? Use one of the "intellectuals" from the readings as an example.

From here the students read a selection from Gramsci's *Prison Notebooks* and discussed the concept of "organic intellectuals." Then they read oral histories of people in a small working-class neighborhood of Philadelphia, conducted interviews on their own with people they regarded as a community intellectuals, and finally analyzed their interviews. The assignment sequence was highly creative and challenging, conceived all of a piece, and not particularly connected to conventional forms such as the "standard college essay." This made for exciting discussions, but sometimes disappointing results. The graduate instructors were often confused about how to introduce the most demanding material—especially the Gramsci readings—and occasionally they were at a loss to grade essays that did not seem to respond very well to the assignment.

As with the earlier meeting, the meeting at Temple focused more on assignments in the host school. The discussion centered particularly on a research assignment written by a DA who was no longer on staff, having taught with us only 1 year between his PhD in composition/rhetoric and an appointment to a tenure-track position. The syllabus centered on an investigation of brand names, advertising, and consumerism in the everyday lives of the students, and required students to read a book on consumerism called *No Logo* by Naomi Klein as well as articles from the *Harvard Business Review* and other materials. About two-thirds of the way through the course students undertook an 8- to 10-page research project on an aspect of consumer culture. Here, in part, is the assignment for that research project:

> Goals for the Assignment
> In the course of completing this assignment, you will learn to:
> 1. Compile and arrange a body of research material into a workable essay
> 2. Connect a body of data to an audience's present interests and concerns.
> 3. Compose a lengthy document that provides information about something with which your audience might not be familiar.
> Assignment Description
> You will learn and write about some aspect of consumer culture that you find interesting. You may decide to report on a movie, an advertising campaign, a place, a brand, a TV show, or a sporting event. Any one of these (and many other) topics is (are) available, but be careful not to choose a topic too large for sufficient coverage in a few weeks. You may want to restrict your topic, for instance, to a particular object, performance, or a commercial.

The assignment introduction goes on for another page, requiring five scholarly citations from at least two different sources and encouraging the use of non-scholarly sources as well. The audience is specified as "the class and myself," and an oral presentation of 8 to 10 minutes is also built into the project. One note that disturbed the CCP faculty and some of the Temple instructors was this one:

> We will cover methods of textual citation and resource use in class. However, you will have to teach yourselves the research tools made available in the university library. I'm glad to help in any way possible, and I encourage you to ask questions or set up meetings if you feel you need additional guidance through the research process.

Format for the paper is stated, including typeface size and kind, and two office conferences and two peer reviews are required. The general guidelines for English 50 call for a research experience of some sort, but this one is probably more elaborate than most.

The discussion on this assignment focused on what participants felt were the abilities students were meant to develop and the skills students were assumed to have when they entered the course. The CCP instructors were particularly sensitive to the assumed skills, which is why they were upset by the idea that students were expected to teach themselves how to use the library resources. They felt that this assignment would overwhelm their students and they wondered what Temple students made of it. Here is the list of assumed skills the group noted:

- Ability to ask for help
- Ability to locate research tools and general awareness of kinds of library resources
- Competence in handling summary
- Understanding the assignment
- Reading comprehension for main points and hidden polemics
- Ability to critique a public performance and maintain critical distance

At first, the Temple instructors did not seem to notice the assumed skills, and they were a bit defensive about the insistence in many of the assignments that students employ theoretical texts like Gramsci, Klein, and authors for the *Harvard Business Review.* But as we talked through the Temple assignments and compared them to the CCP assignments, we developed a consensus that the university tasks tended to emphasize taking a position drawn from a text and using theory as the frame for the essay. Community college tasks, the group agreed, tended to put more of a premium on a clearly stated opinion on a text-based topic, defended in a well-organized structure written in standard English. I summed this up for the group and also confirmed the summary with a group of CCP faculty later on: Generally we could characterize the Temple assignments as more theoretical and the CCP assignments as more formal. Both emphasized "process" along the way, but CCP faculty stressed organization and surface features of the text whereas Temple faculty concentrated on the intellectual framing and cultural context as the students constructed their arguments. At one point in the discussion, someone said that Temple wanted students to learn "the things you can do with texts." Others agreed with that observation and thought it might be different from what students are expected to learn at CCP.

WHAT DOES SPONSORSHIP TELL US ABOUT ALIGNMENT?

The two CCP/Temple assignment meetings—designed to establish the deep alignment Bob Schneider and I had hoped for—convinced me that the reasonable questions Dianne and I came up with in the coffee shop were inadequate to analyzing the assignments we assembled. We were looking at particulars in assignments, but what we finally encountered was a profound difference in orientation, in focus, in a basic attitude toward the task of writing. I needed to find a theoretical lens to help us understand what causes such profound differences. As I looked at these assignments, I began to think about equally profound differences between the curricula in Fields and Somerset high schools, detailed in Chapter 2. I began to consider more deeply what it means to write for composition classes in a variety of institutional settings, all of which claim to be introductory to later academic success.

I take it as given that most teachers at CCP and Temple are trying their best to educate their students. There might be a lazy and cynical person here or an arrogant and insensitive one there, but most instructors at both schools are committed to doing their jobs as they understand the task. Everyone involved has at least a master's degree or is supervised by someone with advanced training, and nearly everyone in this particular instance comes from training in an American English department. Are the students so terribly different in the two schools? Is one program dominated by traditional pedagogy suited to the students and another dominated by social constructivist pedagogy equally suited to the students? Or is perhaps one assignment pretty much as good as another for teaching an equivalent course? After all, when we considered the data on transfer students at Temple, even the CCP students who persisted into upper-level writing-intensive courses at Temple did not really do so badly. Perhaps differences in the two programs do not matter as much as we might think they do.

Patrick Sullivan asks such questions in his 2003 article: "What is 'College-Level' Writing?" He concedes that it is extremely tricky to decide across different contexts what "good" writing is, but he reminds us that we are forced by circumstance and political necessity to assess our students anyway. A question about the utility of training underprepared students is always in the air, and politicians would be all too happy to cut back on support for students who do not easily fit into the curriculum in 4-year schools (see Adler-Kassner and Harrington's review of public controversies in Minneapolis and New York City over basic writing, 61-82). "There appear to be in the political arena," Sullivan says, "very compelling reasons for us to develop a clear, precise, shared definition of what we mean by 'college-level' work" (381). He notes the like-minded efforts of various professional groups such as the WPA's committee that produced the "Outcomes Statement for First Year Composition," and he takes his own stab at the essential qualities of college writing, centered especially on "the ability to discuss and evaluate abstract ideas" (384). But his conclusion is to call for us to "design writing tasks that will allow us to evaluate our students for these kinds of skills" (385), and he urges us to do the additional hard, patient work to establish a dialogue that will accomplish the task of defining writing at this level. It is a brave and necessary call, but when we look closely at the assignments at Temple and CCP, we recognize that more than hard work may be necessary to overcome the obstacles.

Considering the nature of these obstacle further, I returned to the concept of sponsorship I first touched upon in an earlier book, *'Round My Way*, as well as the theory of sponsorship elaborated by Deborah Brandt in *Literacy in American Lives*. An analysis of literacy sponsorship may help us understand the differences we see in the CCP and Temple assignments as well as the curricula at Fields and Somerset discussed in the last chapter. Brandt defines sponsors of literacy as "any agents, local or distant, concrete or abstract, who enable, support, teach and model as well as recruit, regulate, suppress, or withhold literacy—and gain advantage by it in some way" (19). She widens the concept from a function we might commonly associate only with schools and patriotic essay contests in order to factor in the economic nature of literacy, the active role that businesses and government can play in shaping reading and writing abilities and experiences people choose to pursue. She offers us many, many examples of people who grew up on farms and in small towns, moved from one part of the country or another to the midwest, experienced massive changes in technology and workplace demands, all the while growing in their abilities to read and write influenced by the social and economic forces at play in their times. Although individuals do make real choices about how they use literacy in their work and home lives, the field of choice is largely defined by broader social forces:

> The competition to harness literacy, to manage, measure, teach, and exploit it, intensified throughout the twentieth century. It is vital to pay attention to this development because it largely sets the terms for individual encounters with literacy. This competition shapes the incentives and barriers (including uneven distribution of opportunity) that greet literacy learners in any particular time and place. (23)

Brandt's concept of sponsorship allows for a direct link between the types of literacy learning environments available to people in community colleges or urban universities and the demands of the market or the political climate at any given historical moment.

In *'Round My Way* I define sponsorship somewhat differently. Rather than focus primarily on economic pressures, I associate sponsorship with institutional realities that authors represent in their writing:

> The question, as I see it, is not what genre or mode a writer chooses but what institution the writing maintains or elaborates or challenges, and how the writer fulfills his or her role as an author within cultural institutions. It follows, as well, that a writer's authority in a society depends in large part upon the power and influence of the institution that sponsors that writer's authorship. (25)

Here I use "institution" in the way the sociologists Peter Berger and Thomas Luckmann use it, as "a habit which must be formalized in order to be passed on to a new generation" (*'Round* 28, see also Berger and Luckmann 54). My focus in this definition is on disciplinary and cultural realities brought to life by the writing of authors or those trying to take on authority in written language. I go on to analyze the struggle by basic writers to become closely enough identified with powerful institutions in order to feel themselves authors who can derive social power from their sponsors.

Both Brandt and I emphasize the way writers grow and are shaped by larger entities for which literacy serves a foundational purpose. Whether it is the formation of anthropology as a field or the rise of the car dealership as a means of product distribution, writing organizes and represents the work and material existence of these institutional sponsors. But neither of us has said very much about the nature of the institution determining how teachers, as local agents, administer literacy sponsorship under the specific demands of a time and a place. "Neither rich nor powerful enough to sponsor literacy on our own terms," Brandt says in a 1998 article first announcing her version of literacy sponsorship, "we serve instead as conflicted brokers between literacy's buyers and sellers" ("Sponsors" 183). We are "conflicted" presumably because we can often see how certain policies and pedagogical practices serve the purposes of the institution for which we work, but we may not endorse the sort of literacy these institutionally sponsored practices produce (I think, for instance, of the large lecture and the multiple choice exam this budget-saving pedagogy spawns). There is much more to be said about the imprint of sponsors on the practice of teachers, although I only indicate some possibilities here.

In the case of Temple and CCP, we can trace not only the schools' direct investments in institutional sponsorship, but we can understand the types of literacy they favor in terms of their function in the economy. In a palpable way, instructors in the two schools operate under very different sponsoring notions of literacy due to their institutional affiliations, their relationship to market forces, and the history of schooling students bring to the classrooms. Differing labor conditions may also figure in the comparison, but I think this may be less the issue than it might seem. In both institutions the people who teach first-year writing are working very hard, probably carrying too heavy a workload to pay adequate attention to each student they have on their roster. The biggest difference might be between Temple's DAs who, in the academic year 2003-2004, taught three courses (at least one basic writing course with 17 students and two introduction to composition courses with 22 students per course each semester) compared to a full-time faculty member at CCP who teaches four courses a semester with at least 22 students in each class. But the DAs also do not have permanent jobs and, along with their teaching, must search for new jobs, try to publish in order to get out of postdoctoral status, and struggle to maintain a sense of belonging and self-respect in an environment where they are neither faculty nor graduate students, neither part of Temple or apart from it. The labor conditions are not ideal for most instructors in the two programs.

There are some major differences, however, between the two institutions as sponsors of literacy. Dougherty's argument about the contradictory nature of community colleges highlights the complexity of CCP as a literacy sponsor. A community college must produce students who will "plug in" to other programs or employment positions readily. Students come to them, and legislatures fund them, in order to "make them ready," although the readiness often has an abstract character; it might be preparation for an entry-level job in business, for a major in biology at Temple, or for a paralegal program run by a law firm. The teachers in a community college are not directly connected to a department whose purpose is to train undergraduates in the latter part of their careers, and thus they have less allegiance to the disciplinary discourse in English than university instructors—whether graduates or faculty—will have by necessity. CCP students must, above all, be presentable to others outside English 101, and instructors are acutely aware that their students must get what they need now or not at all. Community college faculty cannot afford the luxury of seeing students in the long perspective of a whole college career because it is still quite undecided if the students in their classes will be able to persevere until the degree. Unlike many other community colleges, CCP has a strong commitment to transfer as a major part of its mission, but what happens on the other side of the transfer process is far removed from the day-to-day functioning of faculty and students. The emphasis on students' immediate performance is not so much a matter of vocationalism as it is an artifact of the 2-year school reality: Budgets are extremely limited, teaching counts far more than service, and research counts not at all in faculty work lives, courses are transferable units of credit rather than elements of a larger program.

Perhaps the most poignant moment in Sullivan's article for me was when he questioned one of the major tenets of WAC: "However much we may talk about Writing-Across-the-Curriculum programs or sharing the burden of educating our underprepared students with other disciplines or areas of the college, the fact is that English professors do much of this difficult work" (379). From the perspective of a 2-year college, this sentence rings true. Everyone is working so hard at a 2-year school teaching the classes they are assigned, and students have so little time to get what they need from each course and move on, that the burden for targeted and utilitarian literacy instruction is very much on English teachers. Additionally, a program director at a university would never use the term "English professors" for the people carrying this burden, for few tenured or tenure-track English professors in a university would ever feel that responsibility.

No wonder the literacy has an "autonomous" look to it in a 2-year college. You would have to be a heartless and irresponsible brute not to think about students' skills being crucial for how they will present in the next stage of their journey. Brandt describes the economic pressure on such institutions this way:

> We are inundated with warnings about the new economy, the evaporation of low-skill labor, the need for all workers to become proficient readers, writers, and problem solvers, even as we experience high rates of failure and attrition in public education. This is especially the case in adult basic education and 2-year community colleges, where those taking the full brunt of economic restructuring are typically enrolled. (194)

The expectation of the 2-year college instructor is to "fix" a problem so that the remediated person can function better down the line. I don't mean remediation in the terms basic writing researchers have been fighting against for 30 years; this is an issue that underlies the language of deficit. As Brandt frames it, this remediation is about the economy itself. The 2-year college is designed either to get students back into production mode—as workers in an information economy and as products themselves whose value-added can then be further enhanced by later education or training—or to "cool them out," in the ironic language of Burton Clark, and remove them from serious competition in the labor market altogether.

Of course 2-year college faculty also want to educate their students in ways that resist the pressures of their economic situation. Lewiecki-Wilson and Sommers quote Howard Tinberg, a respondent in their 1999 national survey of community college composition instructors, as asserting: "I consider the teaching of composition to be pound for pound the most important task that any college teacher can undertake. I believe so because I think we comp teachers are in the business of training decent and ethical citizens. Other courses may pay lip service to such ends; we act on them" (443). Tinberg himself has written a detailed account of community college faculty in one school meeting intensively to understand their goals for student writers, the ways they can "offer knowledge that is both specialized and generally useful" (*Border Talk* xiii). Other respondents in Lewieki-Wilson and Sommers' survey report their pleasure at working with the wide array of students' abilities, backgrounds, and ambitions; they see their profession as deeply challenging intellectually. Curricular work like that done by Mary Soliday and Barbara Gleason at the City University of New York indicates that teachers can work against the grain, can address student resistance, and focus on form in effective ways. But even with the best intentions, community college teachers can be frustrated by the experiences of their students with schooling, experiences that have taught students that school is a corridor of closed doors to traverse rather than a palace with many rooms to investigate. CCP faculty repeatedly told me that they felt their students needed more structures for classifying the information and ideas they were encountering, more tried-and-true methods for organizing material and arguments. This often led them to teaching formal writing structures in their courses. The students themselves often come to college asking for the answer to an essentially economic question: What do I have to know to fit into this economic system? Those of good will may want to help students learn to ask for more, but there seems to me little doubt that the driving force in the CCP classroom is the need to get in synch with the economy and the educational system as it currently functions.

Assignment writing becomes a particularly vexed rhetorical problem in this circumstance, because students and faculty do not always share a vision of what school is. For a student with a long history of disengagement in school, the language of an assignment usually translates into nothing more than an exercise prescribed by the teacher and fulfilled by the student. Even under the best of circumstances, the sponsorship too closely resembles a business transaction to allow for greater latitude of invitation on the part of the teacher or interpretation on the part of the student. There exists neither a large store of trust nor a mutual understanding for the teacher–student relationship to depend on, and an assignment is a concrete expression of that relationship. This narrowed relationship can occur in any school, given the nature of most education in America, but it becomes particularly obstructive in a school with few amenities, no dormitories or student unions, precious little green grass, and only a trace of disciplinary presence on campus to connect the reality of the academic field with the reality of the classroom. At a school like CCP, literacy looks like a stamp on a passport before you move on, and it is hard to understand when the border guards want to represent the transaction as something else entirely.

A school like Temple presents another set of contradictions out of which arises a radically different notion of literacy. If at CCP the prized skill is a kind of autonomous literacy that allows students to produce on demand essays of a certain size and shape, at Temple literacy requires that students manipulate the outlines of a theory to mount a critique of a text. Most departmental faculty, outside the first-year writing program, still want students to produce texts that presents a thesis and evidence without errors or digressions. But in any advanced course where the interpretation of texts is required, instructors also want a kind of savvy about the interplay between theory and practice, a sharp ability to recognize irony and subtle argumentation, an awareness of history as the background to any assertion. They want form but they also want theoretical sophistication, or perhaps the willingness to learn what sophistication in later coursework might look like. It may be argued that the students at Temple are more ready for such challenges as first year students than are their counterparts in community college. I am not particularly convinced the differences are that great, but—for students enrolled at Temple—the challenge of being in a 4-year school is that research- and theory-based work is going on all around you; both teachers and students realize they must engage in discourse that constitutes their immediate world.

English 50 at Temple is taught by graduate students, recently graduated PhDs, and adjuncts with a range of experiences in and outside the academy. The notion of literacy that this group has assimilated involves a constant dynamic of challenging and deferring to authority, looking always for the hole in an argument or an unsupported assertion. Processing difficult concepts and applying theory to texts has been a mainstay of many composition programs since David Bartholomae and Anthony Petrosky published their influential book *Facts and Artifacts* and then followed it up with the anthology *Ways of Reading*. Bartholomae has served as a major guiding figure for the Temple writing program over the last 10 years, and his concept of introducing students to academic discourse has been an article of faith with all of us who shaped the program. It occurred to me, however, as I listened to the joint CCP/Temple discussion of the assignments, that perhaps we had gone too far in ushering students into "our" culture, that we had put the prized conceptions of literacy in the research setting above the interests of students in writing classes.

Here, sponsorship both as Brandt defines it and as I do overlap to explain a dilemma for university-based writing programs. Brandt notes that the interests of the learners need not be primary in the way a sponsor shapes a literacy learning environment: "Although the interests of the sponsor and the sponsored do not have to converge (and, in fact, may conflict), sponsors nevertheless set the terms for access to literacy and wield powerful incentives for compliance and loyalty" (19). It is in the interest of graduate students and their graduate faculty to teach a theoretically informed, intellectually challenging curriculum. Every teacher wants to draw on her or his interests to enliven a course, and you don't want people to go stale teaching what they already have read too many times. Yet we must be careful that the nature of our teaching is not more influenced by our need to show tenured colleagues that first-year writing is a rigorous training ground for graduate students and a worthy endeavor in relation to the field from which program administrators draw authority. If Dougherty's critique of community college as too vocational strikes home, it may be the case that university undergraduate programs are too oriented toward the research that fuels the university's measure of status and intellectual substance. As I have noted earlier, this may have a disastrous effect on future faculty who are trained at research universities but may not be prepared to look hard at what students in their regional 2- or 4-year colleges need to learn. It may also cause university-based programs to neglect the study of what students actually do with writing in their lives. Despite all the research the field of composition/rhetoric has done on writing in the workplace and in disciplines outside of English, are we not still teaching a sort of writing that serves the purposes of writing program administrators who hold tenure in research-based English departments?

In Chapter 2, I promised I would return to the differences between the curricula in Somerset and Fields. I said there that I associate the curriculum at Somerset with a need to *control* the classroom environment and give students a specific and limited mastery over a small amount of material. At Fields, there was more of a premium on *continuity*: with the English and American literary traditions, with the sort of writing middle-class students have done in high school for 40 or more years, with the expectations of parents and administrators about what must be taught; with the content knowledge central to the SAT. In the context of sponsorship, this division between control and continuity makes another kind of sense. In working-class and poor schools, literacy is highly linked to control and a certain restricted type of mastery. Following the "autonomous" model of literacy that informs many CCP assignments, prescriptive writing assignments and limited readings facilitate a clipped and shaped literacy at a school like Somerset. The best students are those who can give a short response on time to a particular order, but they are at real risk if they come across larger scale, more open assignments where the writer must structure the answer (see Marshall for a study of the limited value of short answer assignments over essays in a literature class). One is tempted to interpret this in terms of preparation for manufacturing or service work, not college, but the contradiction of the system is that jobs in this country for people who simply follow orders do not pay a living wage and cannot sustain families in a consumer economy. The community college curriculum thus seems a logical next step, moving students through autonomy, introducing a disciplinary knowledge but not connecting extensively with the contexts for disciplinary habits and conventions.

The assignments at Fields are probably no more preparatory for first year writing courses as they are taught at many colleges and universities today than the assignments at Somerset. Yet, the work at Fields High School has a function that serves this sponsorship. Both writing and reading tasks reinforce the notion that literacy is all of a piece with a knowable and consoling history, a history that has produced the substantial buildings and comfortable suburbs that the students and their parents take as their basic reality. Continuity characterizes the literacy because stability in the system is the most important economic and social good to maintain. I marveled at first that the English curriculum at Fields seemed so much like the one I experienced in a suburban high school in Maryland more than 30 years earlier, but really why should I be surprised? A curriculum built on questioning and experimentation, on travel to non-Western countries and service in poor neighborhoods, on artistic principles of composition or socialist critiques of the economy would be counter to the main job of high school in middle-class America. College can do more destabilizing in its curriculum because the ideal college is framed in our system as a place apart, a moment in students' lives when they are removed from the labor market, isolated from their families, able to play out intellectual possibilities with a minimum of danger to economic stability. But high school must reinforce that sense of solidity and continuity to the children, even at the risk of boring them, so that the message comes home clearly: We deserve what we have and it should stay this way forever.

I want to conclude with a word about the data on transfer students who start at community college and finish at Temple. At first glance, the data is somewhat reassuring about transfer students from 2-year schools because they seem to do relatively well at Temple, at least as far as writing courses go. But we should not be fooled by these statistics. The numbers I shared were for students who had made or were still making their "pilgrimage to Zion," as Dougherty calls it; many had overcome the discouragements in the first 2 years, passed the transition to the university, and persisted in their classes at Temple. My concern is for the many students along the way who do not finish their classes at community college, who cannot manage the shift to university, or who cannot hang on to graduate. We should take comfort that some students do persevere and get their degrees, but we can do far better at helping larger number of students gain the education they seek. I keep thinking about the young woman I described in the previous chapter, the highly ranked student from Somerset who decided to start at community college because neither she and nor her teachers thought she was ready for Temple. Very few kids from her Latino neighborhood finish at CCP and go on to Temple, but I would like to see the way much clearer and wider for her and her friends to follow.

I think one idea that a participant identified in the discussion on assignments at Temple may be crucial for paving the way. The effort to teach students to "do things with texts" (to paraphrase J.L. Austin's book on speech acts, *How to Do Things with Words*) is a legitimate crossover point for the interests of academic faculty and beginning first-year students (coincidentally, Joe Harris' has recently completed a writing textbook called *Rewriting: How to Do Things with Texts* that gets at attitudes and abilities students can use without either belaboring the formal or privileging the theoretical). The idea of accomplishing action through words can be a crucial quality for undergraduate education, as students emerge from the passive learning so common in high schools and as they hope to move toward a life of engagement and productivity. Perhaps this could be a point of collaboration between university and community college programs. If deep alignment is to be more than a pretty dream, then we need to identify an attitude toward words and action we collectively choose to adopt, a literacy we collectively choose to sponsor. Coming together across institutional lines will force us to see our divergent concepts of sponsorship and develop strategies that approach alignment as a way of embracing our common responsibilities. As Patrick Sullivan points out, the need for our determining some usable definition of "college-level" writing is absolutely urgent.

4

Alinsky's Reveille

Who serves whom in community-based composition courses? Our field has taken a well-meaning and enthusiastic interest in this combination of writing instruction and service learning over the last few years. Studies in the mid- to late-1990s described courses and institutional arrangements and began to explore the ramifications for composition and English studies (Schutz and Gere; Herzberg; Peck, Flower, and Higgins). Linda Adler-Kassner and her colleagues edited an influential volume in 1997 that signaled the arrival of this new approach as a major pedagogical movement, and in 2000 Tom Deans' *Writing Partnerships* gave us a basic framework for thinking about the cooperative relationship between students and the organizations they encounter in these courses. More recent work has focused on how community-based learning can be sustained over time through faculty research (Cushman), how to address the gap between community and academic discourses (Chaden, Graves, Jolliffe, and Vandenberg) and what contradictions we must struggle with in intercultural inquiry (Flower), each study highlighting strategies for respecting the needs and abilities of participating community partners. In a crucial step toward establishing the institutional structures necessary for sustained partnership, Jeffrey Grabill and Lynee Lewis Gaillet urge us to focus on the interface between writing programs and community partners. Paula Mathieu has written an important book on composition/rhetoric and its "public turn" toward engagement with community partners, and she sums up the challenge succinctly:

"Combining the complex and conflicted missions that underscore the daily life of nonprofits with an often-expanding university mission of service learning makes conditions ripe for disputes and allows connections to be missed, broken, or made in haphazard manners" (89). The need for a balanced and nonexploitive relationship in community-based learning asserts itself insistently in our discussions of this public turn, and clearly at this stage, WPAs must become much more active in developing institutional models that promise true mutual benefits for postsecondary schools and their off-campus partners.

Because the literature is so oriented toward student- and faculty-based outreach into underserved communities, we seldom hear of community-based learning projects initiated by community partners themselves. The Community Literacy Center in Pittsburgh may be one exception (see Peck, Flower, and Higgins), but even that landmark partnership arose as much out of the social commitments of faculty at Carnegie Mellon as out of the community's needs articulated by their Settlement House collaborators. The fact is that universities and colleges seldom develop plans based on suggestions that originate off campus. Faculty and students devise projects based on research into local citizens' needs or approach recreation centers and libraries to house tutoring projects or screening programs. Neighborhood centers with no official link to a university are less likely on their own to take the steps necessary to bring a cooperative project with a university into being: contact the right academic units; work with faculty to develop a plan the center's board would approve; and carry forward the project using university personnel, facilities, and resources.

Neighborhood centers often have energetic and creative people on staff, but they usually face high demand for services, few resources, limited training of support staff, and no time to develop a project with partners in an entirely different work culture like a university. Academics get tenured and promoted for asking questions and proposing interpretations, for publishing and teaching. By publishing this article on community–university partnerships and teaching community-based courses, for example, I add lines to my vita and earn points in the economy of my college and profession. In contrast, directors of neighborhood centers must produce programs and services for their constituents with minimal expense and little room for experimentation, keeping one eye on their Board and the other on funding sources at all times. Manuel Portillo, the neighborhood center director I describe later in this chapter, gains no tangible advantage in his organizing world for appearing in a learned publication; he still cannot get health benefits from the Board of his small nonprofit organization until he brings in sufficient grant money in the next fiscal year.

This difference of time and emphasis stacks the cards toward university-initiated projects that are research-driven and aimed at providing undergraduate and graduate students community-based experiences. As academics passionately interested in literacy—and professionals invested in literacy as the medium of our own careers—we see reading and writing as the heart of our involvement with communities. But organizers see literacy as one of many issues they must address with their constituency, and the people that attend adult basic education programs or welfare-to-work projects see literacy as one of many needs in their lives along with health care, housing, food, child care, and employment. Is there a way that neighborhood centers themselves could pursue an agenda that universities would respond to on terms dictated by the neighborhoods? Can writing programs in particular foster such arrangements? Could a different model of research and outreach support a community-based agenda?

To formulate a new model of community–university connections based more in the latter's reality, we might focus on a theory of action devised for neighborhoods rather than for higher education. Educators tend to imagine their work with students within a traditional pattern—let's call it the "through-put" model. We move students along a path marked by diplomas and certificates, occupy them with reading and writing tasks, determine their achievements with tests or papers. Above all, "through-put" requires that we keep them at desks and tables, in libraries, or at computer workstations, with the occasional field trip or lab to indicate that the learning they do has application in a world outside school. After 4 or 5 years of this, they graduate and move on to jobs or further study. Even most community-based learning courses follow this model; they simply substitute engagement with genuine outside learners for the texts that might otherwise represent the outside world. Cushman notes the prevalence of what she calls the "end of the semester project model of service learning" (59), and this allows for courses with significant off-campus experience to approximate the shape and policy of classroom-based courses. As Cushman is careful to emphasize, this model is by no means wrong or inappropriate, but the traditional approach may not be the most suited for the needs of adult learners in a neighborhood literacy center or children in an after-school program. They need teachers who are not just passing through and programs that appear one year and evaporate the next. They need literacy programs that take into account the array of demands on a stressed community. Most of all, they need tutors who see individual learners as whole people and university partners sensitive to the entire mission of local agencies, not just researchers studying subjects in sites or educators supervising students in field placements.

SAUL ALINSKY: A COMMUNITY ORGANIZING MODEL

Let us consider what a community-based model might look like if it is founded on principles derived from the work of Saul Alinsky, the influential community organizer whose career spanned the 1930s through the 1960s. Long-time organizer and activist Heather Booth has said "Alinsky is to community organizing as Freud is to psychoanalysis" (quoted in Slayton 198). His work can serve as a lens for reorienting our vision, shifting the background setting of our model-building from the campus to the streets.

Alinsky was not an educator, if by that we mean a person concerned with schools and schooling, but he cared a great deal about how ordinary people learn to act for their own good and the good of their neighbors. Like the work of two other theorists who have had a tremendous impact on the field of composition/rhetoric—John Dewey and Paulo Freire—Alinsky's writing is highly suggestive about ways to get students to work together on common projects and take responsibility for their own educational process. Unlike Dewey, however, Alinsky was mainly concerned with organizing disenfranchised people so that they could exercise more political power (or, as Charles Silberman put it "that banding together will give them the capacity to alter the circumstances of their lives" [335]). Unlike Freire, Alinsky said little directly about literacy and more about strikes, actions, and alliances that would shake the established powers from their exploitive and paternalistic habits. Unlike both Dewey and Freire, Alinsky was more a fighter than a writer in his career; his two books on organizing are polemical, sometimes to the point of being obnoxious. Yet Alinsky's commitment to empowering people has much in common with these two better-known 20th-century figures, and his faith in the democratic process resonates with an abiding faith in our field that access to disciplinary knowledge and authority comes through support for students' composing process.

Saul Alinsky was born in 1909 to immigrant Russian Jewish parents living in a small flat of a three-story tenement on the Near West Side of Chicago. His family was not destitute—his father owned a small garment sweatshop in the building where they then lived—but Alinsky grew up in a tough neighborhood where gangs of Jewish kids fought against Polish kids in the bordering slum neighborhood (see Finks or Horwitt for this and much of the following biographical information). He attended the University of Chicago, studying archaeology and sociology in undergraduate school and graduating in 1930. He continued in Chicago's Sociology Department for graduate work in criminology, but, partly because of financial pressures and partly because of his own temperament, he left academic studies to work full time in the field. By the time he had reached his late 20s,

Alinsky had developed a tough but open and effective intellectual style of working with a wide range of people. He had accrued some reputation as a promising young criminologist, and in 1938 he was offered a lucrative job running the Probation and Parole Board in Philadelphia and teaching at the University of Pennsylvania. He decided, however, to forgo the temptations of secure government and academic employment in order to organize on the streets of Chicago (Finks 12-13 and Sanders [June 1965] 44-45).

Alinsky's talents as a community organizer began to emerge when Clifford Shaw sent him in 1938 to a neighborhood on Chicago's West Side called Back of the Yards. Alinsky's biographer Sanford Horwitt describes this place "as perhaps the nadir of industrial slum life," an immigrant neighborhood putrid with the stench of meatpacking houses and stockyards (57); 30 years before, Upton Sinclair had written scathingly about this same neighborhood in *The Jungle*. Alinsky himself said that Back of the Yards "was not the slum across the tracks. This was the slum across the tracks from across the tracks "(Sanders [June 1965] 45). Organizing in the Back of the Yards was a daunting task. On top of the poverty and political powerlessness of the area, the warring factions and relative neutrality of the Catholic Church—the dominant social organization in the area—made the prospects look dim from the start (Horwitt 55).

Alinsky began organizing as he had been trained to do in other in neighborhoods: hang around and get to know the people and resources in the area. In an earlier study of Chicago's "Little Italy," Alinsky had developed a technique for interviewing kids, and 15 teenagers wrote their life histories for researchers with his help (Finks 11, Horwitt 25). But in Back of the Yards, his job was to use his information to organize a juvenile recreation and counseling center under the auspices of Shaw's Chicago Area Project (CAP). What made CAP different from other settlement house programs was that Shaw's approach emphasized "citizen participation." As Horwitt puts it: "When people realized they could change local conditions, Shaw theorized, they would then feel more responsible for doing something about the problems that plagued them" (53). This required Alinsky to develop relationships with all the community's churches and other institutions, in the hopes of getting them to cooperate on CAP. Cooperative effort seemed impossible at first because—although the area was entirely White and eastern European—the Poles, Slovaks, Bohemians, and Lithuanians traditionally did not get along with one another, and their respective churches showed no interests in meeting together, let alone joining hands to accomplish something for all the residents. But Alinsky developed a powerful working friendship with lifelong neighborhood resident and local park director Joseph Meegan, and together they formed the Back of the Yards Neighborhood Council (BYNC), which succeeded in bringing the factions together to fight for the common good.

The BYNC proved a powerful model of what neighborhood organizations could do when they worked together. Developing close ties with labor leader John L. Lewis as well as progressive Catholic Bishop, Bernard J. Sheil, Alinsky built a power base and a national reputation that made him both loved and loathed. Always using Chicago as his base, Alinsky founded a national organization called the Industrial Areas Foundation (IAF) in 1940 (Horwitt 91) and through IAF he or his few organizers led successful organizing efforts in south St. Paul, Minnesota; Los Angeles; Rochester and Buffalo, New York. With the help of future journalist Nicolas Von Hoffman and others, Alinsky organized the Black neighborhood of Woodlawn in the South Side of Chicago. To be sure, they also failed rather spectacularly in New York City's Chelsea district and never made much headway on a project in Kansas City, Kansas. Alinsky's organization trained Cesar Chavez and Chavez later used Alinsky's techniques to organize California farm workers. Alinsky worked with the young Ivan Illich in the early 1950s when the young priest was first starting to be active with the Puerto Rican community in New York City.

Not only did his organizing activities touch many between 1938 and 1970, but Alinsky's thought and writing also influenced many in the field of urban politics and labor activism. The man *Harper's* called "the professional radical" deeply impressed the journalist and economist Charles Silberman, whose popular 1964 book *Crisis in Black and White* offers Alinsky's organizing approach as the main hope for solving the tensions in urban neighborhoods of the time. In addition to his best-selling book on organizing, *Reveille of Radicals*, and his reprise book for a new generation, *Rules for Radicals*, Alinsky also wrote a sympathetic portrait of his friend and mentor, CIO founder John L. Lewis. As *Time* magazine noted in 1970: "Like Machiavelli, whom he has studied and admires, Alinsky teaches how power may be used. Unlike Machiavelli, his pupil is not the prince but the people" ("Radical" 56). Alinsky was one of the outstanding radical, non-Communist figures on the left for more than 30 years of the 20th century.

Throughout his career, Alinsky was often regarded with disgust by the right, wariness by the left, and downright exasperation by many in between. In the 1960s, the conservative *Christian Century* made a habit of attacking Alinsky and his "bizarre, anti-Christian doctrines of power" (1452). Farther to the right, in the late 1960s, the Ku Klux Klan twice picketed his arrival at airports, and the FBI warned him of death threats from the reactionary militia called the Minute Men (Horwitt 539). On the liberal left, *The Nation* said, in a 1946 review of *Reveille*, that "in some parts of the world fascism has made use of exactly this sort of "radical' talk," and *The New Republic* that year said that Alinsky's book "expresses a point of view which runs the risk of developing *away* from the democracy that the author speaks of with such fervor" (both quoted in Horwitt 183). For those farther left, throughout his career "Alinsky's disavowal of a class analysis made him and the importance of his work suspect" (Horwitt xv). The last chapter of *Rules for Radicals*, in which he outlines a campaign to work with the middle class, has the whiff of compromise that New Left radicals must have found repugnant. Moderate critics found his famous dictum that organizers of the poor must "rub raw the sores of discontent" particularly objectionable (*Newsweek* 30).

No matter what audience he addressed, Alinsky was, as his biographer P. David Finks remarks, "hard-nosed, outspoken, and profane; when he wanted to be, he could be loud, bullying, impatient, and scornful of questions he thought stupid or elementary" (266). Like many men of his generation, he was not particularly open to contributions to the work by women (Horwitt 289), and one comes to suspect that his notorious hostility to social work was at least in part a reaction to a profession that women had largely invented, especially in the Chicago of Jane Addams' Hull-House settlement movement (see Horwitt 127). In his books, Alinsky gleefully tells about manipulating and lying to individuals and groups (*Reveille* 106-128), shows disdain for conventional ideas of morality (*Rules* 24-47), revels in conflict and battle with his enemy (*Reveille* 132-54), scorns liberals (*Reveille* 19-23), and takes great pride at being hated wherever he is called to organize (*Rules* 136). In short, he could be an irascible and ornery guy, even to his friends and family.

And yet there is a compelling sweetness to his vision. In *Reveille for Radicals*, Alinsky defines a radical with reference to Revolutionary War-era democrats who "really liked people, loved people—all people. They were the human torches setting aflame the hearts of men so that they passionately fought for the rights of their fellow men, all men" (9). For him, a radical "places human rights far above property rights" (16) and—with an undistracted intelligence "not fooled by shibboleths or facades" (15)—fights both to achieve "economic welfare" and "freedom of mind" for oppressed people (16). Alinsky was never a member of the Communist Party, and indeed resisted any program of principles that might override a more compelling philosophical consistency: "The radical is deeply interested in social planning but just as deeply suspicious of, and antagonistic to, any idea of plans that work from the top down. Democracy to him is working from the bottom up" (17). The straight-talking, unblinking tone of Alinsky's prose can sometimes obscure the complexity of his social thought; he regarded the abilities to compromise and develop relationships as crucial qualities in an organizer, just as he called for organizers to show courage and candor in the face of corporate threats.

From Alinsky's *Rules for Radicals* I have culled a set of principles for community organizing that also make sense for community-based learning approaches in composition/rhetoric. Those with experience in organizing may find these rules commonplace and even old-fashioned, but for the field of composition and those teachers and administrators anxious to develop ties with stressed neighborhoods and failing schools, Alinsky's principles can provide useful guidance. The list is not exhaustive, but I think these principles can help us formulate a new model of university–community connection that is less focused on service and traditional notions of education and yet more effective in promoting productive learning for all involved.

1. Draw on the inevitability of class and group conflict as well as the unpredictability of events for your creativity to invent tactics that fit the moment (19).
2. Be guided by a broadly defined sense of self-interest, taking on multiple issues, and encourage all other participants to do the same (23, 53-59, 76).
3. Try to see every situation in as stark a light as possible, unblurred by ideological imperatives, traditional hatreds, or conventional moralities (12-15).
4. Communicate with others on their own ground, amassing personal experience and solid relationships among the people with whom you intend to work (70, 81-97).
5. Respect the dignity of people by creating the conditions for them to be active participants in solving their own problems rather than victims or mere recipients of aid (123).
6. Shape educational experiences that matter in people's lives by helping individuals identify issues they can grasp and do something about (106, 119, 124).
7. Build the leadership capacity of the group being organized and take as the goal the independent functioning of that community (92, see also *Reveille* 64-75).

These seven principles frame learning in the context of doing. Dewey could have written some of these principles, and Freire could have written others. Yet the community organizer embodies a late 20th-century radicalism Dewey does not, and the Jew from multiethnic Chicago adds an American social context to pedagogy, as Freire could not. Thomas Deans pointed out that Dewey emphasizes education as a means to achieve democratic unity to such an extent that "we hear little about race, ethnicity and cultural difference in Dewey's writings" (35), and he remarks that although "both Dewey and Freire are progressive in their theories and practices . . . only Freire can be considered radical" (41). As radical as Freire's approach to literacy is—serving as the basis for literacy campaigns among the dispossessed of Brazil, Cuba, Nicaragua, and elsewhere in the developing world—in the United States Freire's thought has become so abstracted that his ideas often translate into little more than a preference for discussion over lecture

in college classrooms. His contribution to American progressive educational theory is invaluable, but Freire did not design his literacy programs for the
contradictions of education in American cities, where kids game on
Playstations in unheated apartments with peeling, lead-based paint and
attend schools where state-of-the-art computers sit untouched because no
one has the time or technical knowledge to set them up. Perhaps because
Alinsky is not expressly an educational philosopher, his work provides a
striking challenge to those of us who want to conceptualize the role of literacy education within the context of university–community relationships.

Kate Ronald and Hephzibah Roskelly have noted that "philosophical
pragmatism"—as practiced by Freire, Dewey, and others—"makes experience and consequence integral to epistemology and inquiry" (620). Alinsky
demonstrates this same restlessness to know and to try limits, but he takes
his philosophy to the streets. Alinsky's goal is organizing first and foremost;
even though education was an important part of his overall program, he was
not especially concerned with schooling or literacy. He wanted to make lives
better by bringing people together in a working organization so that they
could change their own living conditions and gain dignity. As he puts it most
succinctly: "Change comes from power, and power comes from organization. In order to act, people must get together" (*Rules* 113). Alinsky has a
bite to him that Dewey and Freire no longer have after so many educators
have borrowed from their work, applied their theories to practice, and
argued their merits and limitations. Alinsky's principles are perhaps more
difficult to domesticate into a pedagogical approach, not because his language is arcane or his philosophy abstract, but because his politics are consistently blunt and confrontational.

At the heart of Alinsky's approach to organizing is his concept of self-
interest. To those who worry that self-interest as a motivational force would
lead to individual greed and communal disintegration, he answers: "The fact
is that self-interest can be a most potent weapon in the development of cooperation and identification of the group welfare as being of more importance than personal welfare" (*Reveille* 94). The proper function of the
organizer, in Alinsky's view, is to identify problems that affect people individually but help them see these problems as issues they can do something
about collectively (*Rules* 119). This requires from the organizer a view of
daily life undistracted by the lure of fast money or political position and a
faith that people will elaborate a program that will be good for all (*Reveille*
56).

Alinsky stresses that nothing can be accomplished without tremendous
effort to build relationships with local leaders (*Reveille* 188), factions in a
group (*Reveille* 125), and indeed anyone the organizer wants to work with
or influence (*Rules* 93-94). However, he also urged his organizers to *disor-
ganize* old and unproductive ways a community works (or doesn't work) in

order to build a stronger, more participatory organization later (*Rules* 116). Alinsky organizers are agitators because they provoke conflict for the purpose of drawing people into action together: "The job then is to get the people to move, to act, to participate; in short to develop and harness the necessary power to effectively conflict with the prevailing patterns and change them" (*Rules* 117). Reading Alinsky now, years after his initial successes in the late 1930s as well as his revival during the radical 1960s, one can feel both the love and hatred the man could inspire.

The picture Alinsky paints of the organizer clashes with the image most of us hold as proper for a teacher. In popular opinion, teachers should not be overtly political, should not manipulate their students, and should not reach beyond the discipline or skill set they are hired to teach. In fact, many of us would feel uncomfortable acting like Alinsky's organizers in the classroom. Yet, we might wish to be more creative and responsive to the particular situations in which our students find themselves, hope to build the leadership capacity of the communities we serve, and desire to communicate based on better knowledge of our students' lives and more respect for their dignity. I am not suggesting that we convert undergraduate tutors into young Alinsky agitators stirring up trouble in schoolyards and street corners. Nor do I urge professors to don leather jackets and give up their tenure to work in storefront literacy centers. Radical fantasies are appealing, but to rush off in that direction is to mistake Alinsky's style for his politics. To me Alinsky is calling for a deeper commitment to change than fantasy allows. He challenges us in post-secondary positions to think like organizers rather than academics when we devise models of university–community relationship.

As academics, even if we want to put neighborhood needs first, we cannot help but start with the demands of our classrooms or the requirements for promotion. But what if we start from the activist's ground in this instance, learning before we act, developing relationships and commitments before we organize classes and set up research projects? When we have established these relationships, we may be able to help the community partners identify problems and transform these problems into issues to act upon, only later considering how students in courses fit in and what university resources could be helpful in addressing the issues. In short, what if we use our research, teaching, administrative, and writing abilities for the sake of the people our students tutor, not only for the sake of the college programs we run? What if the through-put model did not dominate our program designs, but instead we followed a model of long-term investment in the neighborhoods where we work and centers with which we partner? This thinking leads to a model of community-based learning and research in which students and their teachers are not so much providing services as participating in a collective effort defined by academics and local citizens alike.

THE OPEN DOOR COLLABORATIVE

At Temple University in 1998, we started a component of the writing program called the Institute for the Study of Literature, Literacy, and Culture
(Parks and Goldblatt). The College of Liberal Arts supports the Institute
with a very small budget, a stipend for one graduate assistant, course reductions for the director, and in some years reductions for a faculty fellow or
two. Whatever other funding we need comes from grants. After about 4
years, we gave the Institute a simpler name for regular usage: New City
Writing. Changes in the mission reflect the streamlining of the name. New
City Writing is still an academic unit in which scholars and students interested in the cultural formation of literature and literacy can pursue special
projects, but our focus is on community-based writing and reading programs that lead to publications as well as educational ventures where school
teachers, neighborhood people, and university-related people can learn
together. We have published a magazine called *Open City* that collected
writing by homeless people, school kids, and local writers on subjects like
food or shelter. We founded New City Press to publish book projects related to specific communities in the Philadelphia area, such as a series of interviews with residents of an historically integrated working-class South
Philadelphia neighborhood called the Forgotten Bottom (Hyatt), a collection of essays by activist disabled people talking about their lives and campaigns (Ott *No Restraints*), and a bilingual oral history of Mexican mushroom workers in a rural area west of the city (Lyons and Tarrier).

New City Writing works as a partner with local schools and neighborhood organizations. We develop projects with community arts organizations such as Art Sanctuary, serving primarily an African-American population, and Asian Arts Initiatives, a group focused on Asian and Asian
Americans in Chinatown as well as areas in the southern and western sections of the city. We place undergraduates and graduates from courses and
with independent projects in various school and community sites, focusing
especially on writing centers that can be developed and supported by the
organizations involved but can serve as a settled location for visiting tutors
and speakers. We participate in grant writing with our partners, acting as the
administering agents for some grants and providing resources and assistance
for grants held by other groups. Always we try to respond creatively and
cooperatively to needs articulated by neighborhood organizations, and we
try to emphasize institution and leadership building that would allow for
long-term relationships and trust to grow among partners.

As in the composition instruction paradigm shift led by Elbow, Murray,
Sommers, and Perl during the 1970s, community-based learning and
research has shifted focus from product to process because, as Alinsky

would say, the democratic process is paramount. Not that the grants we write and the projects we design are not important—just as the final version of a student's paper matters much more than early process rhetoric admitted—but the unfolding effort to brainstorm ideas, draft grant proposals, revise our sense of what matters to us, and recommit ourselves to collaborative work leads us to stronger final projects than anything that any one of the partners could have devised in our offices alone. Compositionists should recognize the logic of this approach; it is resonant both with the process movement and with the principles of community organizing articulated by Alinsky. Building capacity, forming relationships, communicating across institutional boundaries—these processes ultimately shape the nature of the solutions any community can design and support.

As an example of the way a project might be developed under Alinsky's model, I offer a brief account of Open Doors Collaborative, a cooperative effort among directors of three adult education centers in North Philadelphia and New City Writing. To me, Open Doors suggests a new model emerging at this stage of the community-based learning movement, one that comes from neighborhoods and draws on the university without being controlled by its demands. I entered into conversations with my partners on this project with few expectations and no particular goal except that I wanted to meet some people working at the nexus of ESL, technology, and literacy issues within small agencies in the North Philadelphia community. After more than 2 years of meetings and listserv exchanges and grant writing, I hope that Open Doors will lead to a loose network of programs that could serve as a kind of alternative or preparatory community college. We see a need among people in the neighborhoods who have a desire to try college and perhaps seek a degree but who must take a transitional year or two before they can enroll in traditional postsecondary education. I would not be surprised, however, if a year from now some other formation that my collaborators or I cannot yet imagine may arise from our work.

In January 2002, I called on Manuel Portillo at his office next door to St. Ambrose Episcopal Church in a Latino neighborhood of North Philadelphia. The priest of the church, Father Carlos, had approached Temple's Community Partnerships Office to get ESL teachers from Temple for the Church's new educational program, Proyecto Sin Fronteras, which Manuel directs. Community Partnerships arranged to have a few TESOL students work at Proyecto as a part of their graduate program in the previous year. My colleague Steve Parks had met Manuel at a Temple event, and he praised Manuel and his program. I had also heard of Manuel from an organizer who worked with him in another neighborhood, and I knew Manuel had a strong interest in educational programs that encourage greater civic participation in the community. I put aside everything else one afternoon and went to see him in the Proyecto's office, a converted rowhouse in a portion of North Philly largely Latino but, unlike most of the Latino areas, not exclusively Puerto Rican. Manuel is a slender man, a refugee from Guatemala who left at the height of the government war against dissenters in the mid-1980s. He is intense but a good listener. He had nearly finished a college degree in his country before he had to flee, studied social work in Connecticut and Boston, worked in an organizing campaign for people living with HIV in South Chicago, and then came to Philadelphia in the 1990s to work at various community development jobs.

That first visit Manuel and I talked over hamburgers and coffee at a lunch counter around the corner from his office. He told me about the Guatemalan paramilitary killing his father—a leader in the resistance forces based in the capitol—and kidnapping his nieces before he and his siblings fled the country. I had studied Spanish in Guatemala in 1980, and so at least I knew something of the situation there at the time. I talked about my mother's current struggle with lung cancer, and we discussed the effect that personal traumas have on one's vocational choices. Manuel recounted the problems of a married couple—both doctors from Columbia—who had just asked him for help finding work in Philadelphia. He described the computer literacy class that he himself taught three times a week in the center's computer lab. We shared ideas about teaching and organizing, speculated on why people in the neighborhood wanted so much to "learn computers" and what we could do in response to that strong demand. It turned out we had some friends in common in the Guatemalan refugee community and in the foundation world (despite being the fifth largest city in the United States, Philadelphia often shows itself to be a very small town). We left with no particular plan but the start of a working friendship.

The next time Manuel and I met, my colleague Steve came along too and brought his new baby Jude. Jude was in on the conversation, gumming crackers and magnanimously accepting attention from us and other patrons at the lunch joint. We told Manuel about New City Writing and he told us about his conversations with Johnny Irizarry, a director of a social and educational program called The Lighthouse in the heart of the Puerto Rican community. I got excited about bringing Johnny into the picture because not only had we worked with him closely before on a couple of projects with the Institute, but also he was one of the best known figures in the community arts and cultural organizations of Philadelphia. When he resigned from the Puerto Rican arts organization he ran for many years, the city's main paper ran a front-page article about him, a very rare recognition for a community activist. We had helped Johnny get free tuition to finish a master's degree at Temple during a time when he needed an advanced degree to work with the school district and we needed his guidance to work effectively in the Puerto Rican community. I had always admired Johnny's combination of undying good humor and fierce commitment to social justice, and he

knew just about everyone doing anything progressive in Philadelphia neighborhoods. Johnny and Manuel had been talking about developing an
approach to literacy and education based on the realities of the Latino neighborhoods, an approach with the liberation attitude of Freire but the feel for
economics on 5th Street, the heart of Philadelphia's Puerto Rican community. Steve, Manuel, and I all agreed that working together could really be fun.

Let me pause at this point and glance back at the Alinsky principles.
Stitched into the story about our unfolding relationship with Manuel are
approaches to organizing that differ from what we do in the university. In
school there are classes, schedules, books on a syllabus, concepts to cover. In
a neighborhood there are alliances and enmities, jobs and welfare, abandoned houses and fenced-off gardens. The terrain is less defined and the time
isn't parceled out in 15-week intervals, but the needs are tremendous and the
urgency persists like the stench of 100 old oil-burning furnaces laboring in
winter. Steve and I meet Manuel on his ground, not primarily as professors
representing a major institution but as interested people with lives of our
own. As we talk we learn more about the challenges people around Proyecto
face, what the funding issues are, who teaches and studies there regularly,
how the church relates to the school it founded but must let grow independently. I listen for the self-interest of the neighborhood within multiple
issues, I express my own self-interest in the project, and I try to see THIS
neighborhood specifically as opposed to others in the city or an abstract
concept of poor communities. Most of all I allow myself to be guided by
Manuel, to learn to trust his vision while still recognizing where I have useful observations to add of my own. We are working together to identify
underlying themes that can form the basis of future projects, and both of us
eventually agree that building leadership capacity among the people who go
to Proyecto is a central objective.

Soon after that conversation, I visited Manuel's computer class. Twelve
people worked at fairly up-to-date computers in a little lab on the second
floor. The learners were all women except for one man in his 20s; the women
ranged in age from their early 20s to late 50s and all were Latina except one
older white woman who spoke no Spanish. Manuel introduced me and I
talked a bit about our idea that students need a bridge between where they
are now and the community college or Temple courses they might take at
the beginning of a college career. Two women spoke to me after class about
the possibilities of further links between their computer class and college
programs. Rosa was in her early 30s, spoke English with a strong Spanish
accent—she had come from Venezuela within the last couple of years—and
showed great determination to make a new life for herself and her children.
She wanted to know if we were sending tutors right away to Proyecto. She
had tried community college one semester and decided it wasn't right for
her—too confusing, too much English—but she felt she needed more skills

and a better job, and she was anxious to get started right away. I met her again later that week in Manuel's office. Rosa was dressed for an interview, talking to Manuel about work prospects anywhere in the area.

Isabel was a bit younger than Rosa. She asked questions for herself and others in class, and quizzed me afterward about the admission policy at Temple. It turned out she was from a well-known Dominican family that owned a number of grocery stores in the area. She had gone to high school not far away but had moved to the suburbs after her father was murdered in the course of a robbery at one of their stores. Her sisters had gone to college but, when Isabel got to the city community college, she felt totally overwhelmed by the work her teacher assigned her in the first remedial writing course, although she had earned good grades in her public school. She dropped out, but not before she had battled through two remedial reading and writing courses and gotten credit for the first college composition course; by that time she had met and married a doctor from another Dominican family and was raising two young children in a nearby suburb. She came back to the old neighborhood almost every day, and she wanted to get back to college now, probably at night. Manuel told me later that she was quite capable of doing college work and could pay for it, but she lacked confidence in her abilities at school. Isabel was a powerhouse in her community, raising funds for college scholarships for Dominican students, but her fear of academic work held her back.

At Proyecto later that week, Manuel and I met with Johnny and his assistant director Marta, a young Latina who announced that her aunt had once owned the rowhouse where we were meeting. Also attending were two White women from an adult education program called Urban Bridges. This program was connected to St. Gabriel's, another Episcopal church less than 1 mile northeast of Proyecto in a section of the city called Olney. Felice Simelaro, Urban Bridges' director, and her assistant director Mary Ann Borsuk ran a center that served an extremely mixed community, including Haitians and Puerto Ricans, Cambodians and Africans, with youth programs as well as literacy and technology courses. With a very small paid staff, Urban Bridges depended heavily on the tutoring provided by undergraduates in service-learning classes at a few different regional colleges. Felice and Mary Ann knew a great deal about the range of approaches to adult basic education and also about the support available from the state Department of Education and other governmental and private agencies. Everyone from the three centers had extensive experience with foundations, but no one felt that their center was on very stable financial ground in this period when an uncertain stock market made grant money tight and foundations unpredictable.

We talked about what we would like to work toward, and Johnny spoke movingly about learners needing a curriculum suited to their lives and languages. A small, incredibly energetic man, Johnny is quick to smile but speaks with great seriousness and passion about the work needed in his community. He stressed the need to address the pressures neighborhood center students experience—the urgent demand for marketable skills and serviceable English, the confidence and contacts to get them work outside the neighborhood—but at the same time he felt we had to be committed to building leadership in the community and emphasizing the way people can work together to make things better for all. He clearly had a vision of the kinds of organizations that work best in Puerto Rican neighborhoods, but at the same time his years of cooperative work made him respectful of other opinions and careful not to dismiss anyone.

At this meeting, I took notes on what people wanted us to work toward. The next day I set up a listserv through Temple for the six of us and sent to the list a one-page statement of our purpose and goals, based on my notes from the meeting. At subsequent meetings we talked through the document I had produced. The focus was not only on a "reality-based and transformative" curriculum for information technology literacy, but on an organizing strategy that would enhance the perspective of teachers in these small computer labs and directors of the programs about what adults could learn from the neighborhood environment. One big issue that emerged for all three centers—and others that people knew about in the area—was the need for more qualified teachers to make the best use of the computer labs that they had built with capital grants earlier. We joked about the irony that centers could get money for computers and connectivity, but few foundations or state agencies would pay for the teachers that made those labs useful to the neighborhoods. This was to become a crucial issue for the collaborative to address.

We held a meeting at Johnny's center near the 5th Street hub of the Puerto Rican neighborhood. Here we revised our document to take the focus further off of technology and more on cooperative support and curricular reform. What follows are the first two paragraphs of the document after that meeting:

> The Open Doors Collaborative is a consortium of adult education programs in North Philadelphia concerned with establishing a comprehensive approach to literacy instruction that is reality-based and transformative for learners. We propose to develop teaching and learning practices that engage learners in active civic participation. In addition to sharing ideas on curriculum and policy, the collaborative hopes to share resources in our effort to maintain computer services, attract and retain excellent staff, and buy hardware and software at competitive rates.
>
> As a first project, we will develop a curriculum that promotes critical thinking, independent inquiry, communication skills, and leadership ability within the specific context of North Philadelphia neighbor-

hoods. This curriculum would also integrate the information technology students are learning in the small computer labs that have grown up in many community centers and churches. It could function as a stand-alone course or as a component of a GED program.

We decided to resist the temptation to look for funding from a foundation for the moment. Almost everybody had a story about foundations that asked their organization to follow all kinds of planning and evaluation procedures, only to find that the majority of the money in the grant went to experts who planned and evaluated but added nothing to the work with learners. In my minutes of the meeting, I wrote down this remark from Felice: "The problem is that it's so multilayered that by the time the money gets to the base there's little money left." Everyone agreed that we would not "chase the money" in this new alliance but formulate our plans and goals first, before we began talking to anyone about funding.

I recount the details of our beginnings in Open Doors not because the specifics matter very much to those who didn't live through it, but to illustrate both the complexity and the pleasure of working in partnership across the university–community divide. To make a new organizing effort go, as Alinsky would say, you have to identify the true self-interest of the communities involved and figure out how to get resources to address those needs. You have to identify well-connected leaders with an effective approach to actual problems in the neighborhood. You have to talk through conflicts and negotiate any tensions between organizations that are each struggling for their existence. Our meetings continued through the spring and summer, with the group deciding to stay small; an idea of sponsoring a retreat for North Philly community agencies transformed into an effort to write a grant to support a collaborative project just among our organizations. Felice, who kept Urban Bridges afloat by paying close attention to funding opportunities, ran across a Request for Proposals (RFP) from the U.S. Department of Education that seemed tailored for us. As she said at the meeting where we shifted from the retreat idea to the grant: "We don't want to run after the money, but we have to run our organizations, don't we?" We worked intensively on that grant and, although we ended up not submitting it, we weathered some conflicts across our programs arising from personal styles and organizational cultures. The language we produced for that grant looked like it would work for other grants in the future, but the founding ideas were taking shape with each iteration.

The members of our collaborative came to recognize that the most pressing need for small neighborhood adult literacy centers is more well-trained and committed teachers who know the communities in which they work. This is particularly true where information technology is part of the core teaching skill; the best qualified teachers prefer higher paying work at for-profit trade schools or community colleges if they can't get solid full-time work in neighborhood centers, even if they are sympathetic to the mission of the centers. We developed a two-pronged approach to this problem. First, we would try to get funding for attractive teaching positions—full time and with good benefits—for teachers that our coalition of centers could share. Individual centers may not be able to afford a full-time teacher, but a consortium could share costs, write grants together, and divide the supervisory responsibilities so that all centers would benefit and services to people in the area could increase in scope and quality. Second, we hoped to develop a model of "community educator" on the Latin American model: indigenous educational and health workers trained to provide services to their neighbors by the few educated teachers and health care workers available in the countryside of many poor nations. We felt this model would also work well for technology and literacy training in underserved U.S. urban neighborhoods.

After about 18 months of meeting together, the Open Doors group broke up. Johnny was under heavy pressure from his agency to write grants that would save them, and he no longer had time to meet with us. Felice resigned to pursue other projects, and Mary Ann stayed on at Urban Bridges as it made the transition to connect with a larger social service agency called Episcopal Community Services. Manuel and I, however, continued to meet and develop the concepts. I joined Proyecto's Board as chair and began the job of pulling together community members with little organizational experience and outsiders with expertise but no direct ties to the neighborhood. The Open Doors experience gave us concrete expressions of the problems and possible solutions we could apply to neighborhood literacy centers. I taught a class at Temple where I invited four students from Proyecto to participate, and these Proyecto students became our first class of community educators. Manuel and I are writing grants for Proyecto now that we hope will eventually allow us to go back to our Open Doors partners and develop both the sharing of professional staff and the training of community educators. Additionally, we have worked out a plan for service-learning experiences in Proyecto classes. Community technicians, like community educators, could be paid a stipend to help maintain computer labs in local churches and centers as a means of combining on-the-job training with neighborhood collaboration. I regard the Open Doors project not as a failure but a long-term investment in helping neighborhood leaders identify problems related to literacy and work toward local solutions that eventually will change the way North Philadelphians move through training programs and the way Temple students relate to centers like Proyecto Sin Fronteras.

Perhaps the most compelling element for me of the approach we developed in Open Doors is the shift in focus from individual to collective improvements. This speaks to the last three principles of Alinsky's organizing approach; the shift honors the experience of disenfranchised people while it points toward greater independence for groups and individuals who must see themselves as agents of their own future rather than victims of their history. Manuel has been particularly strong in his argument that, in his own center, the stress should be on how any individual functions within his or her multiple communities. "What are the communities from which you come and to which you wish to return?" he asked a group of his students when I brought composition/rhetoric graduate students from Temple to visit Proyecto. A student I call Lourdes answered by saying she had three communities. One was in the block or two around her house, a micro-neighborhood in North Philly populated by immigrants from the Dominican Republic like herself but also people from Puerto Rico and other Latin American countries. Another was the neighborhood around her husband's little grocery store, a renovated building in an African American neighborhood where the drug trade is intense but where people had been friendly to her and her husband. Lourdes noted that many neighbors there helped her learn English, and now she felt a commitment to make life better in that community, too. Finally, Proyecto itself served as a crucial community for her. She was attending classes there three times a week in computer literacy so that she could help her children with their homework. She said at first she couldn't do more than turn her computer on and off, but now she could set up a system and handle word processing software. She had developed a strong bond with the others in her advanced technology class and wanted to continue working with them. She took great pride in her growing abilities to speak English and manipulate a computer system, but she realized that she had much more to do if she wanted to contribute in significant ways to all these communities. Her own self-interest was intimately tied to the well-being not only of her family but her friends and neighbors who have helped make her life since arriving in this country more hopeful and productive.

Soon after that session, Manuel asked Lourdes to train as a community educator with me. In that role, she worked for 8 weeks writing and reading with my undergraduate senior seminar. We also invited her to join the board of Proyecto. Alinsky would have loved her story, for it illustrates not only the effort to help individuals grasp issues they can do something about but also the way to build leadership capacity, hers and those who encounter her. She is becoming a leader in her home communities, but—believe me—Lourdes' remarks were not lost on the grad students who heard her, either.

LITERACY SPONSORSHIP AND KNOWLEDGE ACTIVISM

But how is this story relevant to college writing instructors and program administrators? What's so valuable about hanging around in North Philly, making fun of foundations and swapping family stories? And what role does a university writing program play in organizing a neighborhood around literacy? Perhaps the most telling question is the one with which I began this article: Who is serving whom? One can never answer the question definitively, even in a single, seemingly static, situation; the worst university–community relationships can change with the weather. A state-funded research university might pay little attention to the needs of poor neighborhoods — or those scholars who interact with them — until a legislator from an urban district takes over the committee that decides higher educational funding. Suddenly, faculty who do community-based work can become important to the university's central administration and the way researchers relate to community needs can come under intense scrutiny. No matter which way the wind blows, the question of who is serving whom needs to be asked again and again.

The question takes on new meaning when we return to the concept of literacy sponsorship. Deborah Brandt stresses the gain that a sponsor receives in having people learning and producing under the particular literacy conditions of the sponsor (*American Lives* 19), but this need not be a destructive or exploitive situation. Much of what I have narrated in the section on Open Doors is meant to illustrate a kind of joint sponsorship of literacy, slowly, carefully developed based on a mutual understanding of self-interest as Alinsky defines it. As long as the partners come to know each other well enough to recognize where they share interests and where their interests diverge, I believe it is possible for them to sponsor literacy jointly for a particular group or groups; all can benefit and none need to feel subordinated or exploited. In this light, however, one must see self-interests coldly and comprehensively. It is, in short, a political act to mount a partnership across levels or sectors of literacy workers. I use the word political because power relations enter into the negotiation. I believe partners need to get to know each other's families, share meals and miseries, but no member of the partnership can forget the differential in power between little neighborhood agency and large university, between national foundation and local literacy center. I focus on these issues in greater detail in the final chapters, but Alinsky's canny analysis serves to deepen what I mean by joint literacy sponsorship because he gives us a calculus with which to figure the self-interests involved in partnership.

I served my community partners with an approach I have come to think of as knowledge activism. My experience, the resources I could contribute, and my noninterventionist approach gave me a certain credibility to participate in the organizational development process. I helped found and nurture the Open Doors Collaborative, and I continue to work with Manuel and Proyecto. A study leave from my university when we first got started gave me time that others in the group did not have, and I have contacts in the city literacy network and foundations that proved useful from time to time. My writing skills allowed me to take good notes and shape them into a document we could rework collectively. My experience with literacy instruction and research helped because I could suggest language in grant proposals that might convince funders. I spoke Spanish passably and taught high school in the neighborhood; this local knowledge allowed me to listen intelligently to the conversation. Most important, I was willing to invest time and energy without being in charge, to build alongside others working in the neighborhood rather than enter the scene with a plan already formed. As Alinsky would have it, I met people on their own ground, observed the situation without preconceived notions of what they needed or who they were. And only under those conditions could we develop a literacy sponsorship that could make knowledge active for people left outside the charmed circle of university knowledge production and conservation.

Another aspect of knowledge activism is that I could bring to bear institutional resources that I had at my disposal for my partners' needs. The Temple University writing program had received grant money to participate in community projects, and I was able to provide some funding to start the community educator training project. I brought graduate and undergraduate classes in contact with Proyecto, and in the last years my Temple colleagues and I have arranged assistantships, internships, volunteer positions, and candidates for jobs funded by other sources, all of which have aided small nonprofit organizations with few resources of their own. I characterize this sort of negotiation with foundations and university administrators in the next chapter as building sponsorships beyond the walls of the campus. For now, let me note that Alinsky's principles operate as useful reminders when knowledge activists begin to draw on their institutional affiliations. University resources, available to us because of our professional (and privileged) positions, must be offered responsibly and cooperatively. It helps no one to give aid without a clear purpose or with no commitment to build relationships across institutions, and it is cynical exploitation to offer resources with hidden agendas based primarily on university-determined objectives.

At the same time, Manuel, Johnny, Felice, and Mary Ann had a store of experiences and allies to share with me. The work they do challenges any narrow understanding of reading and writing confined to the college campus. Rosa, Isabel, and Lourdes reminded me just how broad the spectrum of literacy really is and how high the stakes are for those who do not have full institutional access to literacies of the dominant culture. Brandt has noted that "despite ostensible democracy in public education, access to literacy and its rewards continue to flow disproportionately to the children of the already educated and the already affluent" (*American Lives* 197). This same heritage of class advantage follows literacy educators as well. Unlike college WPAs like me at large research universities, directors of adult education centers do not have tenure or a large institution's budget behind them as they build their programs. Their students and clients often live precariously and must succeed or face welfare cut-offs, unemployment, deportation, or prison. The mission of my partners' adult education centers forces me to conceive of writing and reading beyond the boundaries of undergraduate and graduate curricula, even when I sit in university committee meetings or hold conferences with dissertation advisees. Located only inside my campus, I can either come to believe my job is terribly exalted, the top of the literacy food chain, or I can despair that I make no difference in the lives of anyone. Again, the through-put system defines our consciousness and masks the reality of other community and individual objectives in settings off campus. After every Open Doors meeting I remembered that I function inside an institutional framework for literacy that is merely one among many. This is a recognition I return to later.

In the long run, the shift to a more collective view of education is profound for a college writing program. It can cause us to question the through-put model of education, in which the writing program plays such a prominent part. Of course we want individual students to succeed as they move from general education to major, from wide-eyed (and scared) first-year student to world-weary (and scared) senior. We have a responsibility to help students move through their school careers and be able to function in jobs afterward. But this model is almost entirely focused on individuals developing a knowledge base and skill set. How does a writing program, a general education curriculum, and a department-based major foster a sense in individuals that they are connected to other citizens in large and small ways? How do we in writing programs make manifest our understanding of literacy as social, local, or efficacious beyond having students read articles that say so? The crucial thing is that we need not see our programs as merely forming a conduit; instead we can position our institution as one among many that engage with a wide range of people. When we think of ourselves as members of more than an academic community, our neighborhood connections should be constituted in a way that students encounter partners engaging in substantial work rather than clients receiving aid.

My encounters with Manuel, Johnny, Felice, Mary Ann, Isabel, Rosa, and Lourdes give me concrete moments for understanding Alinsky's "rules." The time demanded to apply these principles overwhelms me occasionally; the conflicts between the needs of different neighborhoods and the real or perceived goals of the university can seem quite impossible to reconcile. Alinsky stresses that conflict is inevitable and out of it must arise creative solutions and greater perspective. At the same time, for all his emphasis on conflict, Alinsky's greatest organizing was built on well-tested friendships. Like organizing, literacy work can be sustained by such friendships even amidst conflict. On the other hand, the specialization and risk-aversion common in university life, the narrow formulations of self-interest and turf protection that seem inevitable in every adult endeavor—these are ways of handling conflict that can exhaust the spirit and wither the mind completely. If we are willing to accept roles as participants or even knowledge activists rather than detached observers or paid consultants, we can reframe for ourselves the sites and texts of literacy instruction through satisfying and reciprocal relationships with our neighborhood partners.

5

Lunch

During the 2002-2003 school year I agreed—perhaps quite foolishly—to chair a task force overseeing the reform of Temple's undergraduate general education curriculum called the Core. The Core grew into an obsession, getting me on campus early every morning and keeping me in the office late nearly every evening. I dreamed about the Core, woke up worrying about it, talked about it to my family over dinner. I neglected writing program work and my own writing, and occasionally I even described Core complexities to my students in the classes I managed to teach. My colleague Bob Schneider, the assistant vice provost for Core and Transfer at the time, became my constant companion. We strategized over lunch about how we were going to organize town meetings with faculty, focus groups with students, and consultations with the university president. I often dropped him off at his house so we could keep talking after we left campus, and we lamented on the drive home over intransigent faculty and the meager resources that made our fine plans so difficult to achieve. Anyone who has led a general education initiative knows that it involves constant attention to politics as well as pedagogy, horse-trading as well as national trends, schmoozing as well as time management. The job cannot help but take over your life.

That year, however, I was also working regularly with Manuel Portillo and others to develop our concept of community educators in adult literacy and technology programs serving North Philadelphia. I regarded those meetings away from campus as great freeing moments. I could engage a set of problems that clearly mattered to the lives of people in need, but I could also glance back at my campus life and see what of it was substance and what was smoke. Manuel and I had lunches together, too, and—like my lunches with Bob about the Core—they were mostly filled with talk of work still to do. Somehow, however, the lunches with Manuel seemed more constructive and promising, despite the fact that North Philly literacy centers have access to fewer resources than the least Core programs at Temple.

In June 2003 I was abruptly relieved of my duties with the Core. The task force had consulted with more than 200 faculty across the university in the course of that year, but a few powerful older faculty apparently didn't like what we had proposed as the outline of a new general education curriculum. I was asked by the faculty senate president to step down at a time when few members of the task force were on campus, and I was told that he didn't even want a final report; whatever we had already produced I could send as an e-mail attachment and the reconstituted committee would carry on from there. He invited me to continue on the committee in a reduced role, but I declined. It was a gift in many ways because I could go back to my work (this book might never have been completed had I continued for another year working on the Core), but I felt betrayed and angry and sad for months afterward.

One development that helped in the healing process was that Manuel asked me to become chair of Proyecto's board of trustees, and I agreed to try the job. I began learning how small nonprofits work from the inside, and this experience affected how I think about writing program governance and resource questions on campus. I want to return to the contrast between academic and nonprofit entities later, but for now I'll just say that the experience made me hopeful where I could easily have become bitter and cynical, recommitted where I could easily have become apathetic and detached. My work in North Philadelphia convinces me that positive change is not only possible but also necessary, and I realize that a complacent cynicism is comfortable but morally indefensible at a time when the gap between rich and poor students is nearly unbridgeable for many.

I call this chapter "Lunch" because it is about relationships that go beyond academia's usual perfunctory committee meetings around a table in a bare room. I want to say that from the most modest intradepartmental project to the largest scale grant proposal involving hundreds of participant in dozens of programs, literacy education depends on a network of relationships that must be carefully nurtured and maintained if students are to grow and learn, if teachers are to feel supported and valued, if researchers are to dig deep into the scene they hope to understand. In fact, I would suggest that the most important job of WPAs is to build and extend the sustaining relationships that make their programs possible. Not that staffing decisions, training programs, assessments efforts, and scholarly writing are not important parts of a WPA's job, but caring for crucial relationships may be the necessary condition for everything else one is expected to accomplish. As I emphasize later in this chapter, these relationships make possible the kind of consciously shared sponsorships that underlie any successful effort at writing projects either across or beyond the curriculum in a particular campus. Building relationships is not particularly glorious work—one will not receive merit raises or awards for great conversations over lunch or coffee— and it can consume a lot of precious time, but relationships can be quietly satisfying and crucially necessary for the health of a program and the wellbeing of its participants. In short, we must build sustaining relationships because we live in the weave of them.

In this chapter, I highlight the role of relationship building for a set of initiatives within and beyond our university campus. I do not present these as exemplars of practice or models of organization; I simply use their histories as cases to illustrate the need for literacy educators to work in collaboration with one another across levels and beyond institutional boundaries. The walls that funding lines and historical precedent encourage us to erect often do much to discourage exactly the sort of learning environments that would best foster literacy abilities. The more we can recognize the arbitrary limits we put on exchanges, consultations, and educational collaborations, the more we can freely invent programs that truly allow learners to use words to redefine their world. In short, I see two possible worlds ahead for college literacy education. In the first one, we continue on the path of specialization, including community-based projects and off-campus research. Specialists in WAC and community literacy and technology and ESL and secondary education grow more distant from one another; they begin to see their interests as so unrelated that one group starts to wonder what it is doing associating with the others, gathered together only by a hodge-podge conference for "composition and communication." In the second world, the one I prefer to inhabit, we continually find ways that researchers off campus feed and are fed by those who remain focused within college courses—we circulate what we know and the sense of field grows stronger. Programs speak to programs, and common purpose sustains us all. We can recognize in our differences that every level, unit, institution, and population has much to teach its neighbors about the character, practices, and potentialities of literacy.

A RETURN TO FIRST PRINCIPLES

Before I begin discussing any individual projects, however, I want to return to the principles I introduced in the opening chapter. I think we're more prepared now to consider these principles on the grounds I discussed in the intervening chapters. These principles take on another dimension when we consider the effort necessary to build and maintain relationships that will make the realization of each possible. In brief, the four principles are as follows:

1. Aim to develop a constellation of abilities that help students become both productive individuals and engaged social beings: access, reflection, and connection.
2. Bring the margins to the center, and recognize that the most stressed students serve as the best guides about what a program can do.
3. Cultivate relationships both inside and outside school to support literacy learning.
4. Continually assess, evaluate, and study the program in as collaborative and imaginative a way as possible in order to gain perspective on the local environment.

If we step back from these principles, we can see that they form a ladder of concerns, each rung leading to the next but each equally important for the climbing. Student abilities stand as the first and most important rung. Despite the institutional demands made by the sponsorship of a community college or a research university, writing programs must take the development of student abilities as their primary motive, but we may not always see how the personal connections developed in the classroom and one-on-one conferences have much to do with the larger and more seemingly bureaucratic concerns of program administration. The common quality, the uprights that attach the rungs one to the other and allow us to lean the ladder against a wall, is the effort to build sustaining relationships all along the way.

I'll take each principle in turn and focus on the nature and character of relationship to which each principle commits a WPA and a program. The first two principles commit us to a more comprehensive view of pedagogy or greater efforts at connecting teachers of different populations of students in dialogue. The third principle leads us to a profound institutional reorientation, away from the autonomous and discrete entities we call schools and colleges and toward a more systematic understanding of whom we teach and when we teach them what. The final principle is about institutional reflection, and it assumes that any literacy organization, no matter how large or small, must recognize itself as an open system. Once we have consider the underlying principles, the specific instances begin to look less like an array of random but well-meaning projects and more like multiple manifestations of a single vision, one built on the diverse and binding human interactions possible among literacy learners and teachers in a broad landscape.

Student Abilities

It may seem self-evident for an undergraduate program to focus on student abilities as its main motive, but it is also easy to become overwhelmed by the list of learning objectives demanded by the collective participants from across the curriculum, in the work force, and in the world of civic responsibility. The field of composition has worked largely under the paradigm of social constructivism for well over 25 years, an era ushered in by the work of such figures as Karen LeFevre, Patricia Bizzell, David Bartholomae, and (after her initial cognitive work) Linda Flower. We have applied this paradigm to assignments and research models, to the analysis of discourse within various professional and disciplinary environments, to teacher training and assessment methods. And yet, we haven't really cracked the individualist mode of American education, in which each student is out to develop his or her own skills to the highest degree. All too often for central administrators, a writing program is judged as good because of its best students' products and poor because of its worst, with little thought about the success of the programmatic orientation as a whole. What would it mean to have abilities centered on relationship building stand at the center of a writing program's effort?

The relational element of literacy is closely examined in Deborah Brandt's *Literacy as Involvement*. She focuses us not on rhetorical concerns of persona and audience awareness but on the underlying imperative in the transaction between writer and reader to "contemplate each other into existence within the confines of a text world" (71). She notes that writer and reader participate in the making of meaning by forming a human relationship through written language:

> What I am trying to convey with an emphasis on "the we," however, might best be thought of as aspects of discourse that belong neither to audience nor persona but to both the writer and the reader as actual presences at the scene of language. "Weness" arises from the mutual recognition that someone is working to write a text and to read a text. Those enterprises are enabled by a developing history of involvement that is a sign not of the other but of the both, and it is this unfolding history that enables the construction of audience and persona to proceed. The emergent ground of the we is a reminder that the writer-reader relationship is not merely one of antagonism or mismatch or role-playing but one of common orientation to reality. (71)

Brandt's gaze here is not on the tricks or manipulations of writer on reader, nor on the resistance readers may put up against ideological or gendered messages offered by writers, but on the unfolding effort of both reader and writer to maintain the text as a ground on which both can meet: "The emerging text is the means by which a writer or reader maintains a grip on reality" (73). That reality is made provisionally each moment by the shared experience of text.

Although Lad Tobin's work does not engage text at the intimate transactional level of Brandt's study, his 1993 book *Writing Relationships* does stress that the social constructivist movement was insufficiently contextual, "overly general or overly technical, the situations far removed from actual students and teachers" (4). He urges us to focus on relationships that develop in classrooms and offices over the writing students do for composition courses. He says we can "help students become better writers" if we look "more carefully than we have so far at the interpersonal classroom relationships—between the student and the teacher, between the student and other students, and, finally, between the teacher and other teachers—that shape the writing and reading processes" (5). This approach makes sense against the background of Brandt's close reading of the literacy experience: Students could learn more about the effect of their words if they write in a situation that highlights the relationships formed around texts. Tobin's contribution to the field has been his insistence that we do more than analyze social forces that impinge on new writers or offer prompts for brainstorming based on research into the cognitive process of writing. He urges us to attend to the quality of relationships developed in the very classrooms that are supposed to be the grounds for literacy improvement.

The problem with Tobin's focus on these relationships is that it tends to freeze our attention on individuals and their specific interactions with one another, and it doesn't easily lead us to connect the social with the psychological frameworks for writing and reading. To some extent this is also a problem in Brandt's analysis because it is difficult to generalize beyond the dyad of writer and reader, even if both positions can be occupied by any number of writers and readers, depending on the text in question. This connection between the individual and the social group to which he or she belongs seems crucial to me, especially if we are to sustain writing programs that not only extend across disciplinary boundaries but also bridge the gap between educational institutions and the surrounding literacy lives of workers and citizens.

Paula Mathieu outlined the history of the "public turn," the tradition within composition to connect student and research writing "with 'real-world' texts, events or exigencies" (1). The successor to Tobin as director of the writing program at Boston College, Mathieu offers a capacious vision of writing inside and outside universities; the many theorists and researchers she identifies as contributing to the roots of this public turn provide a link between the intimate social portrait of literacy in Tobin and Brandt and the much broader questions of public rhetoric. If we embrace a public turn in composition to support literacy partnerships on a larger scale, we still need to keep alive a fine-grained concern for individuals learning to form and interpreting texts. I imagine college literacy based on dialogue and construction, where students learn to compose their own texts within the welter of voices in history, academic disciplines, and current social scenes. Access, critique, reflection, and connection are not a hierarchy of abilities but a mutually reinforcing panoply of skills and habits of mind that make for more satisfying human interaction, especially if the individual has the widest possible sense of whom or what one can engage.

Bringing the Margins to the Center

As Robert Yagelski pointed out, a small but influential line of literacy theorists and scholars, from Paulo Freire to Harvey Graff, have resisted the popular picture of literacy as a matter of basic skills in favor of a more penetrating analysis aimed at "understanding the connection among schooling, literacy, and power" (50). Yagelski identifies a dilemma: Even after we debunk the myth that "literacy leads to individual and social advancement" (51), we still have to reckon with the individual experience of writing as either a way to attain social standing or a barrier to achieving that desired standing. He takes the famous story of Malcolm X learning to read in prison as the exemplar of this dilemma. We want to resist the determinism often implied or suggested by academic discussions of race, class, and gender, but we also want to resist reducing Malcolm X to a folk hero, a "reformed convict who overcame adversity and found success through individual initiative and hard work" (54). His answer to this dilemma is to take into account both the "social and individual nature of literacy" (61), to see reading and writing in specific, localized acts played out across a stage of sweeping political and economic forces.

This strikes me as a productive mindset for writing teachers in a college classroom, but it asks them to operate across a huge range of scale. The teacher, under Yagelski's model, must pay attention to the particular histories and goals of each student but must still understand writing instruction as a matter of initiating students into certain discourses while not rejecting expressivist approaches. The instructor should be able to ground instruction in discursive practices but pay attention to every individual's sense of self that emerges from the work. That's a big bill for even the most experienced teacher; so many first-year writing teachers are either new grad students or contingent workers scurrying from university to college to community college in a single week. How does one bring this mixed economy of pedagogy, this vision combining the social and individual nature of literacy, or what Linda Flower calls the "dialectic of structure and agency" (Flower, Long and Higgins 10), to the level of a programmatic design? How does a writing program follow a vision of literacy that preserves a sense of individual agency but also recognizes social forces that shape and are shaping written language?

My answer to this challenge has two steps. The first—as I outlined in the opening chapter—is to put marginalized students at the center of the writing program, taking their needs and objectives as the defining demands for teachers and administrators to address. The second is to interpret these needs and goals in terms of building relationships rather than remedying deficiencies. Whether the encounter involves learning disabled students in a first year classroom or ESL students at a writing center or adult learners in a neighborhood literacy center, the kind of accommodations marginalized students need are really not so different from the attention exceptional students receive in well-funded honors programs. Students need to feel safe enough to risk being wrong, clear about the expectations of their teachers, and respected for what they know rather than despised for what they can't yet do. It may be that some students need more class time on linguistic features or more direct instruction on reading strategies, but even mainstream students probably can use more attention to details of literacy processing that professors assume they have mastered before they get to college. No one suffers if we apply the lessons learned in basic writing classrooms to the most advanced seminars.

The lessons I wish to apply, however, arise from writing that imagines marginalized students as people with something to say. Thanks to significant work over the last decade, a very thick description of this attitude in relation to basic writing and ESL students exists. Linda Adler-Kassner and Susanmarie Harrington identify an "alternative tradition" of basic writing researchers (including Min-Zhan Lu, Bruce Horner, Laura Gray-Rosendale, and Deborah Mutnick among others) who have questioned the deficit model of remediation and want to shift the focus of pedagogy away from formal correctness and toward a wider understanding of context, power relations, and ideology necessary for excluded people to participate in the discourse of academic and other social institutions (24). A similar tradition can be identified in the work of many TESOL researchers and composition/rhetoric scholars interested in the effect of writers crossing over language barriers (see collections of essays on second-language writing and alternative discourse such as Schroeder, Fox, and Bizzell; Silva and Matsuda; Zamel and Spack). To me, these various voices argue not for abolition of distinctions or special classes (although Ira Shor among others has called for the abolition of "basic writing" courses) but abolition of the marginal status and degrading attitudes toward people who don't easily fit into the American higher educational system.

In a more positive formulation of the challenge, Paul Matsuda says that "everyone in the U.S. academy needs to reassess their assumptions about discourse practices in the academy as they come in contact with unfamiliar discourses" and that "learning from other rhetorical practices can enrich U.S. academic discourse by expanding the socially available repertoire for scholarly communication" (Silva and Matsuda 194). This is a massive project, but I believe that a first step on the way is to allow our thinking about learning environments for marginalized students to influence our teaching of classes populated by students with the White, middle- or upper class profiles that more easily fit into traditional college classrooms. In the same way that feminism confronts traditional university pedagogy and content-driven curricula for men as well as women, programs that address nontraditional learners give us data and experience that can raise questions about how we teach discourse in a range of writing courses, from first-year writing to community-based learning courses to advanced writing intensive courses in ecology. As Ralph Ellison's unnamed protagonist cautions us at the end of *Invisible Man*: "Who knows but that, on the lower frequencies, I speak for you?" (581). All the attendant ironies of that remark in the context of Ellison's novel apply, I think, in the case of basic and ESL writers in writing programs.

One instructive instance of this relationship between marginalized classes and the mainstream involves reading. At Temple, it became clear over the last 3 years that one of the most pressing needs for students in our basic writing class as well as for foreign students in Intellectual Heritage, a general education sequence centering on traditional "great" books, was the need to develop rich and extensive strategies for reading difficult college texts in English. We sponsored seminars on reading instruction and convened discussion groups on how various instructors taught reading. As the conversation unfolded, I realized just how little I understood about reading and how few books I'd read about the subject even though I thought of myself as trained in literacy as well as composition and rhetoric. My field is writing, and although we talked about the reciprocal relationship with reading, very few of my peers in the field of college composition have given more than a nod to the reception of texts. Moreover, my Temple colleagues and I began to recognize that this need didn't stop with basic writers and non-native speakers of English. In other words, this was not a deficit in the students of a particular set of classes but a blind spot in our vision of the program as a whole. Reading is at the heart of what people in the academy do, and yet writing teachers find it just as embarrassing to teach reading—slows us down, can't really do it, they should have learned it in high school—as literature professors used to find the chore of teaching writing when they wanted to teach their specialized form of literary interpretation.

Another area in which attention to the marginalized students will lead to greater strength in the program as a whole is technology. Cynthia Selfe has called for English educators to move beyond a habitual tendency to ignore the deeper implications of technology in American life. She argues that if we don't think hard about computers linked to reading and writing, as well as the ideologies and politics that surround this contemporary literacy, then we become complicit in the inequities such technology preserves: "By paying attention to the unfamiliar subject of technology—in substantial and critical ways, and from our own perspectives as humanists—we may learn some important lessons about how to go about making change in literacy instruction" (134). She wants us to do more than teach students to be good consumers of software and hardware (153); she urges us to develop with our students and others in the culture a critical technological literacy (148), the ability to be reflective and analytical about the social implications of technology intimately linked with literacy. Despite the massive investments the U.S. government has made in the information infrastructure, the poor and people of color remain without significant access to the benefits claimed by the advocates for information technology initiatives that began in the early 1980s: "computers continue to be distributed differentially along the related axes of race and socioeconomic status, and this distribution contributes to ongoing patterns of racism and to the continuation of poverty" (135). If we don't move these concerns to the front of our vision then the entire technology of literacy solidifies around unequal access. The disenfranchised suffer from this arrangement, of course, but those with greater access are cut off from the full import of what they do and say. The meaning of their privileged forms of literacy is hidden from them in the haze of what they have.

The range of experiences with technology that students bring to Temple would be extremely difficult to study. I know a few students come from private schools where they had multiple computers in every classroom and every student had access to computers at home. On the other hand, at Somerset High School, where perhaps a dozen computers connected to the Internet in the library, many Somerset students had no access to a computer at home. Attention to the least technologically experienced students at Temple would force us not only to be much more explicit about procedural knowledge relating to software use, but also would throw us back to ask the questions Selfe urges us to ask about why we do what we do and whose purpose our instruction serves. The more technologically savvy student—who grew up with computers, who knows how to edit video on his or her laptop—may be so embedded in the technology that he or she cannot necessarily see around and outside it. Our least sophisticated students, the ones likely to cut and paste text from Web sites indiscriminately and see all available information as equally credible, may force us to develop a curriculum that can better foster critical attitudes toward technology, greater fluidity and human connection by way of technology, and more democratic debate supported by technology. Our success as teachers of college literacy should not be measured in terms of software and hardware expenditures but in terms of the quality of attention our students develop in our programs. That is clearly a lesson our least prepared students can teach us.

Although I am in favor of maintaining basic writing and ESL classes aimed at particular populations of students, the stratified and segregated model of writing programs often allows for no real dialogue to develop among instructors of different "levels." We saw such segregation at CCP, even within the same department; English teachers congregated and affiliated by the various programs in which they taught. Institutional boundaries certainly discourage dialogue between community college faculty and first-year writing instructors from the university. In Thomas C. Thompson's edited collection called *Teaching Writing in High School and College*, teachers and professors from various projects in Indiana, Nevada, the Pacific Northwest and elsewhere discuss their attitudes toward writing and literacy across school lines, usually over coffee or tea in a neutral space and often because somebody has written a grant or developed a research project to foster the project. These localized efforts—what the Nevada group calls "productively contentious discussions" (94)—suggest that only free flowing conversation among teachers can lead to deep alignment across levels; such conversation can reveal blind spots and flaws as well as unsuspected triumphs in classes we come to see as disparate and unrelated. Because courses for marginalized students are usually the most stressed and the least prestigious, they may be the ones most suited to set the agenda and challenge the rest of us. Teachers and administrators can easily fall into the false assumption that we know what college writing is and what constitutes good progress in learning unless we listen to those who have the most trouble fitting in.

Cultivate Relationships Both Inside and Outside the University

This is the principle most explicitly about institutional relationships across the boundaries of administration, funding, and tradition. I am convinced that some of the hardest problems college students face—substance abuse, lack of motivation or direction, inability to recognize the relevance of what they are studying—come from the isolation and lack of perspective inherent in the segregation of 18- to-22-year-olds in the ivy-covered holding pens we call institutions of higher learning. When I taught in the midwest, those large land-grant universities reminded me of the corn fields that surround the campuses—monocultural environments that need heavy chemical treatments to guard against diseases and conditions that can attack high concentrations of individuals of the same species and variety. When I taught in a small Catholic university and had students tutoring at a maximum security prison, I began to see the similarities between those two seemingly unlike institutions: Both were designed to remove large numbers of employable people from the workforce and both transform young people into adults, for good or ill. Tuition, room and board for one student in a private university costs about the same as yearly upkeep and guarding for one inmate in a top-level state prison. In a highly developed industrial economy, populations of organisms—wheat, cattle, or young humans—are often segregated primarily for the administrative convenience of keepers, growers, and managers. Yet this very segregation undermines the ultimate objective of the venture. Corn must be sprayed and genetically altered to survive this method of cultivation, but the method doesn't necessarily make it tastier, more nutritious, or even more profitable. Prisoners must be herded and controlled at tremendous public expense, only to be released back into their home environment no better able to earn a legal living, participate in civic activities, or navigate the complex social demands of life on the street than when they entered. Young adults absorb a great many resources in pursuit of college degrees they don't necessarily understand or care about. In the end they may leave college either confused about what they want to do next or committed to a vocation they don't love; they often need to be trained on the job for the specific work they do after graduation. It may take them years to appreciate courses they took in college, and much of what they studied may indeed have gotten lost in the haze of new adult freedoms and recreational drugs.

These paradoxical conditions aren't all caused by the institutional arrangements themselves, but the structure inside which growth and transformation take place may determine the outcomes more than we think. To take the ultimate contradictory example, the worst place to go to get better from an illness is a hospital. You arrive in a weakened condition and recover—if you do—surrounded by all manner of toxic agents, loud noises, and overworked experts taking care of a segregated population of very sick folks. Medicine uses the adjective "nosocomial" to refer to diseases such as staphylococcus infections contracted in the hospital because of the hospital environment; we simply accept these conditions as the price we pay for the concentration of expertise, equipment, and resources devoted only to curing the sick. Yet hospitals are certainly not the only kind of environment we could conceive of to treat frail, wounded, or debilitated patients, and perhaps hospitals are not even the most effective model for healing people. They are certainly depressing places to visit, even if your mission is to cheer up an ailing friend.

There can be no easy answers for the challenge of educating today's students in a more open-ended learning environment. Diversity is a common principle to call for in schools and colleges, but it is a difficult factor to manage and benefit from. Even in a school like Temple, with a more diverse undergraduate population than most research universities, few courses really make explicit use of diversity as a resource. Both faculty and students complain about the lack of focus and tendency to "dumb down" courses with students of diverse abilities and experiences, and often the range of experiences and opinions in a given classroom just gets glossed over or ignored. Diversity can only be actively enjoyed when students encounter people as people—not as ignorant peers, potential servants, surly employees, or case studies—outside the traditional campus environment that marks some people as normal and others as aberrant. Encounters themselves aren't enough; people of different backgrounds, life experiences, and abilities must meet on grounds where they come to respect each other. Nor do these encounters have to happen outside the physical bounds of a campus, only that the space be re-defined as legitimate for all kinds of learners. Administrators and faculty need such challenging encounters as much as their students do if they are to maintain a fresh, or less habituated, understanding of education.

The most promising answer to this challenge for universities and colleges, then, is not simply to accept a diverse student population and hire a diverse faculty—these are notoriously difficult goals to achieve, wracked with contention and managed badly by a less-than-committed administration and faculty—but instead to pursue rich and sustained alliances with partner institutions that can build and replenish a truly productive diversity. I remember a class of six city African-American students who had been accepted on full scholarship in the suburban Catholic university where I taught in the early 1990s. I taught them all in a basic writing class. They were bright and hopeful, but they were wary and perplexed by the scene they had entered, and none of them felt safe on a campus that their White counterparts thought eminently comfortable. These six students came from one urban high school because the amiable provost at the time had heard it was the "worst" in the city and so he gave scholarships to the top six students in its graduating class. Within 2 years, only one student of the group was left at the university. The one who survived finally did finish his degree after leaving and coming back. I met him a few years after he graduated, and what impressed me—besides his obvious charm and determination from the very beginning—was that during his later undergraduate years he had made a close connection with a well-known African-American theater company in the city and had gone there to work after graduation. That company, based in a part of town from which he came, had given him a reason for continuing in college despite the strangeness of his campus experience.

Think of the supportive power the university might have had if it could have given those students not only scholarships but an array of connections and work experiences in city settings while they were enrolled at the suburban school. Think of how that might have changed the classroom environment in economics, political science, history, and writing courses not only for the students themselves but for the faculty who knew about the arrangements. Think what challenges to the university might have arisen in the course of maintaining partnerships with local community legal services, welfare offices, neighborhood literacy centers, jails, arts organizations, housing activist collectives. Diversity among individuals in a student population works well when it comes to photos for catalogues and brochures, but only a diversity of institutional affiliations—of literacy sponsorships—will change the environment for learning and knowledge production. Imagine that a faculty member could get tenure not only by publishing in learned journals but by producing successful grants for local organizations and studies for regional planning commissions. Imagine that every tenure decision required at least one letter from a community organization outside the academic world. This is not to say that there wouldn't still be persistent problems with institutional racism or mismatches in educational preparation for students from marginalized backgrounds, but we do choose to work within structures that make the dominant population most comfortable rather than the whole population most educated.

Are even the most privileged students well served by an isolated university? Many in the field of service learning think not, and composition researchers such as Bruce Herzberg, Linda Adler-Kassner, and Tom Deans have spoken out about the value to all students of community-based writing courses. But this principle requires more than classes connected to local actions or services. It commits us to structural changes in the way universities and colleges relate to "outside" organizations. Only structural changes in the way partner institutions connect with one another will bring about the long-term changes that those interested in "service" have called for because, in the case of writing instruction, only structural changes will link the self-interest of schools with those of other literacy educators.

Assess Collaboratively and Imaginatively

Assessment usually comes last in a program description, strategic plan, or grant proposal. The literature on assessment is much stronger on evaluating individual students' writing abilities than on evaluating programs, but we can connect the formative and reflective attitudes of the sort of assessment meant for students with the sort aimed at evaluating programs. In attempting to develop "a discourse that links the teaching and assessment of writing" (164), Brian Huot observed that, "in literate activity, assessment is everywhere" (165). This ubiquity serves as one anchor for his humane and constructive approach to evaluating students' writing, but it can also serve as an excellent starting place for thinking about assessing programs with the purpose of making them better. As Meg Moran has put it, "Program assessment is an effort at improving quality: It's really that simple" (145).

But even while the rhetoric among writing assessment theorists has been toward formative and exploratory evaluation methods, most WPAs and writing instructors still cringe at the thought of assessment because it feels like judgment. I won't try to talk anybody out of that impression here, but I do want to introduce one example of a method for assessing a writing program that emphasizes collegiality, open-endedness, and relationship. I'll call the approach evaluation exchange, and the heart of the idea is to foster partnerships among paired institutions that teach literacy. My reason for highlighting this approach is that it arises out of the emphasis on relationship and illustrates, as well as any instance can, the generative value of relationship as a defining impulse for literacy work.

The idea started when Temple administrators asked us for comparative data about our program and similar programs at "peer" institutions. The definition of a peer institution kept shifting, sometimes referring to other metropolitan universities with similar student populations and funding sources but other times referring to schools that administrators wanted to emulate—usually ones with endowments many times the size of ours. The prospect of using a very limited amount of information to develop a comparison between what we do and what others do seemed unpromising at best to me, and I feared it would lead to terrible misunderstandings and hasty decisions. My colleagues and I began to imagine a different model that would allow for a much deeper engagement as the basis of comparison. We looked around for schools we thought would be like us in demographics, research status, size of program, and also had knowledgeable leaders running high-functioning programs. We then approached a few to see about partnering with us on an evaluation project. Some universities were initially intrigued but couldn't follow through because of timing or money or pressures from within. The University of Wisconsin (UW)-Milwaukee finally seemed like the right partner to engage first, and they agreed to explore the possibilities with us further.

The exchange consisted of reciprocal visits for two administrators from each program going to the other for two days of meetings, class observations, interviews, and dinner parties. Bruce Horner, director of first year writing at UW-Milwaukee, and Alice Gillam, chair of the English Department and former WPA there, came to Philadelphia in November 2003 to find out more about our program and write us a brief report on aspects of the program. Bruce was interested in our syllabus and teacher training, and Alice wanted to find out about our writing center because they were hoping to expand their own. They stayed only two nights, arriving mid-afternoon on Thursday and leaving on Saturday. We returned the visit in April when Keith Gumery, associate director of first-year writing at

Temple, and I flew out to Milwaukee for nearly an identical length of time. Keith was working on the revision of our syllabus for first-year writing, and I was interested both in the particulars of their writing center expansion and also the general plan for writing at the University as well as their recent efforts at developing a graduate program in composition/rhetoric. At the end of our stay we delivered an oral report based on an outline of our observations, and we wrote a more detailed report to send to them a few months later. In that short span, neither side could learn fully about the programs in the partner school but both delegations learned enough to write about what they saw and focus on some particular issues for praise and improvement. The atmosphere of both visits was extremely collegial, and visitors collaborated with hosts about what aspects of the program to investigate closely and what administrative audience to address in writing the report.

One might suggest that, as an assessment, this approach is nearly useless because it was done with such friendly cooperation. Where's the objectivity, the critical edge? How can people who are developing collegial relationships be honest with each other about problems that they see? I would agree that there are probably limits to the honest appraisal visitors can give hosts, especially in this abbreviated time frame. And yet the arrangement also allows for greater honesty and openness that only a mutual and collegial relationship can make possible. As Bruce and Alice grew to know our issues with labor and pedagogy, relationships with college and university administrators, departmental history, staff dynamics and so on, they also shared comparable issues from their program. We were able to show each other a much more intimate view of things as they are lived in the two schools in a way that even the most canny outside observers—sworn to objectivity and given no mandate to share their own stories—could ever have offered us. By the end of the school year, both programs were richer in a perspective that went far beyond any specific recommendation either of us could make.

This evaluation does not take the place of a formal program review, which does have its peculiar advantages, but it illustrates what one can do when one considers literacy instruction in the context of relationships. Bruce and Alice could have visited us as outside evaluators, observing classes and reviewing program documents, but we would never have learned what we did in many conversations comparing our two school experiences, commiserating over obstacles and disappointments, rejoicing over momentary triumphs and long-term goals finally met. One example can stand for the richness of this experience. In his review of our writing syllabus, Bruce questioned the speed at which we covered assigned texts in classes and called for more writing assignments in shorter intervals. When we visited Milwaukee we understood better what his suggestions meant. His own program reads fewer texts and reads them more carefully than ours does, and we got a chance to see how the approach worked in a number of classroom settings. We walked away not quite willing to take up Milwaukee's approach, but Bruce's questions to us became crucial touchstones as we went about rewriting the first-year syllabus that debuted in Fall 2004. This was one of the most satisfying instances of formative assessment we have tried, for it not only gave us insights into our own practice through the eyes of others but it has allowed us to consider our new friends at Milwaukee colleagues in the on-going drama of both our unfolding histories.

This project involved faculty and staff at two similar academic institutions, but evaluation exchanges need not stop there. Some schools have experimented with Writing Boards and focus groups that are composed not only of academics but also leaders from the surrounding neighborhoods and employers from local business or government. I could imagine an exchange between a university or college and a set of community organizations where the visitors observed and asked questions and eventually wrote reports on the campus program, while faculty and graduate students visit the community facilities and reflect on literacy practices there. As is seen in the concluding section, I find these instances of partnership rich and compelling, and if nothing else it makes the dinners and lunches among the people who come to evaluate one another that much more nutritious and tasty.

JOINT SPONSORSHIP: WHAT GRANTS CAN DO TO BREACH THE WALLS

I conclude this chapter by returning to sponsorship as a frame for understanding the complex interactions, or lack of interactions, between and among various types of institutionally based literacy practices and instruction in a given geographical region. In Chapter 3, I introduced the concept of literacy sponsorship for understanding the differences between and among literacy practices at schools and colleges. In Chapter 4, I focused on Saul Alinsky's approach to community organizing as a model for community/university literacy partnerships built on self-interest. I concluded there by suggesting that community–organizing involves a kind of sponsorship that values particular characteristics of literacy practices over others. In this chapter, I have focused primarily on the need for relationships among many educational institutions as the ground for literacy practices and instruction. I conclude here, therefore, by asking how we can reconfigure relationships that emerge from university projects with schools, community colleges, or neighborhood centers into effective joint sponsorships of literacy?

Joint sponsorship occurs when partners across institutional boundaries make an effort to shape literacy instruction and practice following a collaborative sense of self-interest. Alinsky taught that self-interest is not a dirty word; it lies at the heart of much worthwhile public action. In fact, as Alinsky would undoubtedly point out, action taken without a clear recognition of the self-interest of the group can more easily lead to destructive consequences, not only for an organization in a disenfranchised neighborhood but for a school, school district, or city where leadership is not being honest with its constituency about why certain actions must be taken. In order to develop a successful joint sponsorship, all the participants must feel they have an equal voice in the negotiation and that their needs—and the needs of their core constituency—will be fully honored in the partnership. This process takes a great deal of time, patience, and willingness to work through difficult moments when traditions, conventions, historical privileges, or ideological disagreements hamper negotiations. One reason smaller organizations avoid working with universities or school districts is that the difference in bulk is so great; the greater gravitational field tends to pull everything into the bigger organization's orbit, and what counts as up or down is defined entirely in terms of the big organization's central agenda. Those of us who work with or from universities or large school districts must be acutely aware of this gravitational pull and find ways to mitigate its effects.

One way to mitigate the effect of large organizations is to write grants with partners in such a way that all participants feel invested. Often the largest participant, a school district or university, is the most convenient conduit for the grant because they are most set up to handle accounting and payroll, but it is crucial for such grant efforts to be as equal as possible in the writing and decision-making process once the grant begins to function. I offer here two examples of how grant money can support joint sponsorship, but I want to emphasize again that, in order to achieve a secure partnership, relationship must be the primary value. Our culture emphasizes individual accomplishment above communal good in all too many instances, but in joint sponsorship the well-being of the partnership must be a driving purpose in the choices the group makes. Not that individuals and groups should hide or suppress their self-interests: just the reverse. Participants must learn to be clearer about what they really need to stay involved and to honor other partners' self-interest enough that the sponsorship venture becomes worthwhile for all.

John S. and James L. Knight Foundation and the "Literacy Because We Live Here" Conference

In May 2001, a consortium of organizations sponsored a conference that brought together more than 80 college writing instructors, high school teachers, and neighborhood literacy workers at the main branch of the Free

Library of Philadelphia for one day of speakers and small group discussions about the common concerns in their work lives. It was a smashing success, judging by the enthusiastic evaluations of attendees and the lore that has built up around the conference in the intervening years. The conference required collaboration among the Temple University Writing Program, the Philadelphia Writing Project (based at the University of Pennsylvania's Education School), the Philadelphia Writing Program Administrators, and the Center for Literacy (based in West Philadelphia but with sites all over town) as well as additional sponsorship by other organizations. Much of the money for the event came from a grant to Temple's writing program by the John S. and James L. Knight Foundation.

In order to render all the circumstances of this event adequately, I need to recount the history of support from the Knight Foundation for writing at Temple and its environs. Knight grants have been crucial to building our capacity to work inside and outside the Temple campus since their first grant to us in 1999. As I have described elsewhere (see Parks and Goldblatt as well as Chapter 4, this volume), when I first arrived at Temple in 1996 Steve Parks and I began to develop the Institute for the Study of Literature, Literacy and Culture (later called New City Writing). We realized we would need outside money to achieve what we saw as the great promise of community-based work in the urban environment. We also decided on the principle that whatever WAC or Writing in the Disciplines (WID) initiatives we attempted inside the campus should be matched with community-based projects off campus. Always trying to connect outside and inside, always linking Temple students with neighborhood learners, we would move forward by making friends and pursuing projects that made doors where there had been only walls before.

As I was casting about for a foundation to approach, I happened to receive some alumni material from Cornell University that announced a recent grant for their growing writing program. I decided to call up the director of the program, Jonathan Monroe, and we had a friendly chat about what they were doing in their Knight Writing Program (see Monroe). This led to an invitation to attend a conference Knight sponsored at Cornell for a select number of writing programs each summer. At that conference I got to know Jonathan and his colleagues, who were running the most wide-ranging writing program in the Ivy League, thanks in large measure to significant support from Knight. I also began talking to Knight's program officer for educational initiatives at the time, a thoughtful man named Rick Love who happened to be looking for a non-elite institution with which to partner, balancing the funding for Cornell. He encouraged a small proposal from us—a threshold grant, he called it—which they funded in the 1999-2000 school year.

Literacy in Action: Moving On-Line and Off Broad Street, which brought money for a writing and technology initiative on campus and a literacy tutoring program called Project SHINE (Students Helping the

Naturalization of Elders) off-campus, was a 1-year grant of $71,000. Even at that stage we were developing a vision of a larger engagement with the region, although we did not know exactly what we were committing ourselves to with manifesto language like this from the Project Summary:

> Colleges and universities in the United States can no longer afford to stand aloof from the society we study and serve. For over 25 years, writing across the curriculum programs have taken the lead in postsecondary educational reform, and the time has come for writing programs to reach beyond the curriculum and the campus. Academics must recognize how deeply embedded our particular literacy is in the multiple uses for written language employed by community groups, public schools, businesses, government, professions, and the arts. Temple University is committed to an integrated approach to these multiple literacies by extending its Writing Program off campus and on line.

Our partner in the effort to reach outside the university was the Center for Intergenerational Learning (CIL), an agency with offices in a Temple building but with a budget that came (and continues to come) almost entirely from soft money for more than 25 years. CIL had just designed a program called Project SHINE that placed a number of Temple students both in classes and in individual volunteer capacity throughout the city to tutor older adult immigrants preparing for their citizenship exam. I had placed students from my literacy class into tutoring sites through SHINE, and I thought it would be a natural fit.

In a move that we see now as overly elaborate, we created a program called the Community Language Program (CLP) that would serve as the institutional link between the writing program and Project SHINE. We could just have shared the grant with the parent agency CIL, but at the time we didn't think we could be so direct. We found in the course of the grant that not only are proposals easier to write if the rhetoric is simple and objectives clear, but funders like them better. Moreover, once you get the grant the project is so much easier to administer if you know exactly what you have to do and the money flows in the least complicated way.

At the same time we were negotiating with CIL, we decided that inside the university what we needed most was more leadership on technology issues in the writing program. So we developed the idea of a postdoctoral fellowship for a composition/rhetoric scholar with special expertise in computers and technical writing. We had expertise in rhetoric, and composition research, and in cultural theory, but nobody except our undergraduate webmaster knew much about computers. This technology initiative seemed on the face of it to be radically different from the work with Project SHINE, but here is how we summarized the combination in the cover letter for the grant:

Literacy In Action will help contextualize college writing for students and faculty. This initiative will extend our focus on literacy beyond the traditional classroom and move us:

- *On-Line* by bringing a young scholar/teacher to campus in a year-long Leadership Residency focused on the area of technology and writing. This resident will enhance teaching in our well-established writing program and offer workshops for faculty and graduate students in the uses of information technology for writing instruction.

- *Off Broad Street* by establishing the university's Community Language Program (CLP), which will facilitate service learning courses and volunteer efforts to bring college students, neighborhood learners, and school kids together in an array of literacy projects.

On-Line and *Off Broad Street* will grow and intertwine as service learning becomes more technologically sophisticated and technology becomes more service oriented. For this reason, during the grant period the Leadership Resident and the staff of CLP will participate with other faculty from the Writing Program in strategic planning for a fully integrated approach to literacy education over the next years at Temple. (July 28th draft)

The rhetoric of this passage points to a melding of activities that our program still has not fully accomplished, but the goal of having traditionally separated functions for teachers and populations of learners reinforce and extend one another has remained crucial for us over the years. We submitted the proposal in the early Fall 1998, and we heard good news in the following spring. We hired a postdoctoral technology fellow from University of Texas named Ray Watkins late in the spring semester of 1999 and CIL used Knight money to pay for their SHINE facilitator Bob Allen through the next school year. The grant gave us all renewed hope that the direction we had chosen was not only correct but fundable, and College of Liberal Arts Dean Carolyn Adams, an urban development scholar, was extremely supportive of our project.

Steve and I immediately started working on a larger scale, 3-year proposal for Knight that would simultaneously fund community- and school-based projects as well as faculty development, peer tutoring on campus, and on-going program assessment. A key element in the proposal was an endowment for the writing program that would always produce a small income for projects we could fund no other way. We realized that, if we were going to follow a path that cut across the usual institutional boundaries, we were not going to be able to depend on regular funding from any individual school or center, including our own. The decision to seek outside funding proved invaluable to our work beyond the usual academic commitment to curricula because grants brought us a certain respect within our college but at the same time allowed us to pursue projects that nobody overseeing a University's budget could afford to support. Administrators need to think about funding their "own" programs, especially in a cash-strapped, state-related institution; I can hardly blame them for that. Tuition dollars and state funding come mainly to schools with claims for excellent curricula and research agendas on the campus, and administrators gain prestige for the national rankings of programs under their care.

But we were working with a different sense of self-interest, an investment in the whole network of literacy practices that surround and interpenetrate the life of a metropolitan university, even literacies that academics wouldn't normally notice. The more we articulated this vision for ourselves, the more real those cross-cutting practices appeared to us and the more we wanted to promote projects, form alliances, make new friends among teachers and visionary activists in the neighborhoods. As academics, we were like people who see spirits nobody else can see, and we found ourselves in so many conversations that we could barely keep up with all the potential projects. In fact, the world we were encountering was very real indeed—the world we lived in not as academics but as citizens—and as that world became more visible to us in our professional lives, we saw possibilities everywhere. We needed the funds to begin making those possibilities more solid to people inside and outside the academy, but we also needed some guiding principles to make sure we didn't just become overwhelmed with a welter of activity that would add up to nothing. We wanted to do something in this world we inhabit, but we also wanted the work to survive, and that meant our projects needed to be focused and interconnected and self-reinforcing.

The answer, as always, was lunch. Rather than simply sit in our module on the 10th floor of Temple's Anderson Hall, drafting version after version of a proposal, Steve and I devoted many hours of meetings over lunch and coffee—in faculty clubs and college meeting rooms, in corner diners, in downtown delis and cafes—to developing relationships on campuses and in city neighborhoods with people we thought could help us use the money wisely. We were just beginning to make connections for our program, and as we each look back on that time now, we recognize how much more we could have done, but the approach was solidifying itself through a growing number of friendships throughout the city and beyond. We decided to emphasize the community press work we had started to explore, basing our model on work being done in England by the Federation of Worker Writers and Community Publishers, hugely exuberant people that Steve had gotten to know through correspondence and travel, and on the *Journal of Ordinary Thought*, a marvelous community-based journal founded by Hal Adams at the University of Illinois-Chicago. We also decided to build in money for the fledgling Philadelphia Writing Program Administrators (PWPA) in the hopes that a network of professional writing directors would be an invaluable multiplier for any effort to connect undergraduate and graduate students with school kids and adult learners throughout the region. Everywhere there were doors to open and more people to see.

After many drafts and exhaustive negotiating with our staff, community partners, interested faculty, administrators, and development people (not to mention a visit to the *Philadelphia Inquirer*, which, as the largest Knight-Ridder newspaper in the region, had to recommend large grants to the otherwise independent foundation, a practice they no longer follow), we assembled an omnibus grant proposal called *Literacy in Action: Writing Beyond the Curriculum*, requesting $600,000 over 3 years. Cast as a project to enhance and build on the traditional form of WAC, it put more meat on the bones of the first grant:

> We have extended the established conception of Writing Across the Curriculum (WAC) to address the pressing needs of a diverse student body in a metropolitan university with both teaching and research missions. The underlying idea of the grant is that the populations served by Temple University, Community College of Philadelphia, the Philadelphia School District, and other regional partners will benefit from a comprehensive and lifelong-learning approach to literacy. Working together, we can increase the effectiveness of elementary and secondary school writing instruction, adult literacy programs, and civic engagement efforts in neighborhood centers and schools as well as the First-Year Writing Program, advanced writing-in-the-disciplines courses, experiential learning initiatives, and teacher training at Temple. (1)

I include the diagram for that proposal (See Fig. 5.1) here because it gives some idea of the scope of the project we had in mind. Our goal was to develop an infrastructure that would support a flow of services and research inside, through, and beyond the campus, and to have at the other end an endowment of more than $300,000 to support future projects. We submitted the proposal very late in 1999 and received approval of the grant in Spring 2000. Although much depended on the luck that Knight was just then open for a grant related to literacy work at a state-affiliated urban university, I think what was most crucial for our attracting grant money was the depth of relationships from which the work was drawn. One important lesson that we learned in the process is that we should never apply to fund projects that we are not prepared to pursue without the grant, even if at a much reduced level. The projects we promised to pursue were actually already underway when the money began to come in—our partners and we believed in them and felt compelled to find a way for them to happen—and this allowed us to weather the inevitable let down and panic when a grant is suddenly approved, the check arrives, and you actually have to do what you said you wanted to do.

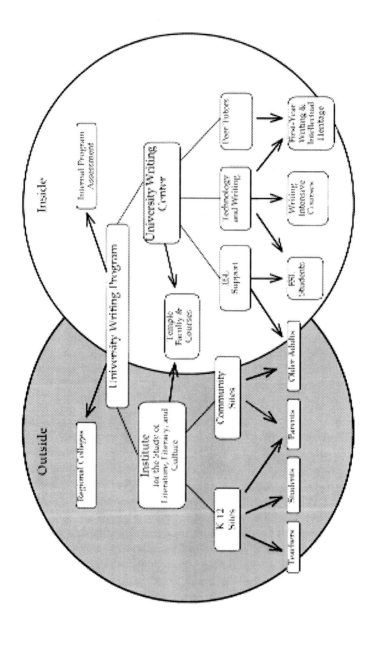

Fig. 5.1. Literacy in action: Writing beyond the curriculum. The groups we serve inside and outside the community.

Although there are many projects I could highlight here, I focus on the May 2001 literacy conference as one example of what relationship building can produce. The conference is not the longest-lived project we funded—it was really meant to be a single event that we hoped would lead to other, different sorts of work—but its effects have lasted a surprisingly long time. I gathered some important lessons about organizing from the experience, and the day of the event was a whopping good time. It was, parenthetically, the last public event my mother attended before she became too sick to go out, and so for me it retains lasting personal value. As a public event, the conference provided a shining moment when people from disparate literacy backgrounds and missions could get together and talk about what they were trying to do collectively.

The opening speakers for the conference were Linda Flower of Carnegie Mellon University, her husband Tim Flower, and their colleague Joyce Baskins from the Community Literacy Center in Pittsburgh. Wayne Peck, the director of the Community Literacy Center, had been invited as well, but at the last minute he couldn't attend. The Pittsburgh contingent spoke about their long-standing work between community and university, and Linda in particular outlined rivaling and other techniques they taught tutors and participants in producing documents that investigate difficult issues of housing and educational policy in the urban neighborhood around Carnegie Mellon. Their plenary session led into concurrent sessions for working groups, where each participant was assigned a group and each group combined people who represented every sector of the literacy continuum from middle school English-language teachers, ESL instructors for schools and literacy centers, college writing professors, school district administrators, literacy workers, and volunteers. After a late box lunch, we reconvened to hear Lucia Herndon, a columnist on family issues for the *Philadelphia Inquirer*, who spoke about her perspective on literacy and then facilitated a general discussion on what people had learned and thought throughout the day. It was still quite a full assembly when we quit at nearly 4 p.m.

The logistics of the conference were handled by Kathryn Zervos, a Temple graduate student in English, and, thanks to her, details for hosting nearly 80 people went off quite smoothly. The heart of the work, however, was negotiating among stakeholders so that no one felt the conference was designed only to benefit or privilege one type of literacy; it had to seem relevant to all constituencies. Although every participant engaged with good will, often perspective attendees wanted to know what such an event would mean to their own particular concerns. We found that activists were simply not used to working with professors, professors had seldom spoken to teachers as peers, and teachers habitually focused their professional attention on their individual classrooms. People were charmed by the idea of meeting others from different literacy projects, but they couldn't quite see what they would get from the experience. Kathryn and I met with the various players regularly to hear their concerns, go over the details of the agenda, and generally help everyone feel they had a stake in the conference.

A relatively new regional organization, PWPA served as one of the official sponsors and contributed some of the most committed participants. We had written into the second Knight grant money for PWPA to use for research, conferences, and other joint projects in the region, and the organization voted to spend its money in 2000-2001 on this conference. The conference has now been stitched into the fabric of the PWPA's history, and it encouraged individuals at various colleges toward community-based work they continue to pursue. Two years after the conference, PWPA became established enough to be named the first local affiliate of the national organization, the Council of Writing Program Administrators (WPA), but at this stage in the organization's development the conference was the organization's first attempt at sponsoring a major public event. PWPA was perhaps its most enthusiastic sponsor, contributing more than half of the advanced registrants; at least 14 college and university writing programs were represented at the event.

But what did sponsorship of the conference mean? The goals of the conference that all the sponsoring organizations agreed on were as follows:

- Gain a clearer sense of the literacy issues that are most pressing for community literacy centers, schools, and college writing programs.
- Build relationships across constituencies.
- Foster long-term collaborations among attendees.
- Pursue literacy as a political issue in the Delaware Valley.

These were admirable goals—quite difficult to reach or to measure over time, but admirable nonetheless. Still, everyone from the largest writing program to the smallest literacy center had compelling organizational reasons for being involved in this event. Without any cynical tone meant, I think we can see the way self-interest drew participants into the event and how an underlying sense of common self-interest evolved from the process. Perhaps more important than all the goals just stated was the development of this common sense of self-interest, because only through that shared conception can any further inclusive, collaborative, or political work arise.

Let's start with the schools. As mentioned earlier, schools have an investment in literacy as a means of asserting control and encouraging a sustaining sense of continuity. Some schools or programs emphasize control over continuity or the other way round, but both values are crucial in literacy sponsorship tied to school. From the perspective of public events, however, schools have a related imperative. The public is always looking to see that their schools are "working," that they are "improving," or "meeting the needs of the kids." In short, they need to demonstrate that they are a functioning unit in the economy, able to produce the next generation of workers and managers who can both take control of the system and value the continuity of past achievements. For this reason, schools are subject to federal No Child Left Behind legislation and much high-stakes testing for the kids and the adults who teach them. The schools occasionally get attention for innovative programs or individual achievements, but at best they are largely taken for granted by the public and at worst they are excoriated for failing to educate young people.

The college sector is under less pressure to produce a standardized product, although there is a growing public concern about what students and their parents get for their tuition. Internally, as I have said earlier, 2-year and 4-year colleges alike need to teach both the form of college writing and a perspective toward theory that students can apply to academic literacy tasks in other fields. However, college literacy is experienced from the outside as arcane, specialized, and often irrelevant to the everyday literacy needs of the economic world. Additionally, even at state-related institutions the general public may feel they are less able to influence the curriculum and policies of higher education than they are with K–12 schools. Writing teachers may be thought embattled because of a perceived lack of writing skills among young people, but professors generally are held in some suspicion because their jobs don't follow the 9-to-5 model that even schoolteachers more or less fit.

Literacy centers employ perhaps the most invisible educational workers. Unlike instructors in schools or colleges, people who want to teach adult basic education are unlikely to find a clearly delineated career path in front of them. Even if prospective teachers know early about adult basic education and recognize they want to teach that population, few graduate programs and even fewer defined avenues exist for entering and advancing in the field. "Literacy" is often understood publicly as the lowest and least prestigious teaching level, and the work is considered remedial, mechanical, highly fragmented, and requiring a bare minimum of pedagogical skill. For those who work in a center, literacy sponsorship in a neighborhood center involves not only decoding and identifying skills but the cognitive leaps to connect adult experience to written texts; some centers go further, developing leadership capacities and a collective investment in the neighborhood as well. But in the public arena, literacy centers have a tremendous stake in educating the general audience about what their work entails and how it connects not only with jobs but citizenship, housing, education, health care, and other issues that directly affect working people. These are goals of their work that stand at the heart of their literacy sponsorship, but they are little understood by people unfamiliar with adult basic education and even by many of the new tutors who come originally to help out "illiterates."

These three sectors of literacy instruction represent sponsors whose work is not only different in terms of content but also method of instructional delivery. In many ways they might seem not to share a common definition of literacy, and what they value about reading and writing can be radically at odds. They attract public and private funding differently, they relate to different sectors of labor, they draw on strikingly different institutions for their authority in public discourse, and yet they do have certain similarities as sponsors of literacy. For one, they are all misunderstood by the general public, one might almost say willfully so. What happens in any classroom from pre-K to graduate school is too often radically reduced to a formula, romanticized, dismissed, or measured inappropriately by reporters, politicians, screenwriters, and bureaucrats. Literacy learning at any level tends to become isolated from the larger flow of money, ideas, and images shared by people not associated directly with education.

Second, they share a concern for teacher training. Most instructors in all three sectors have been trained in some way at colleges or universities, but that training often does not truly prepare practitioners for the jobs they have to do. Teachers at every level as the immediate agents of literacy sponsorship are given some theoretical background and, depending on their sector of instruction, some practical experience, but the sheer weight of enacting the power of the sponsoring institution—be it the university departmental expectation, the K-12 standards mandated by the state, or the competencies encoded in the GED—comes down on them heavily in early years on the job. Teaching can be a lonely profession, and those who survive the isolation of the classroom and persevere often convert the solitude into a virtue and stop sharing what happens day to day with others. Their classroom becomes their domain, and meaningful conversation about fundamental assumptions or pedagogical innovation is all to often reduced to an occasional new trick shared over coffee in the staff room. Underlying attitudes toward literacy can become fixed into rituals, routines, and rubrics; even the most dedicated teacher of literacy at any level can feel cut off from her or his colleagues and profession. University research professors of composition are not immune from this isolation either, for all our yearly conferences and paper production. We relate to our profession so much as a discipline that classroom teaching can become detached from the intellectual pursuits of scholarship and publishing.

I mention only one more shared concern of the three sectors of literacy sponsorship at this conference although one could suggest more. Each of these sponsors must manage the complexity of literacy within the specific parameters of their institutional boundaries. Literacy is by its nature multidimensional and multilateral. Once you teach children to read, they can learn to read wrestling or fashion magazines as well as textbooks on farm policy in the Depression, and once they can write, they can produce comic books about their teachers as easily as they can five-paragraph themes on friendship. The many worlds that literacy touches can be a distraction or an aid to learning, can reinforce lessons or make them seem irrelevant. Many worlds mean multiple audiences and multiple purposes, and this can be a confounding rhetorical demand or a compelling reason for writing. Too often, literacy instruction solves this challenge by narrowing the channel for communication, restricting the band of acceptable texts or topics in order to focus primarily on prescribed skills or strictly defined content. But it is almost impossible to narrow or restrict literacy practice enough to screen out the complexity that writing and reading represent inside or outside the classroom, and a sponsor can kill the excitement and inherent value of literacy by defining it too mechanically and testing it to death.

These shared concerns can be reframed as aspects of a single question, one that fueled the literacy conference in May 2001. How does the literacy instruction these various agents sponsor relate to the larger world around the learners? Whether it is what the non-teaching world thinks of literacy, how teachers are trained, or how the complexity of literacy can be managed, at heart the question involves overcoming the isolation of literacy practices in the classroom settings, the tendency to parcel literacy into semesters and quarters and levels and courses that renders reading and writing inert for all but the most avid language learners. Literacy in this sense is more like water than like cinder blocks; the excitement and refreshment of literacy for learners comes when words and concepts flow and circulates even though blocks are easier to stack, store, and count. The struggle to keep literacy activities engaging and fresh confronts instructors in any school or program, and it is exacerbated by the fact that most teachers of literacy at any level were relatively good at learning about written language in school and thus have little first hand experience of the frustration many beginners face in the decontextualized classroom environment.

This is the design problem that all types of literacy instructors need to solve. Alone, teachers must fight a public perception about K-12 education that packages and measures what they do in fragmented units. Alone, professors must try to reverse the stereotypes of the detached and aloof college instructor. Alone, the literacy worker must contradict those who think the job brutish, menial, and brief. But together we can begin to address the question at its root, raise the public debate about language and how it is learned so that more people see literacy as a palpable presence around them and learning a human behavior that can and should happen anywhere and at any age. Sponsorship in explicitly instructional settings, as distinct from workplace classes or informal on-the-job training, must be especially creative to draw on this common concern for the localness of language use. Learners and teachers will both benefit from this shift in frame, and this is what the conference accomplished at least for a moment and perhaps, in the mind of some of its participants, for longer than that.

Let me conclude this section with consideration of the foundation itself as a literacy sponsor. Foundations, whether large or small, make an investment in individuals or groups when the staff and board feel the grantee can have a beneficial effect on the social or cultural life of a local, state, national, or international scene. Foundations differ in the benefits to society they intend to support. Each foundation has a stated mission, but especially in America the public message about foundations often links philanthropic giving with "democracy," although it is not clear what that means: giving voice and empowerment to disenfranchised people; offering scholarships to poor students; aiding small businesses in economically stressed areas; supporting the mechanisms for free speech, voting, right to bear arms, and other practices associated with the U.S. Constitution. For instance, Dorothy Riding suggests, at the end of her 2004 presidential address to the Council of Foundations 55th annual conference, that philanthropy is the "cornerstone of a healthy democracy." The first principle of belief in the mission statement of the Foundation Center, a major source of information on U.S. philanthropy, reads: "Philanthropy is vital for our democratic society" ("Our Values"). Foundations differ greatly in their methods and emphases for giving, in their underlying conservative or liberal politics; the criteria for granting money may change for a single foundation significantly over time. It would be difficult to hazard a general definition of the contribution to democracy U.S. foundations have made, beyond saying that it seems to entail fostering the well-being of the American political system and the people it serves. Yet the idea of democracy, broadly defined and variously interpreted, seems to lie at the heart of their sponsorship.

This idea of democracy is defined quite specifically in the founding philosophy of the John S. and James L. Knight Foundation. Founded in 1950 with $9,047 to carry on the work of an earlier scholarship fund that honored the two brothers' father, Charles Landon Knight, the foundation had assets of nearly $2 billion at its 50th anniversary, the year they gave us our 3-year, $600,000 grant. The Foundation's *Annual Report 1999*, which includes a picture from a community-based learning class at Temple partially funded by our first Knight grant (45), identifies the Knight brothers' founding interests as "stronger communities, quality journalism and the protection of a free press" (2). Over those 50 years, the Foundation expanded its interests into four areas: community initiatives in the towns where Knight-Ridder published newspapers, journalism, education, and arts and culture. They added a focus on collegiate sports in 1989 when they created the Knight Foundation Commission on Intercollegiate Athletics. Clearly, they defined their mission as having to do with fairness and communication, access and public expression, but they have changed with the times to fit their support for emerging needs as they defined them. As Hodding Carter, III said in the Foundation's Presidential Message in 1999: "For philanthropies, and indeed for all of us, the future simultaneously demands unapologetic grounding in basic principles and an ungrudging willingness to try radically different approaches to dealing with radically shifting realities" (*Annual Report 1999* 4). This concept of holding to founding principles and altering course to fit current events seems to characterize the institution throughout its history. Over time, a flexible institutional culture became a stated value, incorporated into their overarching commitment to the democratic values of free expression and equal opportunity.

In many joint sponsorship ventures—where institutions with separate historical missions, such as a school and a college, agree to cooperate for a common project—a foundation or some other outside funding agent needs to be involved. Grants can be the incentive as well as the bridge for cooperation because they ideally offer both benefits and a common cause to all parties. From the point of view of sponsorship, this is perhaps the most direct contribution to democracy that philanthropists can make: they get people talking to one another and finding conjoint activity (Dewey's term) where institutional affiliations might ordinarily isolate the partners from one another. Even the smallest foundations are too removed from scenes of need to affect change themselves, so they must fund agents closer to actual people and problems. This institutional necessity is in fact a central strength of foundation sponsorship.

The meta-sponsorship that foundations provide, so attractive to anyone who hopes to change a neighborhood or solve a social problem, can itself be a major source of conflict, trauma, and discouragement to partners. Grants are hard to write and even harder to get. It's easy to overpromise when you don't have the money and easier still to make enemies when you do. Foundations themselves have agendas that organizations—particularly smaller and less sophisticated community groups—cannot easily recognize, anticipate, or satisfy. The most well-meaning foundation program officer can misunderstand the pressures on agencies that apply for grants; the larger the foundation, the wider the gulf between them and the tiny groups that can make things happen in neighborhoods. For this reason, big foundations (who give large individual grants and hold huge assets) tend to work with big organizations as primary recipients or as agents for a network of recipients, whereas smaller foundations (who tend to give small grants drawn from modest endowments) become wary of institutions like universities or school districts and prefer to work directly with activists or organizers in storefront-size agencies. The culture in a large foundation has much more in common with the culture in a university than it does with that in a neighborhood literacy center. In short, the institutional character of the players in a joint sponsorship can affect the outcome of a partnership, and the institutional character of the granting agency is not negligible in the dynamic.

When we first began to work with Knight, our developing philosophy meshed with thinking current in the Foundation between 1997 and 2000. Our ideas for enhancing communication and literacy, as well as our approach to communities in a city served by a Knight-Ridder paper, coincided with initiatives our program officer Rick Love believed in. Putting aside the fine language of any foundation's mission statements, the nature of its sponsorship is often strongly determined by the interests of individual program officers because the rhetoric must be interpreted to be applied. This seems counter to my point above about the institutional character of partners, but really it is not. A foundation is neither a tool of an idiosyncratic individual nor a faceless bureaucracy applying rules according to an unknowable calculus. The corporate entity elaborates a mission and individuals administer policy according to their personalities and persuasions as well as the distinctive culture of the organization. I see no reason to be cynical about this arrangement. To assume that a compelling mission statement would directly translate into automatic support for every project that fits the sentiments expressed would be not only naïve but self-centered. At the same time, to assume that one could simply sweet talk a foundation officer into support for your pet project would be foolish and ultimately self-defeating.

A larger problem shadows the relationship between potential grantee and foundation. Even the smallest foundations don't really fund individual projects just because they are worthy projects. Foundations fund projects that suit their overall giving strategy; the larger the endowment, the more ambitious the strategy for change can be. Large foundations become major players in regional, national, and international arenas, and they have very explicit ambitions to influence policy and development in their target areas. People or local organizations develop ideas for funding because they think their particular constituency needs a specific program or piece of equipment. A school wants a new playground, a center wants a computer classroom, but a foundation must see these discrete projects as part of the fabric they are trying to weave. A playground may be worthy but doesn't move forward the agenda of Foundation Y, or a playground may not be the most pressing need for a school but fits exactly the vision of outdoor physical culture being promulgated by Foundation X (I'm not commenting on corporate giving here because I have less experience with this world, but some of the same observations seem to apply). Again, I don't identify this dynamic cynically. It makes sense within the current economic and social system, for better or worse, that a foundation with a stake in the growth and well-being of a region should have a plan to improve that region according to its own definition of growth or well-being. Smaller organizations and stressed neighborhoods may be helped or shut out by this dynamic. University people have an obligation, in my estimation, to understand how foundations give in great detail and participate to the extent that we can bring benefits to a range of partners and influence foundation agendas where that seems most necessary. I recognize my position opens me to the charge of accommodating to established powers, but I see far more immediate utility in participating critically in the system as it is than in remaining ideologically pure and having fewer resources to help my neighbors. We must remain in constant contact with partners who can keep the work most productive and vital, but we cannot afford not to know who to call when a worthwhile project needs to come into being or to survive.

In our case, on the first two grant proposals to Knight the particulars in our institution matched the agenda of the Foundation, and they agreed to sponsor us as we sponsored the various projects inside and outside the Temple campus. In some ways we did not fit what they were funding at the moment—particularly their effort to change the climate for writing in elite institutions by funding Cornell and its summer conference—but the emphasis on flexibility that grew up in the Knight Foundation culture along with their stated commitment to democratic values probably served us very well. On the other hand, particularly on the large second grant, we acted as the primary recipient and eventually the primary sponsor of literacy projects, the ones with the money from Knight. We negotiated less with partners in writing that second grant because we were hoping to have money not only for current projects but for future partnerships and yet unrecognized ventures. The negotiating challenge was in making the conference and other projects work collaboratively, but we had the money on hand to prime the pump. In our third grant from the Knight Foundation, the *Community Arts and Literacy Network* (CALN) project to which I turn now, the sponsoring negotiations grew trickier all around even as the project's mission become more focused. Our first grant was small scale and with one outside partner, but the vision was wide-ranging and somewhat ill defined. Our second grant led us to partner with many organizations, gave us an opportunity to test our vision in streets and classrooms, but concentrated more of the funding and forming power in our hands. The third grant returned to a narrower focus, but this time we understood the nature of our vision better and were prepared to enter into more equal partnership with other institutions. In the third grant we were building a network, which made for more tension and drama, but the lessons about joint sponsorship have been richer as the potential for truly democratic action grew more promising.

Building the Community Arts and Literacy Network

When I began to talk to Rick Love in the latter part of our 3-year grant period about possible projects for a next grant, he told me that the Knight Foundation was changing its focus again and he was himself moving on to a new position at another foundation. I was sad for the relationship we had established over the 3 or more years we had been communicating by phone and mail—I never actually met him, although I felt he understood our project better than most of our colleagues at Temple—but of course I was also concerned about the possibility that the Foundation would not be interested in supporting us further without him as our advocate. For a while there was no real replacement officer for us to deal with at Knight; I reported to Rick's former assistant who was filling in as the Foundation reorganized. Then I heard, to my dismay, that Knight would no longer have an education section in their organization. About that time, a grant program officer at another large foundation, a Temple alumna who had been extremely supportive of our first steps at grant writing, suddenly stopped returning my phone calls and seemed to disappear from the scene. I heard from another friend at a foundation that the new trend in funding was against giving money to university-based programs, and I began to fear that our work would be choked off because we had gone out of style.

This is not meant to be an in-depth study of the world of foundations, nor can I really recount a behind-the-scenes history of the Knight Foundation's changes over the years 1998 to 2004. I write from the point of view of a grantee looking toward a large organization for funding. Ordinarily, those of us applying for grants can know little—outside of phone calls to program officers and what can be gleaned from annual reports—about the politics inside a foundation. Part of the nature of the sponsoring relationship with funding sources is that grant writers feel lucky when they receive money but then, when it's time to go to the well again, they feel mystified about how to get more funding in a changing but inscrutable climate. There is an addictive quality to the situation. You see possible projects before you, and you yearn for money to pay for them, but at the same time you feel ridiculous pushing a button at the door of a building where the bell may be disconnected or the door itself sealed for good. Of course, this emotional state becomes heightened if you don't have tenure or even a stable organization around you; a grant writer for a small agency feels the frustration acutely, hoping to bring in enough money to keep the lights on and his or her own paycheck coming in.

The needs of foundations and granting agencies revolve around the continuity and evolution of their agenda, the clarity of their mission among other comparable institutions. Their sponsorship not only upholds the best interests of the system from which their assets come but also the stability of the foundation itself. This is a logical extension of the foundation concept, and I cannot quarrel with it. Upholding the system may mean supporting those who challenge it or at least address its inequities, and many foundations continue to search for new ways to recognize and respond to more radical challenges or deep economic crises within the scope of their mission. As he had in 1999, Knight Foundation's Carter, in his 2003 President's message, once again emphasizes flexibility in choosing which projects to fund:

There is no clear ideological or political road map on this subject, no infallible text. The circumstances in which we take on the work are fluid. A constant ebb and flow in how the public views and is willing to finance the role of government; new, unexpected factors such as the great flood of immigration of the past 20 years; changing mores and the surfacing of demands for change that sharply conflict with the clear moral imperatives of other Americans: All of these and numerous other threads are part of the warp and woof of contemporary life. They inevitably affect Knight's decisions about what we can most usefully support and what is, for the moment, less important or undoable given our limited resources. (*Annual Report 2003* 4)

It's almost comical, from a grantee's point of view, to hear the president and CEO of one of America's largest foundations refer to their "limited resources." Yet from Carter's point of view the remark is not only perfectly reasonable but also grounded in cold institutional reality. Ideology may or may not limit their options, but cash reserves certainly do. By definition, a foundation cannot fund everything and cannot even fund most of what needs funding. A sum of $90.4 million in 2003 grants by Knight is actually a pitifully small amount to address problems of "democracy" in the United States; that sum would not be enough to address all the needs for 1 year in the state of Pennsylvania alone. In a compelling way, the grantor and the grantee develop their relationship in the context of limited resources and an urgent demand to make choices, even though the scale and context of those choices may differ radically between the two.

Despite the fact that the organization of grants had changed at Knight, we decided to try again to submit a grant once we could determine their new criteria. The Foundation had refocused on journalism, an area where we knew we couldn't compete. It also "significantly deepened its ties to its communities," creating a Community Partners Program that "promised greater resources . . . directed over a longer period of time to a locally recommended, tightly focused set of community investments" (*Annual Report 2003* 46), deploying eight program officers to oversee initiatives in 26 locales. This seemed to us a promising avenue, and it would force us to integrate our efforts even more with other community organizations. Our first step was to invite Julie Tarr, the new program officer for the Philadelphia area, to visit our offices in January 2003 and review what we had done with our earlier grants. Julie was amendable to the visit, and she not only listened to our report on projects over the last years but helped us brainstorm what would fit Knight's new direction. She was careful and wary about committing to anything, but she did ask us questions that gave us an idea about what the Foundation was looking for at that moment. I made some follow-up calls to friends and acquaintances who had been working with Knight in the city under the new internal structure, and we slowly began to form a plan we thought might appeal to Knight but at the same time serve the purposes of all involved. Steve Parks took the lead on this grant because I was still deep in the throes of the general education reform that year.

Julie seemed most excited about the idea of building a network with community arts organizations that would also connect them to schools. She had recently attended a presentation on a long-term grant project called *Culture Builds Community*, funded by the William Penn Foundation and evaluated by a group at the University of Pennsylvania's School of Social Work called the Social Impact of the Arts Project (SIAP). SIAP gave an extensive assessment of the way funding had strengthened the grantee community arts organizations, expanded cultural participation in their local neighborhoods, improved the community-building capacity of grantee organizations, and contributed additional unanticipated benefits to the region. The report was strongly positive, and it highlighted relationship as a crucial element for the survival and growth of community-based initiative, providing "the first empirical documentation of the role of networks of relationships in sustaining the community cultural sector" (Stern and Seifert ii). Julie felt that Knight would do well to follow up on the *Culture Builds Community* results by supporting a network that could grow over time. We had already started some work with two arts organizations in North Philadelphia, Art Sanctuary (AS) and Asian Arts Initiative (AAI), and we had strong connections to Philadelphia school district schools overseen by Temple Partnership Schools. Julie knew our partner arts organizations and thought our potential three-way network (see Fig. 5.2) had promise.

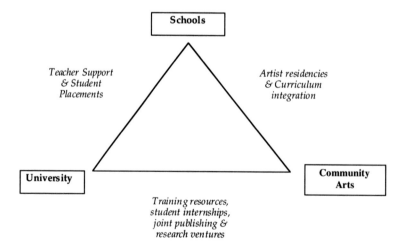

Fig. 5.2. The CALN Partnership Triangle

I will not go over the complex negotiations over six months that result-
ed in a two year, $325,000 CALN grant we submitted to the Knight
Foundation in September 2003. We received the grant in late Winter 2004,
with a start date of January that year. We held meetings at Temple, off campus, even in our homes to try to develop a trust among us all and a core idea
that every participant could benefit from and support politically and profes-
sionally. At one point we engaged an organization called Executive Service
Corps of the Delaware Valley, retired executives who consult for free to
non-profit organizations looking to define their mission, and with their help
we began to get our conflicts and misunderstandings out on the table and
resolve many of them. Due to the time frame for this grant, much of our initial organizational work had to be done with the hope of receiving money
but the promise of none, and by the time we received the money we were
expected to have our collaborative plans already well underway. As it turned
out, that precarious process worked for our group. I want to consider now
why it worked for us and what we learned about joint sponsorship as a
result.

First of all, we had two excellent partners in AS and AAI. AS was
founded and is led by Lorene Cary, a well-known novelist and an adjunct
instructor at the University of Pennsylvania. AS' mission is to bring the
finest in African-American arts—writing, dance, music, film, visual art—to
people in North Philadelphia in collaboration with the Church of the
Advocate, an Episcopal church with a great activist tradition and a grand
French Gothic building hung with murals. Gayle Isa directs AAI, a center
that offers performances and classes as well as a training program for practicing artists who want to learn how to teach in schools and community centers. Gayle is an experienced arts activist who brings to her work an insis-
tent commitment to the arts as a way to empower people and not as a way
to separate out elite practitioners. Both Gayle and Lorene lead their organizations with a high degree of democratic investment from their staff and the
people they serve, and both brought to the initial discussions patience to
cooperate willingly tempered by a fierce sense of their organizations' self-
interest. Both organizations needed money for operating expenses and new
projects, but neither would follow a plan that didn't further their own established agenda. AS and AAI may be smaller than Temple, but neither one
could be bought, bartered, or bullied by a cadre of college professors, even
if the professors carried along a bag of money. Lorene and Gayle were
friendly but independent partners.

Second, we were building on significant collaborative experiences with
both organizations that made the new project seem like the logical next step.
Our colleague in the art and art education department, Billy Yalowitz, had
been developing annual performances in cooperation with AS artists for 3
years before we entered into the CALN project, and Billy became a princi-

pal investigator with us on the grant; this brought Temple's Tyler School of Art into the picture. Along with professional musicians, poets, and dancers, Billy and a graduate student in urban education, Karen Malandra, aided by Temple undergraduates, had been working with local high school students in an afternoon program at the Church of the Advocate. This student group came to be known as the North Stars. They study African dance and drumming and learn to recite aloud poems they compose; they work every year toward a multimedia presentation called the North performances, each one centered on the history of North Philadelphia within the larger epic of African-American history and art. At AAI we had supported a writing group for residents in Philadelphia's Chinatown. We also had begun to support the publication of an oral history project centered on the diversity of people—from older stalwarts in the community to bicultural youth—who lived or worked around Chinatown (see Sze). Both community organizations knew we weren't intending to lord over anyone or take a deep cut of a grant, and we knew we could trust them to follow through with solid programming on any plan we collectively designed.

Third, the triangular structure of our collaboration had benefits for each partner on every side of the triangle and a flow of expertise that moved in all directions. We hoped to bring arts programming into school curricula that lacked local richness, but the point was not "enrichment" but a true deepening of the literacy experience for the students and the teachers. It would employ accomplished artists and bring them in contact with school kids, undergraduates and graduate students, and adults in the neighborhoods and the partner educational institutions. It would help pay for administrative costs that burden small organizations, and it would help us sustain our community publishing venture, New City Community Press. It would make manifest a connection we all felt between literacy and art work, between people's real concern for social justice and the cultural capital that is too often kept on reserve at libraries, college classrooms, and up-scale galleries. This was another example of breaching institutional boundaries, and it illustrated clearly the benefits that flow in all directions when you open doors in the traditional walls.

Work like this brings multiple tensions into play. Despite our initial good will, and the good fortune of a significant amount of money to fund our projects, we had much to learn about each other's organizations, about the pressures and reward structure with which each partner had to contend, about how our personalities could harmonize and clash. I cannot tell individual stories here because any narrative would sound like telegraphic gossip about people you don't know—like reading *People* magazine about spats among celebrities from a country you've never heard of—and very seldom is prose more meaningless than that. I offer this brief overview of internal organizational tensions each partner managed during our final year. AAI experienced significant staffing turnover and began a hunt for a new building while mounting a major public installation. AS scrambled to receive and fulfill multiple grants while presenting a year-long series of celebratory events for the poet Sonia Sanchez. Tyler's Community Arts established a new curriculum and recruited students under a new dean. New City Writing spun off the New City Community Press (formerly New City Press) as an independent entity while the Writing Program underwent program reviews, administrative traumas, and the advent of a new general education plan. Steve Parks left Temple for a different university just as we were starting to develop as a network. Lorene and I both had books to finish and classes to teach. Nicole Meyenberg and Karen Malandra, administrative assistants being paid a pittance for the work they did, kept us centered on the terms of the grant and often smoothed out wrinkles caused by partners going off in opposite directions. Through it all we talked—face to face or by phone, in whole group or in smaller clusters—not always with crystal clarity or perfect patience, but with just enough mutual acceptance to make decisions that moved our work forward.

Our biggest challenge, however, was not forging trust among ourselves. In my view, the most difficult design problem was how to work with the schools. At the time we wrote the grant, we still had high confidence that we could work with the set of schools that had been entrusted by the school district to the supervision of a unit attached to the Temple University president's office. We regarded the staff in that school partnership office as highly competent and devoted to the children, solidly committed to the work outlined in the grant. We had principals and one or two teachers from at least two K-8 schools meeting regularly with us, and a promise that a middle school near Temple's campus would become a high school for the arts in the next years. But soon after we received the grant, things started to fall apart with the schools. The principals stopped coming to meetings, some key partnership staff left for other jobs, the head of the partnership seemed to be backing off on his involvement with the grant. Then we found out the school district had decided to close the school we thought was going to become a high school. In a trend that reminded us all too much of other promising projects with the school district, this one went down hill quickly.

What I came to realize is that our model for working together as collaborative partners did not match the model school administrators had for working with outside contractors, particularly around art. We saw ourselves as developing plans together with teachers and principals, learning about institutional imperatives and brainstorming the best projects for everyone involved. But school people don't have time for deliberation and experiment. They have kids to teach, tests scores to improve, buildings to maintain. They need to pay a fee for services, or at least have a grant pay providers for specific performances or workshops or in-service training.

Our hope for long-term, sustainable relationships seemed impractical and indulgent in an institutional environment where principals could be gone in a year and yearly progress was the most powerful currency; even social studies had begun to seem a needless luxury that detracted from time on task for math and reading skills. They wanted "art," but it needed to be in discrete packages that could be plugged in to curricula driven by test preparation and definable outcomes.

Luckily, however, our partners had already developed solid relationships with public schools in North Philadelphia both inside and outside the partnership. I also worked hard to maintain our relationship with the Temple-affiliated schools, and I found a willing ally in Walter Jordan-Davis, the development officer for the partnership. He and I met regularly over coffee at Temple's Student Activity Center, talking about all the possible projects we could do, talking about how this work fit into the larger contour of our professional lives. While principals have come and gone, support for these schools wavers and surges at the whim of District administrators, Walter and I were able to prepare the way for projects in the schools. We tried to focus on specific "deliverables" that the schools could use with little disruption to their days. The North Performances were perhaps our best export to the schools because AS already had the mechanisms in place to bring presentations and workshops into the schools and bring students to matinees in the Church. New City Writing designed and offered a creative writing workshop at a local not-for-profit bookstore, Tree House Books, for fourth graders at one of the partnership schools. AAI planned a big school outing to their Chinatown In/flux installation, but unfortunately the trip was cancelled by a snowstorm. While the school side was never our strongest component, we were able to maintain the triangle and build on a record the arts organizations had compiled with teachers and administrators.

Here's how we stated our mission to ourselves after almost 2 years of working together:

To develop a model arts and literacy network in North Philadelphia that functions to make, sustain and transform relationships among community arts organizations, Temple University community-focused programs, public schools and other educational partners. By creating programming together we benefit participants and challenge lines of social division.

Goal 1: Create a network infrastructure
- Build conduits to each other's resources and programs
- Augment the work that is being done in existing organizations
- Incorporate mutual training opportunities between organizations
- Challenge each other's understandings of knowledge, power, and relationships

Goal 2: Design and implement a set of models using arts and literacy as a form of community expression, education, and political efficacy.

- Design and implement curriculum for applied classroom and community-based event uses
- Provide mentorship and professional opportunities for teaching artists and classroom teachers involved with network programs
- Support and develop undergraduate service-learning courses and graduate research courses that can support the work of CALN partners

Goal 3: Expand and institutionalize the avenues through which organizations, neighborhood residents, public schools, artists, universities, and students can use arts/literacy to engage in civic debate and participate in neighborhood reform.

- Organize and attend public forums and academic conferences focusing on the work of CALN members and interests
- Produce documentation focusing on the pedagogical, historical, and artistic work of CALN members
- Make available formalized models/research for other public schools/community organizations wishing to integrate into their organizations

Goal 4: Sustain a responsive self-governed vehicle that continues beyond the existing funding stream.

- Develop strategic financial planning
- Invite other North Philadelphia members into the network
- Utilize external evaluators to assess CALN activity (process/product) and make available research for future governing
- Tap into Temple students for internships

Goal 5: Shape Temple University in a way that allows it to be more responsive to organizations and individuals in the surrounding neighborhoods.

The goals are extremely ambitious, but the effect on us of our regular meetings has been profound. We attended each other's functions, supported cross-organizational events like an Asian American Hip-Hop conference, which won a Governor's Award in 2006 for the collaborative work of AAI and AS. New City Community Press contributed to the publication of the oral histories from Philadelphia's Chinatown in a book called *Chinatown Live(s)* (Sze), and that book later served as the text for a sculptural installa-

tion in AAI's 2005 community-based show called Chinatown In/flux.
CALN sponsored presentations in local schools by the North Stars, and
both community arts organizations worked successfully with Philadelphia
youth in their after-school programs. Tyler School of Art developed materials for its community arts program partly with CALN funds, and undergraduates from their program attended CALN events and learned from
CALN-sponsored artists. The Tree House workshops helped New City
Writing develop a more positive connection with the Temple Partnership
Schools, parents and kids, and business people in the immediate neighborhood. The final goal of shaping the university—the most difficult one for all
of us to agree on, and the least elaborated strategically—still remains to be
fulfilled in a meaningful way. We had our share of tension, distrust, and anx-
iety between and among the partners, but we are discovering more and more
reasons why it is in our self-interests to work together.

In March 2006, CALN organized a conference for approximately 60
participants to put questions about community arts and literacy to artists,
activists, funders, teachers, and students. This was perhaps the most satisfying moment of the grant period, for we had a chance to recognize, in the
presence of others who do this sort of work, that indeed we had learned
something about how to work together and could share these lessons with
others. I talked about work with the schools, contrasting our desire to facilitate collaborations among artists, teachers, parents and students while the
schools expected a client–provider relationship because they have too many
demands and expectations on them to take a slower, more exploratory
approach. Gayle highlighted the challenges of working across the power differential between a university and a small organization, how slowly a university can change and how little even tenured faculty can influence the university's choices. Lorene talked about the arts as providing an alternate view
of literacy from the one tested and tested in classrooms, "a breakthrough of
the divine," she called literacy informed by expression, group history, and
personal growth. Billy talked about the way his work with AS made him
want to find projects that spoke out of his personal community commitments, and he pointed to a theater project he is developing with Palestinian
and Israeli actors as a consequence of his directing the early North performances. We facilitated groups for those who wanted to pursue the topics we
each had raised, and then we offered afternoon sessions for issues the participants wanted to pursue.

In the final hour of the conference, we asked three guest speakers who
had listened to the day of presentations and workshops to reflect on what
they heard. The video of these talks reflect much about the overall concerns
during the day's discussion. Jan Cohen-Cruz, an artist and scholar of community arts from New York University, started off sharing with us a broad
array of resources across the country, such as the clearing house Web site for

this work (communityarts.net) and the site for an exciting multimedia organization in Appalachian Kentucky (appalshop.org), as well as conferences people could attend. She noted one theme of the conference was the desire to make community arts not only a job but also a way of life. As one example, she said that in her own artmaking she sought out people who knew more than she about specific elements of a community's life, such as tenant organizing or the history of New York's Lower East Side. This allowed her to step out of the typical professor's role of expert: "I like having a practice at the heart of my life that makes it easy to be the one who doesn't know anything." Pepon Osorio, an installation artist and MacArthur grant recipient who had recently joined the faculty at Temple, talked about his own experience with the pressure of making art in neighborhoods. He regretted always having to make relationships quickly and then move on, like a squatter in a place not his own. He recognized the need to create long-term relationships within which art could be made slowly, carefully, "passing on a vision more than a project."

Deborah Brandt, the third guest and the scholar whose idea of sponsorship so influences the approach I take in this book, identified the problem we faced as a struggle for a predominant definition of literacy in our economic moment:

> We are seeing the ascendancy of a definition of literacy for work, for productivity, that lies behind so many of the literacy policies, standards, and tests that we see in schools now. Because of our current system, the economy needs more and more workers who spend more of their days manipulating symbols—usually print symbols and other kinds of graphics. Our schools are getting caught up in meeting the inexhaustible demand for this form of literacy. . . . But I also saw today an articulation of a different definition for literacy. Lorene Cary of Art Sanctuary was talking about the arts, communication, and literacy as a breakthrough of the divine, as a method for healing, as a way for political expression to occur when other avenues are not available. Many people today have linked literacy with free expression, self-expression, human development, the right to be. This has been a definition of literacy that has brought great things to the society at various times, and it's getting pushed away. ("Understanding" 26)

This distinction between literacy for production and literacy for expression and development remained in the minds of many who attended. The editor of an independent investigative newspaper on the schools, Public School Notebook, attended the conference and later asked to publish a transcript of Brandt's remarks in order to emphasize her point about the link between a narrowed conception of literacy and the obsession with standardized testing represented by the Bush Administration's No Child Left Behind campaign.

ONE INSTITUTION AMONG MANY: WHAT DOES JOINT SPONSORSHIP PROMISE?

What does the CALN experience tells us about joint sponsorships of literacy? Unlike in the first Knight grant, we were working here with multiple partners, each with a distinct sense of self-interest and a set agenda. Unlike the second grant, where we were the primary recipients and our cooperative efforts followed from a working principle rather than an imperative built into the funding, in CALN the Temple writing program was one among many organizations needing to work together for the sake of the funding but also for the sake of the idea of a network. Like the Open Doors project that I described in Chapter 4, CALN could not be a creature of any one center or any one constituency. Like any project, its originators want it to thrive and grow, but this project will not be considered fully successful unless it can demonstrate that other arts organizations, other schools, and other colleges can participate in and shape the concept, as we tried to do in the conference that ended the grant.

When I look at the map of the blocks around Temple University, I am humbled by the richness of institutional life around us. Figure 5.3 shows only schools and centers where we have developed cooperative projects, most related to CALN. Many other public, private, and church-related schools are not plotted on the map, and the map does not register established and storefront churches, health centers, museums, or home child-care centers within blocks of the university. It does not include funeral parlors, mom and pop stores, diners, bodegas, beauty parlors, and nail salons; nor does it locate youth, elder care, or prisoner outreach services in the neighborhoods. In all of these, people use their literacy and could learn more. The university—for all its dormitories and laboratories, its elevators and furnaces, its parking lots and practice fields—is just one organization among many in North Philadelphia. Temple may be one of the city's largest employers, may produce more trash than anybody within 20 blocks, may fix more broken noses and cracked teeth than any hospital on our side of town, may own more books. Yet, when it comes to developing partnerships and fostering a living relationship to reading and writing in North Philadelphia, Temple must work together on an equal footing with others invested in this place.

One value embedded in the way we sponsor literacy in the academy is that our particular language should be readily distinguished from the common speech of conversation, newspapers, magazines, and Web sites. Our written documents are meant to be more precise, more reasoned, more contextualized in history and theory; our literacy is distinctly learned and learnéd. This attitude toward language—laudable for its ambitions but sometimes laughable for its arcane jargon and pomposity—has the effect of separating

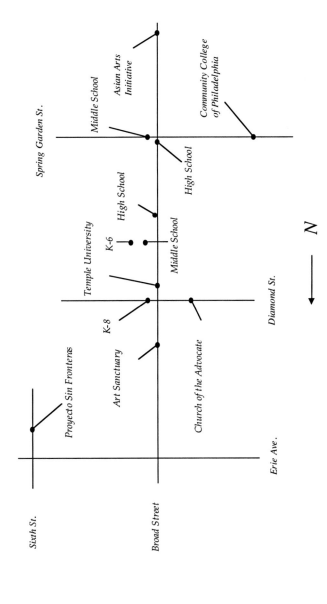

Sixth St.

Proyecto Sin Fronteras

Broad Street

Art Sanctuary

K-8

Temple University

Church of the Advocate

Erie Ave.

Diamond St.

K-6

High School

Middle School

High School

Spring Garden St.

Middle School

Asian Arts
Initiative

Community College
of Philadelphia

N

Fig. 5.3. One Among Many Partners

us from other literacy sponsors. Joint sponsorship between a university and other literacy venues can seem to academics like an attempt to "water down" ideas or research methods. In some instances it may force simpler language and simplified concepts, as in some high school textbooks (though this may be the result of commercialism and special interest pressures more than the reading level of teenagers). In other instances vocationalism may put form above intellectual exploration, as in some community college classrooms. Of course we want an institution in a society to be devoted to critical review and close observation of the natural and social world, historical precedents for modern events, creative processes in the imaginative arts, technical invention in the practical arts. But I wonder if the real fear in academia about joint sponsorship between universities and surrounding organizations is not based on a less selfless impulse.

We can return at this point to the competing models of the research university and the metropolitan university with which we started in the introduction. Jerome Ziegler has characterized this tension in more specific terms as that between a traditional liberal arts faculty with "their views about the centrality of research and graduate education in their disciplines" and faculty "concerned with professional training, and education, and 'outreach'" (Ziegler 224). In order to engage in the kind of joint sponsorship I have been describing, a university partner must choose a role that shifts its function away from one model of knowledge diffusion and allies it with another, less prestigious model. I doubt that in either case knowledge is truly less complex or demanding, only that the complexity and demand are different in character and standing. It is frightening to put theory to the test in a neighborhood or school, daunting to explain a concept to funders rather than to disciplinary colleagues, and downright maddening to hassle with the bureaucracy of a school district when you feel you know better. But as we have discovered in the CALN negotiations, community organizations are challenging the university to change its ways: to be more accessible to the people in its geographical home and, in the process, to transform the nature of the university's mission and self-concept.

When I look at my year with general education through the lens of my work with schools, community colleges and neighborhood centers, I see a different struggle than the one I thought I was fighting. One day I chaired a meeting where sixty science professors showed up mad as hell because they thought I was leading the move to reduce their lab science requirement from two courses to one. They made all kinds of ridiculous statistical arguments that had nothing to do with what students actually learned or how they would learn it. I walked away no more convinced either way on the one-course-or-two question, but I was profoundly perplexed by the blind religious fervor these scientists showed over an issue that they might have approached as a challenging empirical problem. That year I was trying to get warring faculty units to recognize what they had in common and how they could help all undergraduates learn skills and knowledge they would need beyond college. I thought the real obstacles were the old heads who didn't want to change or the partisans who were trying to carve out the most turf possible for their particular programs. My perspective was limited by the frame of the university, defined by the literacy sponsorship of an unassailable academic establishment. But I developed a different point of view attending meetings in church basements and stuffy upstairs offices, watching events in airy performance spaces or ill-ventilated middle school gyms, observing lessons in dingy community college classrooms or the brightly tiled auditoriums of high schools designed in the 1950s.

I realize now that general education was simply too embarrassing for my colleagues to address directly. They thundered and postured and fulminated because they had very little substantive to say. To pay attention to general education is to pay attention to teaching stripped of its privileges and disciplinary authority; thinking about what undergraduates should be able to do when they leave college runs counter to what the modern university requires us to be. Universities drive local economies with their research and their land use policies, they sponsor sporting events that attract thousands of fans, and they confer legitimacy to avenues of inquiry or professional practice that mainstream culture considers vital. I am not suggesting that research universities cannot develop reasonable undergraduate curricula, but the whole process of paying attention to that level of literacy runs counter to the current nature of the institution and its functions. General education provoked abstract ideological debates and pointless political maneuvering because anything else would unmask the extent to which the institution does not invest in the daily experience of undergraduates in classrooms, library carrels, and computer workstations. Teaching students, until they are safely ensconced in their discipline, is done by contingent instructors, and engaged intellectual service is lost in the pomp and circumstance that transmogrifies "what I say" into "what is known."

Like general education, literacy partnerships with community-based organizations foreground educational processes that universities cannot afford to make a priority. Academics need not hide what we have learned when we work with others outside the academy, but we should question our apparent expertise, question our inclination to think we know what's right and why we value some kinds of literacy over others. Arts organizations help us re-evaluate verbal language as only one communication medium for understanding human experience or exploring imagined space. Speakers of languages other than English challenge American ethnocentric language habits. Foundations force us to enter the national debate on literacy and economics while senior centers in immigrant neighborhoods initiate us into the drama of aging in a strange country. Dialogue across language users can help each of us maintain, as Carter from the Knight Foundation says, "an ungrudging willingness to try radically different approaches to dealing with radically shifting realities" (*Annual Report* 1999 4). We learn to see these shifting realities only through the eyes of all our partners in a particular place, the place we share.

6

On Circulation

But if we believe that writing is social, shouldn't the system of circulation—the paths that the writing takes—extend beyond and around the single path from student to teacher? ("Made Not Only in Words" 310-11)
    Kathleen Blake Yancey

This book has been a long time in the making. It started in 2001, when I received a leave to pursue a question I hardly understood: How do writing activities leading up to and beyond the college curriculum connect with writing on campus? As I collected data from visits to schools, community colleges, and literacy centers, my mother grew very sick. She died in April 2002, just as I was completing an early draft of the first few chapters. I read Dewey and Alinsky that year as though I had never heard of them before, searching for a new way to see what I had been doing by intuition for nearly 10 years. Since my study leave, Temple has raised its admissions standards and re-examined its approach to general education, writing included. I did not always feel happy with the direction the institution was taking, and yet my love of Philadelphia and the students who find their way to Temple kept me here. I don't know if I'm any wiser now than when I started this book project, but I am older and a little more circumspect about what can happen to large-scale visions. Still, I remain convinced of this overall assertion: A framework for literacy sponsorship that includes multiple partnerships within a region will serve most postsecondary schools better than a traditional view of writing contained by campus boundaries.

Some of the most enthusiastic advanced readers of this volume have asked me for more concrete suggestions others can use to make programs in their home communities and neighborhoods. Throughout the previous chapters, I have tried to lay out some principles to guide others in the creative work of designing programs and engaging with partners, and I have tried to account for projects we've done over the last few years at Temple. In these final pages I suggest ideas and directions that others might consider for work on their own terrain. I worry that occasionally I have come across as too cheery, too ready to minimize the immense problems that cross-institutional work encounters in addressing social justice issues. For this reason, I begin with the very real obstacles that lie in the way of literacy sponsorship beyond the college curriculum. Organizers and educators must learn as much as possible about what blocks or limits their work, but at the same time we must see these limitations as features of a landscape within which we move.

One persistent problem for community-based partnerships is the fragility of the small nonprofits that carry on much of the important work in troubled neighborhoods. One organization with which I work, for instance, recently experienced an extreme cash-flow crisis: Grants had been promised but the checks had not arrived while salaries, bills, and insurance premiums went unpaid. You want to throttle a slow bureaucrat somewhere in a government office, or berate a clerk who mislaid a check request, but this is the perpetual frustration of nonprofit work. Every little agency experiences crises like this; some survive, whereas others fold. The staff makes do, the work suffers, and there's always another grant to post. A sewer pipe breaks, the church that owns the building has no money to pay a plumber, and so the office staff ignores the stench till a parishioner can fix the leak for free. A heat wave hits, but the center can't afford air-conditioning, so they toil on with humor and bottled water. A secretary has to be fired because she shows up 2 hours late for a week—she secretly got a job in a factory but hasn't had the nerve to tell the director she works till 1 a.m. every night—and no one can take time to hire a new employee. Heck, the organization can't afford a secretary anyway, no matter how much they need one.

As a deeply invested observer at a nonprofit, you see these scenarios unfold all the time. If you have a tenured job in a university, you want to reach into your pocket and pick up the tab, but you know that won't solve the structural problem. You want to fix the leaks or buy an air-conditioner, but you don't know enough rich people to foot the bill, and even a sudden cohort of donors wouldn't change the basic circumstance. Hurricane Katrina taught us the simple lesson that poor people don't have the cars to leave a city when the mayor says go, and they can't easily return just because the rains stop and floodwaters recede. Small tornadoes, or the moral equivalent, hit low-lying neighborhoods and unsteady farms every day; the system just never seems to have enough to help the people most in need. If you work with small nonprofits, you have to deal with the shortages and shortfalls best you can and still show up every Monday morning.

On the higher education side, other sorts of vexations wear at people who try to engage in community partnerships. Sometimes you find colleagues or administrators simply don't understand, or see their own agenda as precluding connections off campus. Consider these hypothetical situations. A college financial officer turns back your reimbursements because he doesn't see why you're working with "those people." What are we running, a philanthropy? The star professor, who moans about the sins of rightwing politicians, tells her graduate students you are turning the university into a community college. The provost, who swears publicly that he is committed to community outreach, cuts an entire office of school and community partnership because it doesn't belong in his portfolio. The dean dismisses your grants as "mere" service. If you have tenure, you try to laugh it off as so much distraction, but at night you dream of students in class with their backs to you or alleyways leading nowhere. If you don't have tenure, you're expected to walk away from projects your superiors think too risky. Even friends shake their heads and suggest you take a year to focus on something more productive.

If we compare the urgent pressures and demands on community nonprofits to the political hassles in a university, complaints from the campus sound like whining. Recounting the little nicks or painful slaps of academic life can be tiresome to anybody who doesn't work for a dean. My point is not to make light of the challenges in a college setting; I just don't want to accept them as reasons for paralysis or endless further study. We know this work can be frustrating, thankless, or futile at times. Some activists become bitter, or self-righteous, or angry, or self-serving, or all of these. Some make speeches at parties when everybody else wants to talk about the movies. Some work harder and harder and stop sharing their worries even with their life partners. Others drink or eat or smoke too much and delude themselves that they're relieving stress. I don't have an answer to any of these emotional traps, but I do believe in seeking out sources of support and love in sustainable relationships that make living and working possible. Without being maudlin or romantic, I simply report that allies, friends, students, and family have helped me recognize when I am obsessing or losing perspective. They make jokes, or pat my back, or talk baseball, or just listen. Students and adult learners employ their literacy with a vigor that continually brings me back to the pleasure and immediacy of teaching, and even a few stolen hours for my own writing life revive me. The urgency of the work never dissipates, but allowing urgency to engulf me helps no one.

In the remainder of this chapter, I consider three questions out of the many one might ask about this work. These questions hardly exhaust the possible concerns, nor do the answers settle the matters they address. The first sounds like a cross between Lenin's famous question, "What is to be done?" and the practical teacher's query to the theorist, "But what'll I do on Monday morning?" The second speaks to the struggle for equilibrium and survival inside your home institution while you pursue work off campus. The third points toward the need for caring but critical assessment. I present questions I have heard in a number of settings—not just in metropolitan universities but also in selective colleges with idyllic rural campuses as well as underfunded suburban 2-year schools—and I offer answers that aren't really answers, recognizing that readers most need to develop creative responses to their own special circumstances.

1. What literacy sponsorships will work beyond the college curriculum?
2. How do we contribute to our home institutions while engaging off-campus partners?
3. Are these efforts worthwhile?

I am sure readers will have more questions, but let these serve as representative of the constant inquiry necessary to sustain community literacy work from a college or university base.

My short answer to all three of these questions follows from Kathleen Blake Yancey's Chair's Address in March 2004. Among her many prescient observations, she notes how important "patterns of circulation" (300) can be for understanding literacy learning and practice. Comparing circulation to activity theory as Charles Bazerman and David Russell define it, she traces the way texts grow and transmute as they move across media, institutional setting, time. She highlights intertextuality, "a conversation that we invite students to join," which "occurs through genres and is really many conversations, with texts circulating in multiple, interrelated ways" (312). This is exactly the conversation I mean when I define literacy to my undergraduate teaching students as "the ability to engage in a conversation carried on through written language," but she emphasizes the conversational character of literacy with a singular passion and urgency. In her account of our curricular and instructional practices, she warns against isolating print from the Web, first year from graduate school, service learning from advanced composition. Programs and projects must raise questions for each other, resonate, or interleave; learning here begets learning there. I take her charge quite seriously, and I hope this book contributes to the reframing she calls us to undertake. Undergraduates tutoring senior ESL learners, elementary students visiting college writing centers, community college instructors meeting with university graduate TAs, speeches turning into video turning into print broadsides—teaching and research in one corner of town should inform what is possible in another. Let us explore and extend the idea of circulation inside and outside the college campus.

WHAT LITERACY SPONSORSHIPS WILL WORK BEYOND THE COLLEGE CURRICULUM?

Community-engaged projects should arise from the needs and aspirations of the partners with whom we work. The key to developing new ideas is to listen closely to what people in neighborhoods, centers, and schools say they need or want and then develop ideas with the staff and volunteers from those sites. At the same time, those of us who work in writing programs or education schools have knowledge and experiences that give us something valuable to add to a conversation about literacy-based projects. The balance between listening and contributing, responding and inventing—always monitored and adjusted by critical reflection and lots of open conversation—determines the quality of a successful partnership. Not to say that some projects don't go on too long because of the sheer persistence of one partner, nor that well designed, egalitarian programs don't get washed away because of funding failures or staff conflicts. But in order to have a chance at building a sustainable program that genuinely serves its target population, the higher education partner must work with care and flexibility. Decisions need to be driven by mission rather than ego.

Two ideas developed over years in composition seem highly promising in off-campus settings: writing centers and community publishing. The work described by Tiffany Rousculp at the Community Writing Center (CWC) sponsored by the Salt Lake City Community College demonstrates the power and flexibility of a writing center located off campus and devoted to the writing of people not enrolled in the sponsoring college. Rousculp situates her academic writing about the project within the network of composition/rhetoric scholars associated with community literacy, but she and her staff have overseen the development of programs in the CWC that suit a variety of needs in a range of settings not normally associated with the academy. Her 2006 article reports that, in addition to coaching and composing space provided in the Center, the CWC supports writing in small nonprofit organizations and sponsors the DiverseCity Writing Series that publishes work from eight local writing groups. As she notes, the CWC started by modeling itself on the Community Literacy Center in Pittsburgh described by Peck, Flower, and Higgins (Rousculp 69) but evolved an ambitious and activist publishing agenda that goes beyond Thomas Dean's model of "writing *with* the community" (Rousculp 74). They take the issue of intellectual ownership seriously, revising program guidelines to give more and more autonomy to the groups with which they collaborate (78), and they make every effort not to interpret the work they publish in a way that might appropriate the individual writer's language and experience into a larger, school-defined frame (79).

I find the work at Salt Lake City Community College an exciting model of engagement that should be possible for many institutions. Rousculp makes the point that the CWC has been supported by the school's administration since its inception in 2001 because the center "has met the needs of the community college as well, thus securing its continued funding" (75). The community college publicly promotes values such as community involvement, economic development, creativity, and cultural diversity (77) and, like many other 2-year schools nationally, it sees service-learning programs as consonant with the overall mission of the institution (75); the CWC extends that commitment in a vibrant new direction. Following a similar approach, state-funded teaching schools like West Chester University in Pennsylvania as well as research institutions like University of Wisconsin-Madison are extending their successful college writing center experience to schools, libraries, and other public sites. This is an extremely promising trend. At the same time, however, we must keep asking ourselves what these projects aim to accomplish: general goals such as "increasing involvement" or "helping people develop their voices" isn't focused enough either to sustain funding, convince municipalities or individuals that the projects will matters to them, or guide strategic planning. I suspect that community-based centers, which sometimes start with admirable intentions but vague goals, will eventually need measurable results within the realms of economic development, political empowerment, job training and placement, as well as professional development to attract funding consistently and garner public support over time.

Writing centers in public schools tend to have more prescribed goals already in place because school administrators have limited tolerance for programs that take up time and space but don't contribute to direct learning outcomes or teacher support. In a framework that takes into account a range of literacy experience in a region, writing centers in community colleges, 4-year colleges, or universities would be linked with writing centers in schools and neighborhood literacy centers. In many ways school writing centers could serve as the crucial outposts in a writing center network, especially if staff circulate through the different environments the range of centers represents. Centers can be places where individual instructors gain perspective on writing pedagogy and literacy learning that they can encounter nowhere else. Just as a writing center in a college allows staff to see writing as it is practiced throughout the curriculum, a network of centers can teach a young tutor or a tempered comp/rhetoric veteran the similarities and differences in literacy learning across age, class, race and task differences. An English graduate student, for instance, who has tutored 3 years in the university writing center may choose to take a year to tutor in an urban elementary school center if that is open to him or her. The job may look like an easy gig before he or she starts, but the student walks away from the year a humbler and wiser teacher. Even if the student goes on to a career teaching college literature, he or she now understands at a much deeper level how reading is first acquired and what the challenges are for young readers in stressed neighborhoods. What Kathy Yancey calls "circulation" is the crucial consideration here— how lessons learned in one spot in a system of sponsored literacy projects can be applied and incorporated into the functions and theory in other areas. Circulation of tutors and staff among centers can enhance the effectiveness of the whole system.

When we turn from the center idea to its cooperative component, community publishing, the capacity for circulation grows while the challenge to maintain focus becomes more intense. Paula Mathieu has written probingly about the uses of community publishing for both undergraduate students and dispossessed people, and she warns that "turning to the streets necessitates a serious re-examination of the work we do as teachers, writers, and scholars" (116). One example of this challenge to follow a reflective and articulated mission is the trend Rousculp describes in the DiverseCity Series to increase autonomy for writing groups and hold off on interpretation of texts by academic editors. Rousculp notes that DiversityCity Series tries to sell the anthologies they publish at readings and consignment shops (74) in order to defray some of the costs of publication; they give away more copies through authors and organizations. Nothing wrong with this in the early years of developing an effective approach to engagement, but quite frankly why would a foundation or state agency continue to fund a college or university to oversee an activity if the individual groups are mostly autonomous? Why not simply give the groups money directly, or fund a collective of local organizations and cut out the intermediary? Yes, we want to avoid being exploitive and co-opting in the way we package and gloss community-based writing, but beyond the first exhilaration of hearing their stories read in public and appear in print, what do new authors get for their involvement in a noninterventional press sponsored by the academy? What can a university or college add to the partnership? Some foundations have already begun to ask these questions.

When our press (first New City Press and later New City Community Press) produced our first publications, we also had only a modest plan about how to distribute our texts. We started with two issues of a magazine called *Open City* and then published a collection of interviews, *The Forgotten*

Bottom (Tarrier and Hyatt), conducted by anthropology undergraduates in a small Philadelphia neighborhood soon to be wiped out by urban renewal. We celebrated these publications at the time, but almost immediately we recognized that printing new authors wasn't enough. The problem of distribution hit us full in the face: we still have hundreds of copies of *Open City* and *The Forgotten Bottom* sitting in storage, with no way to get them into the hands of new readers. A press needs to bring its writers to the public—that's what a publishing house purports to do—and we won't stay in business long if we can't sell at least enough books to prove to funders that we've got a viable plan to put our books to work for the authors and the communities. I don't mean we must only take on projects that will sell. When our editors and board of trustees commit themselves to a publication project now, we require a plan for distribution and community utility that assures the book a reasonable chance at an active life after it is in print. This goes beyond a traditional marketing plan. The idea is to give readers and authors a method for using the books in their lives, as a model for neighborhood school projects or a tool for organizing data collection or a text for training teachers to understand their students' lives. The authors themselves should be developing not only their writing skills but also their abilities as editors, managers, publicists. Our great fear is that good books will sit inert on a storeroom shelf or mute in the back of a vendor's window display.

We have had the most success with *Espejos y Ventanas/ Mirrors and Windows*, a bilingual collection of interviews with Mexican mushroom farm workers who live and work in Kennett Square, an area west of Philadelphia. The editor/translator/interviewer, Mark Lyons, has become a fierce advocate for the book, regularly representing it at immigrant education conferences and university teacher training programs throughout the country. Through Lyons, and others connected to the Press, the book has made its way into the hands of Spanish language students, immigrant workers, teachers using ethnography in English and social studies units, organizers working on the U.S.–Mexican border. Lyons designed curricular material to accompany the book and developed a script for public dramatic readings of the text. He has a long history with the mushroom workers' union and returns periodically to Kennett Square to talk to folks about the book and their current struggles. He holds down a demanding day job as a physician's associate in a health center serving the main Latino neighborhood of Philadelphia, but he has devoted a considerable amount of his own time to the project out of a passion for oral history, storytelling, and social justice. Lyons became a one-man marketing campaign, and his dedication to the farmworkers who told their stories in *Espejo* has brought out the book's far-reaching potential to touch and transform others. We are rapidly approaching the time when we will have to go into a second printing, though the technology of on-demand publishing may eventually lighten the risk to the Press.

The sort of success *Espejos* has had depends in part on our "interpreting" the interviews in the book, although none of the interpreters involved were professional academics. Lyons and journalist Leticia Roa Nixon provide an historical and political introduction to the oral history process in this community, while the prefatory poem by Mexican diplomat Enrique Cortazar and the afterword by the Chicano poet Jimmy Santiago Baca give the book a greater cultural context. If we had simply handed a set of interviews back to the collective group of workers, they would have had little way to use the collection. Another book we published, *No Restraints*—a collection of writings by disability activists about life within their community and personal circles in Philadelphia—nearly sold out on the basis of word of mouth and the public reputation of its editor, Gil Ott. Like Lyons, Ott was not an academic, although he was an extremely well-read and widely published poet. In this book project, his strongest credential was his long history as a literary activist with homeless people, his professional involvement in the disabled community, and his personal struggle with chronic illness. Both for *No Restraints* and *Espejo y Ventanas*, New City Community Press acted as a sponsor for the gathering and shaping of the texts, using editors who would be fully accepted by the participants, as well as arranging for funding, design, production, and promotion of the book. Publishing is expensive, and it requires that the authors involved put considerable effort into their contributions. To get the book out to a reading public demands that somebody or some committee shape its form and articulate its meaning at least enough to make it accessible to an audience.

I started by saying that the writing center and publishing ventures offer a promising method to extend university-based services to the surrounding community. If we think of these two approaches as having a "tactical orientation" in Mathieu's use of that term (xiv), then they can have tremendous power and utility as long as they attend to the local and maintain creativity and flexibility. Combining these two tactics by using a center to generate texts for publication can be promising but tricky. In significant ways, the mission of a center conflicts with the undertaking to publish, particularly books. A center sets out to improve the practice and process of individual writers who seek help, whereas publishing requires selection, editing, and a conscious decision to make a product with a particular look and tone that to some extent subordinates the individual to the group. That conflict need not tear the two components apart; the energy of a genuine writing project and purpose to strengthen both individual and group voices can fuse center and publishing functions. To my mind, the center's function is especially crucial because the imperatives of running a business, even one expressly designed to generate no profits, can detract from the pressing mandate to help every writer grow.

New media may provide tactical approaches for resolving this apparent conflict. Not all projects need to become books, and in fact much community writing, whether initiated by individuals or groups, may be better off appearing first on well-designed Web sites that can evolve in response to immediate changes in a neighborhood or region. We are beginning to see this with organizations like the Neighborhood Story Project in New Orleans, where Hurricane Katrina's devastation is slowly being processed in terms of the life stories of youth who lived through the catastrophe: "In the aftermath of the destruction, we are in the process of re-envisioning our work and our city. We are beginning to organize an oral history project about people's lives in New Orleans, their experiences with the storm, and their hopes for the future" (http://www.neighborhoodstoryproject.org/katrina.html). New media—content prepared for web, video, or cell phone technology—can get at experience much more quickly and effectively than print. A writing center can initiate the process, working with authors at the initial stage when experience connects with written language, and books have their place in a much later, more elaborated stage. In the intermediate stage, however, new media literacy projects allow for the immediate circulation of reactions to catastrophes or windfalls and help writers come to terms with the obstacles and joys in their lives.

HOW DO WE CONTRIBUTE TO OUR HOME INSTITUTIONS WHILE ENGAGING OFF-CAMPUS PARTNERS?

Perhaps the hardest part about pursuing projects off campus is protecting and maintaining commitments to our own college or university when we are not around as often. Alinsky would call the process of understanding those home commitments a matter of recognizing the organizer's self-interest, but Brandt might add that self-interest also characterizes the literacy sponsorship possible for an individual agent as well as the larger institutions he or she serves. Remember that Brandt's definition of a sponsor of literacy specifies that the person or organization "gain advantage by it in some way" (19). We can identify conscious conspiracies and unexamined double standards that allow one group historically to maintain control over another through higher education, but sponsors also operate for gains that are not necessarily shameful or discriminatory, such as conserving knowledge traditions or opening up access in order to transform dysfunctional habits of mind. Whether we see this from Alinsky's or Brandt's point of view however, developing a strategy for maintaining your home commitments strikes me as crucial not only for keeping your job but also for clarifying your planning process with partners who must act equally in their own self-interest.

Successful literacy work in a postsecondary institution requires two sustained investments. The first involves the quality of writing instruction and learning on campus. Even if you are hired specifically to develop community partnerships—and very few of us have that luxury—the well-being of students at your home institution must be a major factor in program calculations or eventually the institution will eliminate community engagement as irrelevant to its mission. A college or university, even at a major research center, must rank the learning outcomes of its students highly, in most cases above the learning of people not paying tuition. The second investment grows out of the commitment higher education faculty owe to their own learning and research, no matter what their institutional affiliation. University faculty on tenure lines ordinarily must publish to fulfill their obligation to the mission of their sponsoring institutions and their disciplines. But instructors or professors at 2- or 4-year colleges also derive their authority and intellectual identity from their respective fields of study. If we do not configure our community engagement work as having a research dimension, then projects can become mechanical and unexamined over time. I do not mean merely that we should be tinkering with programs each year, hiring the best teachers and tweaking the curriculum or supplemental texts. We need to reconsider purposes, measure effects, and incorporate new theoretical models all the time, leaving our certainties out in the rain to soften and break down for next year's planting.

Yancey's notion of circulation contributes to both the student and the faculty literacy commitments in postsecondary education. Investment in one place can have a profound effect elsewhere if the system is structured to allow for circulation of insights, techniques, or counter examples. Students in a first-year writing program need not be engaged in community-based learning to get the benefit of projects other students are doing. Perhaps their TA taught writing to teens during the summer and now has a better grasp of why students resist his assignments in the fall. Perhaps the head of second-language writing recently learned about video production working on a documentary in an immigrant neighborhood, and now she has brought back an enthusiasm for visual analysis to the curriculum. Perhaps, through a series of colloquia for community college and university instructors, university lecturers begin to rethink the abstract language in their assignments while community college faculty begin to assign more and varied readings in their classes. Perhaps the autobiographical essays that prisoners write in a criminal justice class offered through the university become texts for on-campus students in a writing intensive class studying perspectives on the American penal system. I have myself not had experience with professional or business writing—and thus have not written about that sector of composition in this book—but clearly a major step for writing programs is to link first-year, professional, business, and technical writing more directly to corporate offices, laboratories, and government agencies in a far more fluid and experiential way than the usual internship arrangement can sustain. The potential for challenge and growth through the exchange of written, visual, virtual, or oral texts seems limited largely by the structural elements of a system that facilitate or discourage greater circulation.

From the student learning perspective, then, maintaining a commitment to quality requires flexible administration and a willingness to foster rich conversations that actually lead to change. However, I do not want to minimize the very real problem of time management. Attending neighborhood meetings, visiting schools, consulting with foundation program officers or state bureaucrats—all necessary background work to community engagement—takes a tremendous amount of time. I hope that eventually community literacy will become as indispensable in any composition/rhetoric program as first year writing or classical rhetoric. Having more faculty, as long as they make it a habit to talk to one another, usually enhances the reach for all. However, I would warn against the temptation to depend on experts to handle exclusively one or another literacy activity. Even with a community literacy specialist on staff, others interested in writing should have experience off campus just as everyone should know a bit about program administration. Circulation encourages open architecture for knowledge exchange and questions the departmental segregation and turf battles common in American universities and colleges.

We need literacy research in every setting. We need to know what happens to learners of all ages and educational levels as they come in contact with one another, how writing develops in situations other than conventional classrooms, and what challenges reading presents to young and old communicators when they shift attention across a variety of media, audiences, and purposes. Retaining college students until they graduate is a major problem throughout the United States; this problem alone justifies a great deal more cooperation in research and alignment across levels than is commonly found. The field needs to dust off its founding commitment to empirical study, not with an attitude of rigid positivism but with a sense of creativity and pragmatism as well as a critical eye for productive new qualitative and quantitative methodologies. Researchers must learn how to investigate questions of composing and problem posing in order to guide future teachers, and scholars must develop overarching conceptions that do more than tap the prestigious theories of the day. Longitudinal composition studies such as those at Stanford, Harvard, or the University of Massachusetts-Amherst could also be designed and carried out across multiple sites and levels, could draw researchers from a variety of instructional settings—pre-K to college and factory floor to senior center—in order to learn about writers and readers as they transform or stagnate, achieve or fail in systems that may just as easily gridlock as interlock.

Yancey describes circulation in terms of genre shifting and media crossing, and this fluidity of form may offer a new approach to the conundrum of faculty "productivity." Publication, as measured by lines on a curriculum vitae, has come to drive life in research institutions and colleges looking to move up in national rankings. Schools where publication is not required of faculty are classified as lower in public discussions of quality. Within those schools, faculty who do not publish may grow wary of or hostile to those who do because publishing scholars may be looking down on their peers or trying to "write their way out" of their current jobs. If we step outside this commodified system where nearly everybody feels inadequate compared to somebody else, we need to ask what values should we uphold in all good schools. It seems to me we want to encourage substantive intellectual growth for every teaching assistant and adjunct as well as every visiting, assistant, or full professor. Publication stands for knowledge, sophistication, and prestige, but it can only go so far to represent the deepening understanding we hope to see in most faculty, especially in relation to their teaching.

Of course, faculty coming up for tenure or promotion, unemployed instructors looking for full- or part-time positions, or graduate students building their CVs are not positioned to call for change in the accepted system of ranked publications and preferred presentation venues. Understanding doesn't quantify very well, and wisdom barely registers in citation indices. However, the publication landscape has already begun to change through the inexorable logic of circulation. Legitimate publishing venues now include online journals, largely because these journals are read and cited by people in the field. Book publication grows harder and harder to come by in the humanities, and even the strictest administrators know we lose valuable faculty in failed tenure decisions every year because many bright people cannot balance the demands of publishing, teaching, and faculty politics. In our small corner of the academic world, if established scholars and researchers who study community literacy or first-year writing or professional communications start to discuss their work in crossover or transformational forms, discussing the urgent issues not only in academic venues but in activist newsletters, radio interviews, press releases, and Web site texts, perhaps these will begin to seem more legitimate for new faculty as well. This approach may make a stronger impact than academic publications can on the public view of a given college or department, and perhaps on the national rankings of schools with exceptional community engagement programs.

Grant writing may also offer a valuable new avenue for demonstrating the accomplishment and standing of faculty involved with literacy projects. Grants have long served as a measure of faculty production in the sciences and some social sciences. The high-risk grant game is not a racket humanities faculty should rush to join, but as part of a whole portfolio of work for promotion, for instance, a grant might become a valued component. In colleges that are less driven by research, faculty may find that work beyond the campus can become highly valued if it attracts funds for enhancing the mission of the college and the learning experiences of students.

We will have to call for a revision of the criteria for faculty productivity over the next few years. Administrators and departmental committees must see a person's work not merely in terms of the traditional triad of teaching–research–service but in a more holistic sense of a person's intellectual and disciplinary goals, how the whole person thinks and acts on her convictions and philosophical orientations. Nontenured faculty will have to be valued for their professional growth and their contributions to curricular design and community engagement. Perhaps this sounds impossibly optimistic, given the brutal politics of tenure and employment in contemporary higher education, but the current evaluation system simply doesn't guide faculty at most levels toward the work that the contemporary university needs to accomplish. Senior faculty perpetuate the system by serving on promotion and tenure committees or making new hiring decisions; we can begin to take new factors into account. Circulation provides a positive form of resistance to the rigid and dysfunctional qualities of academic practice.

ARE THESE EFFORTS WORTHWHILE?

I can hardly end by answering this question "no." Still, I don't hasten to answer "yes," either. Worth is local, and efforts at community engagement cannot be broadly accepted or rejected. Temple, like other metropolitan universities, is historically bound to the city and crucial to the region's economic health as one of Philadelphia's largest employers. A metropolitan university really must sponsor programs for surrounding neighborhoods and connect with local institutions, large and small. We cannot wish the city away, although I have known administrators who tried. The university initiates and maintains a full roster of activities rooted in city and suburban realities—hospitals, podiatry clinics, intergenerational theater, economic development projects, community college transfer agreements, summer youth programs, day-care effectiveness studies, a public radio station, a student newsroom, preservice teachers in the schools, landscape architecture interns in the arboretums—by which Temple is constantly shaping and being shaped by Philadelphia and its adjacent counties. Yet every project we undertake requires effort we could put somewhere else, outside or inside the campus. Every hour of meetings or planning or presentations is precious and could be used in a different, possibly more productive way. For this reason, there remains a need to assess and reflect continually, to judge the value of our efforts on more than a single metric. In this work there is no bottom line because a program or project has multiple ways to fail or succeed.

The CALN project described in the previous chapter provides a particularly good example of this complex calculus. We spent $324,000 over 2.5 years. What did we have to show for it? The money went into the publication of a couple of books, helped fund a large art show in Chinatown and 2 years of North Star performances, produced workshops in schools, teacher development seminars, and matinees for kids. We have video documentation for our programs we could never have produced without the grant. It forced four organizations to find ways to work together where they had little reason to cooperate before. It paid for a 1-day conference for about 80 people to talk about arts and literacy; most of the participants had not met each other before, and so new connections formed over lunch and workshop deliberations. Did Knight get its money's worth? Was it a good use of my time when I might have been putting more thought into a new writing intensive course in the nursing school or more energy into critiquing one of my graduate students' dissertation proposals?

Yes, CALN was worth the trouble for me and worth the money for Knight. I always look back on any project and see how we could have accomplished more: better planning, more participants, more school programs. I certainly feel that at times I could have been more attentive to this or that detail or, more importantly, met more often with my partners. But this work beyond the college curriculum has pushed me to factor other realities into my life as a college writing director, as a composition researcher, as a poet, even as a father and husband. CALN not only brought the struggles and visions of Chinatown and North Philadelphia into Temple writing, it forced literacy to share space with the arts in the way we imagined programs and projects with the schools. I am convinced that new media will make a vital contribution to writing programs in and outside the university, but CALN also convinced me that drawing, dance, music, and other traditional media deepen our understanding of how human beings make meaning through symbol, color, shape, sound, and gesture. As an amateur organizer, I see the way cultural events and works bring people together, helping them explore and express the issues that matter to them most. I cannot speak for my partners in the grant, but I suspect they too learned new perspectives on what they do and what potential partnerships can offer. Not to be ignored in this calculation is that a set of relationships and institutional successes now register in our institutional memory. We know we can pull off partnerships up and down Broad Street, the boulevard that runs up from City Hall through the Temple campus, with North Philadelphia laid out on both sides, all the way to Cheltenham Avenue at one edge of the city. Any one project proves nothing; every project must renew the bonds between city and university. But I'm happy to start over each time with a little more experience, a few more fellow Philadelphians to call on as friends and allies. After all, it's our city.

Bibliography

Adler-Kassner, Linda, and Susanmarie Harrington. *Basic Writing as a Political Act*. Cresskill, NJ: Hampton P, 2002.

Adler-Kassner, Linda, Robert Crooks, and Ann Watters, eds. *Writing the Community: Concepts and Models for Service Learning in Composition*. Washington, DC: American Assn. of Higher Education, 1997.

Alinsky, Saul. *Reveille for Radicals*. New York: Vintage, 1946.

_____. *Rules for Radicals*. New York: Vintage, 1971.

Ahlburg, D.A., S.L. DesJardins, and B.P. McCall. "A Temporal Investigation of Factors Related to Timely Degree Completion." *Journal of Higher Education* 73.5 (2002): 555-581.

American Association of Community Colleges. "Community College Fact Sheet." http://www.aacc.nche.edu/Content/NavigationMenu AboutCommunityColleges/Fast_Facts1/Fast_Facts.htm

Astin, A.W. *What Matters in College? Four Critical Years Revisited*. San Francisco, CA: Jossey-Bass, 1993.

Bartholomae, David. "Inventing the University." *Literacy: A Critical Sourcebook*. Eds. Ellen Cushman, Eugene Kintgen, Barry Kroll, and Mike Rose. Boston, MA: Bedford/St. Martin's, 2001. 511-524.

_____. "Writing with Teachers: A Conversation with Peter Elbow." *College Composition and Communication* 46 (1995): 62-71.

Bartholomae, David and Anthony Petrosky. *Facts, Artifacts, and Counterfacts*. Portsmouth, NJ: Boynton-Cook, 1986.

_____. *Ways of Reading*. 7th Edition. Boston, MA: Bedford/St. Martin's, 2004.

Bazerman, Charles, and David Russell, eds. *Writing Selves, Writing Societies: Research from Activity Perspectives*. Fort Collins, CO: The WAC Clearinghouse and Mind, Culture, and Activity. 1 June 2004 <http://wac.colostate.edu/books/ selves_societies/intro.cfm>.

Berger, Peter and Thomas Luckmann. *The Social Construction of Reality*. New York: Anchor-Doubleday, 1967.

"Best National Universities and Liberal Arts Colleges." *U.S. News & World Report* (30 Aug 2004): 94-100.

Bizzell, Patricia. "Power, Authority, and Critical Pedagogy." *Journal of Basic Writing* 10 (1991): 54-70

Brandt, Deborah. *Literacy as Involvement: The Acts of Writers, Readers, and Texts*. Carbondale, IL: Southern Illinois UP, 1990.

_____. *Literacy in American Lives*. Cambridge: Cambridge UP, 2001.

_____. "Sponsors of Literacy." *College Composition and Communication* 49.2 (1998): 165-185.

_____. "Understanding the Collisions between the Arts and Literacy." *Public School Notebook* (Summer 2006): 26.

Brooke, Robert. *Writing and Sense of Self*. Urbana, IL: NCTE, 1991.

Carey, Kevin. "A Matter of Degrees: Improving Graduation Rates in Four-Year Colleges and Universities." Washington, D.C.: The Education Trust, 2004.

Chaden, Caryn, Roger Graves, David A. Jolliffe, and Peter Vandenberg. "Confronting Clashing Discourses: Writing the Space Between Classrooms and Community in Service Learning Courses." *Reflections* 2.2 (Spring 2002): 19-39

Clark, B. "The Cooling Out Function in Higher Education." *The American Journal of Sociology* 65.6 (1960): 569-576.

Cohen, Arthur M. and Florence B. Brawer. *The American Community College* (2nd Edition). San Francisco: Jossey-Bass, 1989.

Cope, Bill and Mary Kalantzis, eds. *Multiliteracies: Literacy Learning and the Design of Social Futures*. London: Routledge, 2000.

Crowley, Sharon. *Composition in the University*. Pittsburgh, PA: U of Pittsburgh P, 1998.

_____. "Reimagining the Writing Scene: Curmudgeonly Remarks about Contending with Words." In *Contending with Words: Composition and Rhetoric in a Postmodern Age*. Patricia Harkin and John Schilb, eds. New York: Modern Language Association, 1991. 189-197.

Cushman, Ellen. "Sustainable Service Learning Programs." *College Composition and Communication* 54.1 (2002): 40-65.

Deans, Tom. *Writing Partnerships: Service Learning in Composition.* Urbana, IL: NCTE, 2000.

Degnan, James and Tim Walsh. "Undergraduate Matriculated Students Who Leave Temple University." Report to Vice President Tom Maxey. Philadelphia, PA: Temple U document. September 2001.

Dewey, John. *Democracy and Education.* McMillan, 1916. Free Press, 1944.

———. *Experience and Education.* 1938. New York: Touchstone, 1997.

———. *How We Think.* 1910. Mineola, NY: Dover Publications, 1997.

———. "My Pedagogic Creed." *School Journal* 54 (Jan 1897): 77-80. Reprinted in *John Dewey on Education: Selected Writings.* Ed Reginald D.Archambault. Chicago, IL: U of Chicago P, 1964. 427-39.

———. "The Way Out of Educational Confusion." Harvard UP, 1931. Reprinted in *John Dewey on Education: Selected Writings.* Ed. Reginald D. Archimbault. Chicago: U of Chicago P, 1964. 422-26.

Dougherty, Kevin J. *The Contradictory College: The Conflicting Origins, Impacts, and Futures of the Community College.* Albany, NY: State U of New York P, 1994.

Drake, Alexis. "Influences on Good Students' Decisions to Leave Temple University." Report submitted to the Provost. Philadelphia, PA: Temple University document. April 2004.

Durst, Russel. *Collision Course: Conflict, Negotiation, and Learning in College Composition.* Urbana IL: NCTE, 1999.

"Episcopal Editor Denounces Saul Alinsky." *Christian Century* (November 15, 1967): 1452.

Ellison, Ralph. *Invisible Man.* 1947. New York: Vintage International, 1995.

Enos, Theresa. *A Sourcebook for Basic Writing Teachers.* New York: McGraw-Hill, 1987.

Fishman, Stephen and Lucille McCarthy. *John Dewey and the Challenge of Classroom Practice.* New York: Teachers College P, 1998.

Finks, P. David. *The Radical Vision of Saul Alinsky.* New York: Paulist P, 1984.

Flower, Linda. "Intercultural Inquiry and the Transformation of Service." *College English* 65.2 (2002): 181-201.

Flower, Linda, Elenore Long, and Lorraine Higgins. *Learning to Rival: A Literate Practice for Intercultural Inquiry.* Mahwah, NJ: Erlbaum, 2000.

Foundation Center. "Our Values." http://fdncenter.org/about/;jsessionid= TJYTQ1COIOGRGP5QALRSGXD5AAAACI2F

Fox, Tom. "Change and Complicity." *College Composition and Communication* 49.2 (1998): 256-259.

"The Gadfly of the Poverty War." *Newsweek* (September 13, 1965): 30-32.

Giroux, Henry. *Border Crossings.* New York: Routledge, 1992.

Goldblatt, Eli. '*Round My Way: Authority and Double-Consciousness in Three Urban High School Writers.* Pittsburgh, PA: U of Pittsburgh P, 1995.

Goldblatt, Eli and Steve Parks. *Literacy In Action: Moving On-Line and Off Broad Street.* July 28 1998 draft for the Knight Foundation. Author's collection.

_____. *Literacy in Action: Writing Beyond the Curriculum.* Jan 25, 2000 draft for the Knight Foundation. Author's collection.

Grabill, Jeffrey T. and Lynee Lewis Gaillet. "Writing Program Design in the Metropolitan University: Toward Constructing Community Partnerships." *Writing Program Administration* 25.3 (Spring 2002).

Hansen, Kristine. "Serving Up Writing in a New Form." *College Composition and Communication* 49.2 (1998): 260-64.

Harris, Joseph. *A Teaching Subject: Composition Since 1966.* Upper Saddle River, NJ: Prentice Hall, 1997.

_____. *Rewriting: How to Do Things with Texts.* Logan, UT: Utah State UP, 2006.

Hathaway, Charles, Paige E. Mulhollan, and Karen A. White. "Metropolitan Universities: Models for the Twenty-First Century." *Metropolitan Universities: An Emerging Model in American Higher Education.* Ed. Daniel M. Johnson and David A. Bell. Denton, TX: U of N. Texas P, 1995.

Heath, Shirley Brice. *Ways with Words.* Cambridge: U of Cambridge P, 1983.

Herzberg, Bruce. "Community Service and Critical Teaching." *College Composition and Communication* 45 (1994): 307-19.

Horwitt, Sanford D. *Let Them Call Me Rebel: Saul Alinsky—His Life and Legacy.* New York: Knopf, 1989.

Huot, Brian. "Toward a New Discourse of Assessment for the College Writing Classroom." *College English* 65.2 (2002): 163-180.

Hyatt, Susan, ed. *The Forgotten Bottom.* Philadelphia: New City P, 2002.

Jones, Donald. "Beyond the Postmodern Impasse of Agency: The Resounding Relevance of John Dewey's Tacit Tradition." *Journal of Advanced Composition* 16.1 (1996): 81-102.

Knight Foundation Annual Report 1999: The First Fifty Years. Miami, FL: John S. and James L. Knight Foundation, 1999.

Knight Foundation 2003 Annual Report. Miami, FL: John S. and James L. Knight Foundation, 2003.

Lewiecki-Wilson, Cynthia and Jeff Sommers. "Professing at the Fault Lines: Composing at Open Admissions Institutions." *College Composition and Communication* 50.3 (1999): 438-462.

Lyons, Mark and August Tarrier, eds. *Espejos y Ventanas/Mirrors and Windows.* Philadelphia: New City Community Press, 2004.

Marshall, James. "The Effects of Writing on Students' Understanding of Literary Texts." *Research in the Teaching of English* 21(1987): 30-63.

Mathieu, Paula. *Tactics of Hope: The Public Turn in English Composition.* Portsmouth NH: Heinemann, 2005.

McLeod, Susan and Elaine Maimon. "Clearing the Air: WAC Myth and Realities." *College English* 62.5 (2000): 573-583.

McLeod, Susan and Eric Miraglia. "Writing Across the Curriculum in a Time of Change." *WAC for the New Millenia*. Eds. Susan McLeod, Eric Miraglia, Margot Soven, and Christopher Thaiss. Urbana, IL: NCTE, 2001.

Miller, Richard. *As if Learning Mattered: Reforming Higher Education*. Ithaca, NY: Cornell UP, 1998.

Monroe, Jonathan, ed. *Local Knowledges, Local Practices: Writing in the Disciplines at Cornell*. Pittsburgh, PA: U of Pittsburgh Press, 2003.

Moran, Meg. "Achieving WAC Program Assessment." *Assessing Writing Across the Curriculum*. Eds. Kathleen Blake Yancey and Brian Huot. Greenwich CT: Ablex, 1997.

The Neighborhood Story Project. http://www.neighborhoodstoryproject. org/.2006.

Newkirk, Tom. *More Than Stories*. Portsmouth NH: Heinemann, 1989.

Ott, Gil, ed. *No Restraints*. Philadelphia, PA: New City P, 2002.

_____. *traffic*. Tucson, AZ: Chax P, 2001.

Parks, Steve, and Eli Goldblatt. "Writing beyond the Curriculum: Fostering New Collaborations in Literacy." *College English* 62.5 (2000): 584-606.

Pascarella, E.T. and P.T. Terenzini. "Predicting Freshman Persistence and Voluntary Dropout Decisions from a Theoretical Model." *Journal of Higher Education* 51 (1980): 60-74.

Peck, Wayne C., Linda Flower, and Lorraine Higgens. "Community Literacy." *College Composition and Communication* 46 (1995): 199-222.

Penrose, Anne. "Academic Literacy Perceptions and Performance: Comparing First-Generation and Continuing-Generation College Students." *Research in the Teaching of English* 36.4 (2002): 437-461.

Phelps, Louise Wetherbee. *Composition as a Human Science*. New York: Oxford UP. 1988.

"Radical Saul Alinsky: Prophet of Power to the People." *Time* (March 2, 1970): 56-57.

Riding, Dorothy S. "The State of Philanthropy." Council on Foundations 55th Annual Conference Plenary Session. Toronto, Canada, April 26, 2004. http://www.cof.org/Content/General/Display.cfm?contentID=1571

Ronald, Kate and Hephzibah Roskelly. "Untested Feasibility: Imagining the Pragmatic Possibility of Paulo Freire." *College English* 63 (2001): 612-632.

Rose, Mike. *Possible Lives*. New York: Houghton Mifflin, 1995.

Rousculp, Tiffany. "When the Community Writes: Re-envisioning the SLCC DiverseCity Writing Series." *Reflections* 5.1 & 2 (Spring 2006): 67-88.

Sanders, Marion K. "The Professional Radical: Conversations with Saul Alinsky." *Harper's Magazine* (June 1965): 37-47.

Schell, Eileen and Patricia Lambert Stock, eds. *Moving a Mountain: Transforming the Role of Contingent Faculty in Composition Studies and Higher Education*. Urbana, IL: NCTE, 2000.

Schneider, Robert. "Transfer and Philadelphia High School Students at Temple University: A Fact Sheet." Philadelphia, PA: Temple U document, 2000.

Schroeder, Christopher, Helen Fox, and Patricia Bizzell. *ALT Dis: Alternative Discourses and the Academy*. Portsmouth, NH: Boynton/Cook-Heinemann, 2002.

Schutz, Aaron, and Anne Ruggles Gere. "Service Learning and English Studies." *College English* 60.2 (1998): 129-149.

Selfe, Cynthia. *Technology and Literacy in the Twenty-First Century*. Carbondale, IL: S Illinois UP, 1999.

Silberman, Charles E. *Crisis in Black and White*. New York: Vintage, 1964.

Silva, Tony and Paul Kei Matsuda. *On Second Language Writing*. Mahwah NJ: Lawrence Erlbaum, 2001.

Slayton, Robert. *The Back of the Yards: The Making of a Local Democracy*. Chicago: U of Chicago P, 1986.

Smith, Jeff. "Students' Goals, Gatekeeping, and Some Questions of Ethics." *College English* 59.3 (1997): 299-320.

Soliday, Mary and Barbara Gleason. "From Remediation to Enrichment: Evaluating a Mainstreaming Project." *Journal of Basic Writing* 16 (1997): 64-78.

"Somerset Language Arts Course of Studies." Philadelphia, PA: Somerset High School document, 1994

Spellmeyer, Kurt. *Common Ground: Dialogue, Understanding, and the Teaching of Composition*. Englewood Cliffs, NJ: Prentice Hall, 1993.

_____. "Response: Testing as Surveillance." *Assessment of Writing: Politics, Policies, Practices*. Eds. Edward White, William Lutz, and Sandra Kamusikiri. New York: MLA, 1996, pp. 174-181.

Stern, Mark J. and Susan C. Seifert. "*Culture Builds Community* Evaluation: Summary Report." Social Impact of the Arts Project. Philadelphia, PA: University of Pennsylvania School of Social Work. Jan. 2002.

Stewart, Susan. *Crimes of Writing*. Durham NC: Duke UP, 1994

Street, Brian. *Social Literacies*. New York: Cambridge UP, 1995.

Sullivan, Francis J., Arabella Lyon, Dennis Lebofsky, Susan Well, and Eli Goldblatt. "Student Needs and Strong Composition: The Dialectics of Writing Program Reform." *College Composition and Communication* 48.3: 372-92.

Sullivan, Patrick. "What is 'College-Level' Writing?" *Teaching English in Two-Year Colleges* (2003): 374-390.

Sze, Lena, ed. *Chinatown Live(s)*. Philadelphia, PA: Asian Arts Initiative and New City Community P, 2004.

Tarrier, August and Susan Hyatt. *The Forgotten Bottom Remembered: Stories from a Philadelphia Neighborhood*. Philadelphia, PA: New City P, 2003.

Thompson, Thomas C., ed. *Teaching Writing in High School and College: Conversations and Collaborations*. Urbana, IL: NCTE, 2002.

Tinberg, Howard. "An Interview with Ira Shor—Part I". *Teaching of English in Two-Year Colleges* (1999): 51-60.

_____. *Border Talk: Writing and Knowing in the Two-Year College*. Urbana, IL: NCTE, 1997.

Tinto, Vincent. "Colleges as Communities: Taking Research on Student Persistence Seriously." *The Review of Higher Education* 21.2 (1998): 167-177.

Tobin, Lad. *Writing Relationships*. Portsmouth, NH: Boynton/Cook-Heinemann, 1993.

Walvoord, Barbara. "The Future of WAC." *College English* 58.1 (1996): 58-79.

Westbrook, Robert. *John Dewey and American Democracy*. Ithaca NY: Cornell UP, 1991.

Yagelski, Robert. *Literacy Matters: Writing and Reading the Social Self*. New York: Teachers College Press, 2000.

Yancey, Kathleen Blake. "Made Not Only in Words: Composition in a New Key." *College Composition and Communication* 56.2 (2004): 297-328.

Yancey, Kathleen Blake and Brian Huot. *Assessing Writing Across the Curriculum: Diverse Approaches and Practices*. Greenwich, CT: Ablex, 1997.

Zamel, Vivian and Ruth Spack. *Negotiating Academic Literacies: Teaching and Learning Across Languages and Cultures*. Mahwah NJ: Lawrence Erlbaum, 1998.

Ziegler, Jerome M. "Winds of Change: The University in Search of Itself." In *Metropolitan Universities: An Emerging Model in American Higher Education*. Eds. Daniel M. Johnson and David A. Bell. Denton, TX: U of N. Texas P, 1995.

Author Index

Subject Index

Printed in the United States
87256LV00003B/505-600/A

9 781572 737693